THE SCHOOL MUSIC
ADMINISTRATOR AND SUPERVISOR

Catalysts for Change in Music Education

ROBERT H. KLOTMAN

School of Music
Indiana University

PRENTICE-HALL, INC., Englewood Cliffs, New Jersey

PRENTICE-HALL INTERNATIONAL, INC., London
PRENTICE-HALL OF AUSTRALIA, PTY. LTD., Sydney
PRENTICE-HALL OF CANADA, LTD., Toronto
PRENTICE-HALL OF INDIA PRIVATE LIMITED, New Delhi
PRENTICE-HALL OF JAPAN, INC., Tokyo

To Janet, Paul, *and especially* Phyllis, *my most reliable supporters and distinguished critics*

ACKNOWLEDGMENTS

The author wishes to acknowledge his sincere appreciation to the following music administrators who have made their materials available to him for use in this text:

DEWITT ASHER, Director of Music Education for the Akron, Ohio Public Schools

PHILIP FULLER, Music Curriculum Specialist for the Fairfax County Public Schools, Virginia

WILLIAM KOERPER, Director of Music Education for the Detroit, Michigan Public Schools

LOUISE ROSSI, Music Coordinator for the Warren, Michigan Consolidated Schools

BURDELL SELL, Music Consultant for the Columbus, Indiana Public Schools

ELIZABETH HAYS WHITE, Director of Music Education for the Oak Park, Michigan Schools

CONTENTS

INTRODUCTION, 1

Chapter 1
THE PROCESS OF ADMINISTRATION AND SUPERVISION, 5

Chapter 2
THE PURPOSE AND FUNCTION
OF SCHOOL MUSIC ADMINISTRATION, 13

Chapter 3
TRADITIONAL PATTERNS OF
ORGANIZATIONAL STRUCTURE AND BEHAVIORS, 24

Chapter 4
DESIGNING AND PLANNING CURRICULA, 33

Chapter 5
THE IMPROVEMENT OF INSTRUCTION FOR CHANGE, 46

Chapter 6
PERSONNEL PRACTICES, 60

Chapter 7
EVALUATION AND THE PROCESS OF CHANGE, 77

Chapter 8
SCHEDULING AND ITS IMPLICATIONS, 90

Chapter 9
BUDGET AND BUSINESS, 100

Chapter 10
KEEPING THE COMMUNITY AND SCHOOL INFORMED, 125

Chapter 11
THE CHALLENGE OF ADMINISTRATION, 135

Appendix A
PUBLIC SCHOOLS ANNOUNCEMENT
OF ADMINISTRATIVE OPENING, 144
ANNOUNCEMENT OF SUPERVISORY OPENING, 147

Appendix B
A CHECK LIST FOR THE EXAMINATION
OF CURRICULUM GUIDES IN MUSIC, 150

Appendix C
EVALUATION CRITERIA: MINORITY TREATMENT, 153

Appendix D
RATINGS ON TEACHER COMPETENCE MEMORANDUM, 155

Appendix E
THE VOCAL MUSIC PROGRAM, 157
THE INSTRUMENTAL MUSIC PROGRAM, 160

Appendix F
OUTSIDE ENGAGEMENT FORMS, 234

Appendix G

CODE FOR UNDERSTANDING AND COOPERATION
BETWEEN SCHOOL AND PROFESSIONAL MUSICIANS, 165

Appendix H

PUBLICATIONS, 169

Appendix I

PROMOTIONAL FORMS
FOR MUSICALLY TALENTED STUDENTS, 171

Appendix J

LETTER FROM MICHIGAN EDUCATION ASSOCIATION, 177

Appendix K

SPECIFICATIONS FOR INSTRUMENT PURCHASES, 178

Appendix L

SPECIFICATIONS FOR PIANOS (CONSOLE STYLE), 201

Appendix M

TABLE OF ALLOWANCE
FOR FAIRFAX COUNTY SCHOOLS
ADOPTED DECEMBER 12, 1966, 205

Appendix N

PPBS SAMPLE BUDGET, 208

Appendix O

APPLICATION: MUSICAL INSTRUMENT INVENTORY, 216

Appendix P

DATA PROCESSING FOR
INSTRUMENTAL MUSIC LIBRARY CATALOGS, 228

BIBLIOGRAPHY, 238

INDEX, 243

INTRODUCTION

Education is a cooperative enterprise shared jointly by the schools and the public. When conflicts of interest arise, however, the ultimate decision rests with the public. This is axiomatic. In a democratic society, the voters elect their representatives to Boards of Education, and they, in turn are obligated to carry out the mandates of the public. The people's responsibility is to strive to maintain the best possible education for their children by supporting positive board of education action. If it is not forthcoming, then the people should elect members to the board who are sympathetic with their views. This is the democratic process.

The board of education, in turn, selects the proper administrators to implement the program desired by the community. As the community and its aspirations change, so must the purposes and objectives for education be altered within the community. It is in this sense that the enlightened administrator becomes a catalyst for change. Incidentally, in the context of this text, the use of the terms "administrator" and "administration" refer to male or female directors and supervisors with administrative responsibilities. However, when the responsibilities or references deal with supervisory concerns, then the individuals will be identified as "supervisors."

A recognized principle of change is that "all change is not necessarily progress, but one cannot have progress without change." The administrator's function is to determine whether or not the proposed change is desirable—that is, whether or not it is in the best interest of the child and the community or will impede learning rather than contribute to it. Education has long been accused of changing for the sake of change to create the impression of being "up to date." Too often educators have been eager to grasp at gimmicks and panaceas, and some may even have listened to soothsayers. They have been accused of being reactors rather than visionaries and planners. This can no longer be tolerated. "Accountability" has become a part of the educators' common parlance. They must

1

plan in such a way that their decisions and results may be measured and upheld in the court of public opinion. Change and progress are not accidental. They are the result of careful planning and systematic procedures that are designed to achieve recognized desirable goals.

It is essential that one understand this concept of school administration if one is to assume the role of leadership that accompanies the responsibilities for administering and supervising the school music program. A music administrator must realize that his actions and judgments will affect the music education of an entire school system, and therefore, he cannot ignore the need for appropriate decision making.

There are definite skills and techniques that are essential to the development of a competent administrator and supervisor. It is no longer sufficient that he be a faithful teacher who has put in his required years and is now ready for a special reward in terms of an administrative appointment. Competent administrative leadership is crucial for the survival of music education in our schools; to develop individuals who are prepared to accept this responsibility requires special study and examination.

It is the purpose of this text to define those skills and techniques necessary for the development of a successful school music administrator. Actually, one cannot isolate the responsibilities of music supervision and administration. They encompass every facet of the school program—testing, classroom teaching in all areas, human relations and community relations, psychology, etc. They are complex assignments of overlapping, interwoven responsibilities that include curriculum planning and evaluating for the improvement of instruction. The assignment may require of the individual a quick value judgment when guidelines may or may not exist, or infinite patience when time can be an asset rather than a detriment. Music administrators must keep abreast of curricular developments and innovations not only in the field of music, but also in related areas if they are to be the educational leaders for their department. They must be sensitive to current issues confronting their schools and interpret the music program in light of these issues as confrontations and demands arise.

But even this aspect of the job is only a segment of the administrative responsibilities. Administrators must be able to exercise sound economical judgment in preparing a budget or recommending expenditure of funds. They must work within the context of the school personnel practices when making or recommending assignments. Administrators and supervisors must be active in recruiting competent teachers. And if this is not sufficiently complicated, music supervisors and administrators must be expert in scheduling classes to protect the time allotments available for music in the schools and must deal with personality conflicts that occur between teachers, between teachers and administrators, and among administrators themselves. They are frequently called upon to interpret the music program in light of school policies and maintain appropriate school-community relations when the opportunity presents itself. They are the educational leaders in music; they are the instructional leaders in music education; they must provide educational leadership in the curricular field of music. Many of the examples cited in this text will be from recent experiences gained in Cleveland Heights, Akron, and Detroit. Therefore, one might construe this text as being only "big city" oriented. Such is not the intent. The basic principles apply whether in a rural area, a small community, or an urban area. Only the degree to which they are utilized and the manner in which they are applied will vary. Small communities as well as large cities need guides and procedures for developing programs. Suburban areas are affected by city concerns. Every situation is unique, and yet all are closely related as the part of a mosaic which we euphemistically call "national patterns."

Personnel problems exist in the rural area of our society as well as in our big cities, and administrators need guiding principles to assist them in dealing with such concerns. Ethnic studies in the current climate are as important in suburban areas as they are in the inner city.

"Relevance" implies wide-spread applicability as it relates to the social-political period of our times, and music education is not exempt from the responsibility of keeping music in the mainstream of contemporary life. This does not, however, imply merely doing certain music just to be "with it." Musical activities are governed by a school's philosophy. The process directed toward achieving its philosophical goal is built on specific objectives. If the purpose of music education in a school is to teach students how to analyze, organize, and perform music, then activities will be directed toward analyzing, organizing, and performing. And if the music used has wide-spread applicability related to the social-political period of our time, then and only then does it become relevant. Unless the music lends itself to the basic goals, it is irrelevant. The responsibility for directing, guiding, and educating the staff so that music education is in the forefront of current thought rests with the administrators and supervisors in the music department.

As we become more computerized and better organized through systematic planning, it will be necessary to consolidate and combine efforts so that smaller units will offer the same opportunities provided by larger or more wealthy communities. The challenge under these conditions is to retain the identity and unique qualities of the smaller districts. It is only by knowing the pitfalls as well as the advantages of modern planning that we can administrate for desirable change, progress, and even efficiency without undermining the unique individual characteristics of the school and community.

In a society that places a high premium on function and materialistic gain, it might be tempting to imitate successful management procedures of business. In some school systems it has even been suggested that "educators" be replaced by successful business executives. This can be a dangerous direction for education and particularly education in the arts and humanities. Such ideas often occur in a transition period to assuage criticism but do little to solve the needs for educating children. A better solution is better *educators*, who understand what is needed, how to plan to accomplish their desirable goals, and how to implement such programs. Some of the solutions will be found through organizational techniques of business and government, but one cannot rely on them as panaceas for solving human dilemmas. In the final analysis, administrative judgment must prevail, and this is entirely dependent on how it affects learning.

Chapter 1

THE PROCESS OF ADMINISTRATION
AND SUPERVISION

All processes in administration and supervision are guided by an individual's basic philosophy which will assist him in decision-making. It is a philosophy that is evolved out of many and varied experiences and is in keeping with the social and educational philosophy of the times. Inherent in this governing philosophy should be a dedication and commitment to progress and growth for students and teachers who are involved in today's music education. It must have survived the test of practice and time and still be able to be upheld in the arena of current public debate and examination. To be functional, such a philosophy must be sufficiently flexible to adjust to changing times and maturing opinions. Just as times and situations change, certain characteristics of one's philosophical position will mature and adjust to these changes.

A philosophy for an administrator or supervisor is not acquired solely through academic investigation. It must be tempered in the crucible of time and developed through a series of classroom experiences as well as administrative opportunities. It does not evolve out of sterile test tubes but is founded on mistakes as well as successes in actual situations. In short, no matter how well one understands the process of administration and supervision or reads all of the available material on the subject, one does not become an instructional leader in music—for that is the role of music administration—until one actually participates in the administrative process, whether in the classroom or behind a desk. In a sense, a part of the process is actually growing on the job. One does not "arrive" with the administrative or supervisory appointment. Rather, one merely passes into another phase of one's education.

Lest this be interpreted to mean that only experienced music administrators should supervise or administrate music programs, the author hastens to add that one acquires this experience by beginning in the starting blocks even as a raw beginner. Anyone who exhibits promise and competency in music and in working with people is entitled to the opportunity of entering the field.

Administrating and supervising a school music program is in a sense a clinical type of operation that will vary with each situation and each individual. There are those who may insist that every administrative decision can be reduced to some scientific principle. "If one can argue that science gives birth to application, so also can one argue that just as often it is art, practice, and technology which give birth to science."[1] Ideally, the decision-making role in administration should be based on a scale balanced between application of scientific principles and human, artistic concerns.

As a physician diagnoses his patients' ailments, so must the music administrator diagnose and prescribe corrective measures for his school music program, including preventive action that will keep his healthy, successful program from succumbing to inertia and complacency. In addition, the role of the chief administrator in music and his supervisors is to be able to communicate with those above and below the line and staff relationships, to be able to plan programs that require foresight, and to be able to "plan ahead." They guide and direct the school music program as its instructional leaders. Their central function is to coordinate the efforts of everyone involved in working toward their goal of an appropriate music program for all the children in their schools as well for the entire community.

As implied earlier, administration and supervision are dependent upon skills that a competent music educator develops in working with people, both within and outside the educational structure. Although attempts have been made in the past to compare and analyze administrators in education with those in industry, it is, under certain conditions, as improper as comparing apples with flywheels. Students are not products that can be counted or measured immediately as one can count apples or flywheels. We are dealing with people and aesthetic values, and they need time to grow and mature. They present variables that cannot always be predicted. Behaviors can be identified and measured, but aesthetic quality and aesthetic judgment cannot. We should be able to account for behavioral learning but not lose sight of ideals that are inherent in the art and cannot be immediately measured. There are some experiments such as the "Indiana-Oregon test" which attempt to measure aesthetic judgment, but even these efforts lack sufficient validity. There are aspects of the school music management such as budget planning, scheduling, school construction, analyzing enrollments, inventories, gov-

---

[1] Robert H. Roy, The Administrative Process (Baltimore: The Johns Hopkins Press, 1965), p. 2.

ernment projects, and several others that may utilize management techniques and systems planning. A sensitive administrator, however, will distinguish between those areas that rely on management techniques and areas in education where this does not apply.

"SCIENTIFIC" APPROACH TO
DECISION MAKING AND PROBLEM SOLVING

Historically, one can trace ideas of scientific management into educational philosophy with the turn of the twentieth century, when business and industry emerged as the most influential and prestigious forces in our society. In addition, with the rapid growth of urban areas which were a result of mass immigration from Western Europe, efficient tactics and procedures had to be developed to accommodate the rapid expansion in school systems, and the success of business and industry in their manipulation of human resources seemed to be a logical exemplar for educators to emulate.

In 1910, Frederick Taylor introduced a system of "scientific management" to the business world that resulted in a new executive concept for school administrators. It led to a "cult of efficiency" with emphasis on scientific business skills for operating a school in a business-oriented society. This type of thought dominated educational administrative thinking until 1929, when the public became disenchanted with business and industrial practices as a result of the economic collapse of the nation.

During the period that followed, there occurred a revival in the concept that the school administrator's major concerns were educational and instructional rather than "business." Daniel Griffiths suggests that this idea may have resulted from a reawakening of social conscience stemming from the depression.[2] It certainly must have influenced a concomitant trend—the utilization of human dynamics in school administration and school management.

In the 1950s, the human relations element continued to dominate administrative thoughts, but attempts were being made to develop a "scientific basis for school administration, under which theory served as a guide to administrative action."[3] However, this still presented certain dilemmas. Theory varied considerably between individuals and communities, and so many human variables were constantly injected that it

[2] Raymond E. Callahan, *Education and the Cult of Efficiency: A Study of the Social Forces That Have Shaped the Administration of the Public Schools* (Chicago: University of Chicago Press, 1962), p. 2.

[3] H. W. Handy and K. J. Hussain, *Network Analysis for Educational Management* (Englewood Cliffs: Prentice-Hall, Inc., 1969), p. 2.

was almost impossible to formulate a consistent, definitive position for an existing theory.

More recently, as a result of the scientific successes in putting men in orbit and on the moon, a closer look was taken at another form of scientific management which was identified as system analysis or operations research. There are many terms used to identify the various systems approach at this writing, and there will be many more post publication. Two techniques currently in use in some school programs for solving problems are "Program Evaluation and Review Technique" (PERT) and "Critical Path Method" (CPM). These systems are direct transfers from military and business operations. They are technically referred to as operations research and system analyses and are planned to realize the optimal solution for *systems problems*. However, these may function only if there is a set of interconnected complexes of components that are functionally related to each other. Where this relationship does not exist, the operations research system breaks down. Therefore, the entire procedure is based on a careful systems analysis whose prime objective is to improve system or interconnected performance.

If properly understood and properly utilized, a systems approach for solving some problems can be implemented, but these problems must be tightly structured. Because of the nature of music and music educators this can present almost unsurmountable obstacles and perhaps even an undesirable approach to problem solving. The nature of the art of music and music instruction is filled with variables designed to enhance the art forms. Under certain conditions and in certain areas of music education, a systems approach would be a futile and wasted effort.

A competent music administrator will utilize systems planning where it is functional and desirable. There are areas where it can be useful and areas where it does not apply (see pages 33 and 34). Since successful systems planning is dependent on careful structure, a consistent approach or methodology needs to be devised to bring structure to units that might otherwise be poorly structured. As guidelines for structuring such conditions, Optner suggests the following seven steps:[4]

1. The problem process must be flow-charted, showing at least the principal decision-making points.

2. Details of the principal decision process must be described.

3. The principal alternatives and how they were generated must be demonstrable.

4. The assumptions pertinent to each alternative must be clearly identified.

[4] Stanley Optner, *Systems Analysis for Business and Industrial Problem Solving* (Englewood Cliffs: Prentice-Hall, Inc., 1965), p. 21.

STEP I: PREPARE A FLOW CHART

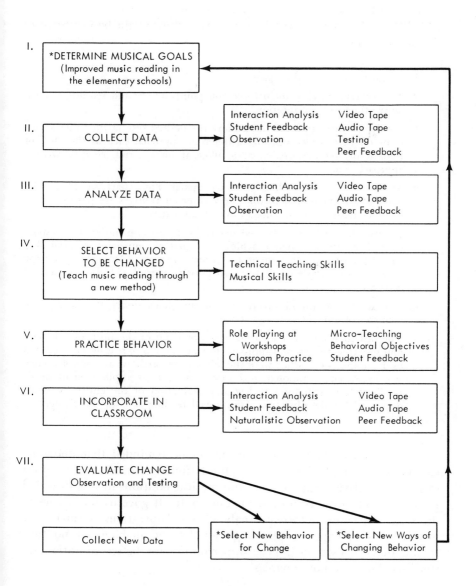

THE PROCESS

SOURCES OF INFORMATION
AND TOOLS

I.
*DETERMINE MUSICAL GOALS
(Improved music reading in
the elementary schools)

II. COLLECT DATA

Interaction Analysis   Video Tape
Student Feedback   Audio Tape
Observation   Testing
                         Peer Feedback

III. ANALYZE DATA

Interaction Analysis   Video Tape
Student Feedback   Audio Tape
Observation   Peer Feedback

IV. SELECT BEHAVIOR
TO BE CHANGED
(Teach music reading through
a new method)

Technical Teaching Skills
Musical Skills

V. PRACTICE BEHAVIOR

Role Playing at   Micro-Teaching
   Workshops   Behavioral Objectives
Classroom Practice   Student Feedback

VI. INCORPORATE IN
CLASSROOM

Interaction Analysis   Video Tape
Student Feedback   Audio Tape
Naturalistic Observation Peer Feedback

VII. EVALUATE CHANGE
Observation and Testing

Collect New Data

*Select New Behavior
for Change

*Select New Ways of
Changing Behavior

5. The criteria by which each alternative will be judged must be fully stated.

6. Detailed presentation of data, data relationships, and the procedural steps by which such data were evaluated must be a part of any solution.

7. The major alternative solutions and details to explain why other solutions were eliminated must be shown.

For example, if a concerted effort is being made to improve music instruction for the purpose of improving reading skill in the elementary school through a new approach, a systems concept might be instituted in the following manner:

1. See flow chart, preceding page.

2. The asterisks mark principal decision points and would require detailed description and specification.

3. Should the new approach not achieve the desired results, then the department might consider utilizing a different approach such as the Orff, or Kodaly, or Manhattanville, or a different book series, creative writing approach, etc.

4. At this point, the architects of the system flow chart would require detailed information as to why the various alternatives are possible. This includes observable advantages and disadvantages.

5. Criteria should be specific and determined by those individuals responsible: Does the alternative achieve the goal of improving reading skill without destroying enjoyment and interest in music? Does it expand the repertory to include music from all periods as well as from a variety of cultures?

6. The sixth step would involve all of the items under the heading of "Sources of Information and Tools."

7. The last item on the system analysis would be in the form of summary and report as to why one approach to teaching music reading was selected over another—i.e., what were the advantages or disadvantages of a creative approach as opposed to a strictly traditional application of music reading? It is actually a review and evaluation of the entire "system," organized for the objective of improved reading skill in the elementary school.

As a word of caution, readers should be reminded that under no circumstances should basic philosophical thinking be altered to adjust to systems analysis. Philosophical and musical positions dictate direction for music and music education for our youth. It governs the nature of the system structure. "Systems analysis" and "operations research" are merely tools to expedite planning and decision making. At no time should they be used to impede opportunities for better education for students. They are not panaceas!

THE "HUMAN" APPROACH TO DECISION MAKING

One of the difficulties in administration and supervision is to develop the ability to perceive oneself as others do. Perception is a form of behavior, and if the administrator or supervisor cannot see himself as others do, then he may lose actual contact with situations that require decisions affecting these situations. So often individuals in roles of leadership are called upon to make quick decisions with little opportunity for lengthy research and investigation. They must then rely on their empirical observations and a prevailing philosophy that will dictate a position. No one wants to make an incorrect decision or be accused of poor judgment. Logic may seem to be the proper process for such decisions, but unfortunately things are not always logical as *we* perceive them. Because of the many variables that exist in an administrative decision, directors and supervisors in charge of programs in music education need to develop antennae that will assist them in recognizing these situations.

Many administrators, to avoid making an error, will avoid a decision. This, in a sense, is tantamount to a negative decision and represents a type of action. Deferment of action may be desirable under certain circumstances, but it must be based on careful thought and judgment. It is in essence a form of decision. There are, however, times when action is absolutely necessary and a measure of administrative risk involved. A competent music administrator will assume this risk and make a necessary decision based on as many facts as are available, including his understanding of the existing variables.

If one reads this book expecting solutions, he will be disappointed. There are no absolute solutions for all problems. No one can be a successful administrator by merely reading a book, any more than one can play the violin by reading a text on how to play. One can only measure administrative results in relation to the time and context of the existing society. In a sense, each one's success will be measured by his ability to function in difficulty.

> "This is true, most decisions are easy and most results not critical. But, infrequent as they may be, there *are* difficult decisions to be made and critical results to evaluate, and it is here that the administrator and his supervisors stand or fall."[5]

Thus, the process of administration and supervision is acquiring basic knowledge and skills involving music and music education, develop-

[5] Robert H. Roy, *The Administrative Process* (Baltimore: The Johns Hopkins Press, 1965), p. 2.

ing a guiding philosophy that provides direction for the individual and the schools, possessing the necessary ability to deal with people in the positive sense, knowing the technical information available to assist in arriving at decisions, and constantly testing and evaluating all of these areas in the clinic of the classroom and the total school environment.

The process should be so organized that being a part of it will enable the school music administrator or supervisor to understand and make decisions which will provide the best possible education in music for the students and their community. It will permit them to direct, manage, and operate an effective program in music education. An appropriate process will encourage those involved to commit themselves to developing excellence in the music department for the benefit of the students and the entire school music program.

In the final sense, the ideal music administrator is not one who regards himself merely as a "manager" but one who is involved in *creative decision making*. He should envision himself as one whose major function might be to alter the course and direction of future music programs. His decision will be based on scientific and artistic experiences of the past as well as those being developed for the future.

Selected Articles For Supplementary Reading

AcKoff, Russell L., "The Meaning, Scope and Methods of Operations Research," *Progress in Operations Research Series,* I, (1961), 3–34.

Elsbee, Willard S., Harold J. McNally, and Richard Wynn., "A Look Ahead at School Administration," *The National Elementary Principal,* XLVI No. 5 (April, 1967), 40.

Leonhard, Charles, "Philosophy of Music Education," *Music Educators Journal* (September–October, 1965), 58.

Mannis, Daniel B., "What Kind of Music Educator Are You?" *Music Educators Journal* (March, 1971), 32.

Chapter 2

THE PURPOSE AND FUNCTION
OF SCHOOL MUSIC ADMINISTRATION

The singular purpose of music administration and supervision is to provide musical and educational leadership. This aim should govern virtually every action taken by the individuals involved. Indeed, one cannot separate the terms "music" and "education" as though they were two clearly independent functions. All teachers of music, whether in a concert or in a classroom, are responsible with varying degrees for both functions as they affect their students. The school music administrator and his staff are concerned about the combined concept, "music-education," as it affects the total school population. The terms are interdependent and interrelated. In this sense, decisions referred to as "solely educational concerns" will have a corollary or related effect on music and vice versa. Therefore, decisions should be made and courses of action pursued in light of this dual concern, and the administrator will have to assume responsibility for the weight or emphasis given at a particular time to a specific choice.

The term "leadership" conveys different meanings to different people and is affected by different circumstances. The dictionary defines the word "lead" as "to guide by example; induce to a course of action, persuasion or thought; direct by influence." Leadership is defined as "the ability to lead." Underlying these definitions is the implication of movement. Thus, the term "leadership" in this context means providing the necessary action or catalyst to move individuals or a group in the direction of problem solving and achieving mutually acceptable, desirable goals. To accomplish this action the following concepts need to be considered.

1. *Change occurs through changing the behavior of people.* There are many types of changes—in the conduct of daily teachings; in values, perceptions, and understandings, and even in skills. By altering one or more of these factors, the music administrator is effecting change. It may occur in the behavior of an outstanding teacher with years of service or

13

with a neophyte struggling to succeed. An example of this kind of change occurred in Detroit through the use of an MENC–Ford Foundation composer-in-residence. A teacher in an "advantaged" suburban area of the city had rejected a composition by the composer as being too difficult for his students. A teacher in an inner-city school who was close to retirement was then approached and offered the music with the challenge that it was described as being too difficult for the "advantaged" school. This teacher was selected because she was an outstanding musician who had always done excellent work but had been quite conservative and traditional in her programming. She accepted the challenge and gave a beautiful performance of the composer's manuscript. She later confessed privately that she had agreed to do the composition because she felt so inadequate when dealing with contemporary music and did not wish to admit to this weakness. She also felt that working with the composer would be of tremendous value for her students and she didn't want "her inability" to deprive them of this opportunity. The significance of this incident was that in the few years that remained prior to her retirement, the teacher who performed the work included a contemporary piece on each of her remaining concerts—a significant change in her behavior. Similar examples have occurred in other communities where CMP composers have been placed.

2. *Leadership is not always observed or measured by overt behavior or manner.* It is far more significant that it be measured by the quality of ideas rather than the quantity of programs. As much leadership may emanate from behind a desk as on a speaker's platform or a podium. One can exhibit good leadership if his ideas are carried out successfully by others, who receive appropriate credit. After all, one of the major functions of administration is coordinating the ideas and efforts of members of the staff toward the achievement of their goals.

3. *Leadership is dependent upon value judgment in establishing priorities.* It involves decisions that affect programming, organizing, and shifting responsibilities. One could devote his entire time to "housekeeping" chores without being confronted with any decision making that would effect change in the school music program. A good music administrator must learn to choose what needs to be set aside as well as what should be pursued. This decision will be based on how he envisions his role as the music education leader in his community.

4. *The music administrator should serve as a catalyst to stimulate rather than inhibit the activities of all of those who are a part of the school music arena.* In this sense leadership becomes a function that provides the necessary interaction to promote change. Too many rules exist within departments that prohibit action rather than encourage initiative. Often teachers hesitate to suggest imaginative innovations for fear of

ridicule or disapproval from superiors. It is better to be critical of things not attempted than to be overly concerned about unsuccessful experiments.

5 *Change does not occur unless there is a disturbance or imbalance within the group.* Complacency is not conducive to change. The role of leadership requires that the music administrator or his supervisors shift the direction of balance so that a weakness in the program becomes a matter of concern or a source of disturbance to those involved. Those affected may then interact to restore the balance within the group and remove the cause of irritation.

For example, string programs have generally suffered in most communities. Where an active, interested school administrator has expressed a concern and a desire to ameliorate this situation, action has been taken to improve it. In most of these cases, strings were able to survive and even stronger programs were developed. In some instances the catalyst might be the personality of the teacher, but someone has to express concern and provoke the necessary imbalance in the existing structure if the program is to improve.

6. Finally, *the school music leaders should evaluate their own effectiveness in terms of how well they have achieved the established goals of the community, school, and staff while maintaining rapport and group support in relation to item 5.* In addition, is there evidence of growth and competency by teachers and members of the general staff? It is even conceivable that periodically the department might distribute a questionnaire to their staff which would enable their teachers to react without recrimination to current practices and services emanating from the central music office. Unless there are avenues for interaction, the music administration is not always aware of the true impact of its programs as they exist in the classroom.

In any music department, it is difficult for the level of performance to rise higher than the capacity of the individual in that department who carries the greatest authority, prestige, and influence. Competent individuals are seemingly unable to function at their best when, over long periods of time, they are frustrated and held down by weak leadership. It is for this reason that competent leadership is so crucial to the success of a music department.

THE NATURE OF
MUSIC ADMINISTRATION AND SUPERVISION

The nature and function of music administration and supervision will vary according to the size of the community, its goals and aspirations. It will also vary according to the place assigned to it by the current educational leaders. None of these items remains in a fixed position. The times and a changing society will alter them. Their position will be adjusted periodically according to the effectiveness of the school music program.

If one has a superintendent or chief administrator who feels that the entire focus of a particular program needs to be centered on "basic skills," then to maintain a successful, acceptable music program, the aims and objectives established for music will emphasize basic skill learning expressed in behavioral terms. In one junior high school electronic pianos were installed in a general music class to improve reading skills in music because the school had made a commitment to raise the general reading level of its student body under a government-funded program. Coordination of the eye and ear with tactile response contribute to better reading habits. Thus a valuable musical instrument was made available to the students. Numerous creative projects and musical learning experiments that went far beyond the original purpose of improving basic reading resulted from the acquisition of the electronic pianos.

Most communities both large and small are heterogeneous with homogeneous pockets. In larger communities the terms used may be "inner-city" or "outer-city." In rural areas there will be consolidated school districts and county systems. The function of the music program will differ even within these communities. This does not imply that one program is better than another because its function under certain circumstances is different. The music administration must respect and consider differences, whether they be ethnic, racial, or socio-economic. It must maintain a sufficiently flexible structure that will permit the music program in all parts of the community to grow and flourish under these diverse conditions rather than inhibit one area by imposing the attitudes of another upon them, unless they be beneficial to that area.

An inner-city area populated by Blacks may be more preoccupied with the "Black image" in music than a predominately white segment of the community. This need should be supported and given the utmost assistance. Although the degree of emphasis may differ, it does not exclude the predominately white area's responsibility to educate itself regarding the contribution made by Blacks to the total music scene. Here one must make a judgment as to degree of involvement. In the Appalachian areas of our country, there exists a rich "folk" culture that should be explored in a similar manner. Virtually every section of our country and every segment of our community could be given as a similar example.

There is also a direct relationship between the effectiveness of the school music program in the classroom and its relevance to the music that the students hear outside the school environment. This includes rock, soul, electronic, aleatoric, avante garde, etc. Sensitive music administrators must help teachers devise ways and programs for relating this music to the classroom experiences if the schools are ultimately to achieve the stated aim—to include the 80 percent of the student body that rejects "music education" in today's high schools.

In their positions of leadership, the music supervisors and directors must implement and facilitate the work carried on in the entire school program—the activities that contribute to the actual learning that occurs in the classroom. They must provide the necessary articulation between levels of instruction, across disciplines, between community and staff, and between staff and school administration. (When a social studies department in one community prepared a brochure commemorating Martin Luther King Day, the music department provided a section in the publication devoted to significant music in this man's life.) In many school systems, such as Parma, Ohio, Related Arts programs and Humanities programs were instituted because of impetus created by music departments.

The school music administrator and his supervisors represent music education as it is envisioned by the school administration, the professional staff, and the community—i.e., they are employed or promoted on the basis of how they appear to these people, and they are responsible to them. The music administrator becomes the unifying force for school music in his school system. Through proper processes, he gives the music program a unity of purpose that is so essential for growth and development within the schools.

To improve the instructional program, the music education leader will conduct or assist his supervisors in organizing in-service programs, meetings, clinics, and workshops. His major effort will be directed toward developing a better climate for music learning.

He will help formulate and set up procedures to review general policies and procedures relating to the music education department and the total staff and community. Working closely with the personnel department, the music director and his supervisors will assist in staffing the schools with competent personnel who will, in turn, carry out the objectives of the school music program in the classroom.

DELEGATING AUTHORITY

Too often music administrators find it convenient to devote much of their time to fulfilling perfunctory, routine duties. As indicated earlier, these matters may be handled by a competent individual who has had some experience in the mechanics of office and music department management. The chief music administrator must do much more. He must assume the responsibility for developing leadership and introducing innovations within his department. To do this he must indulge in creative, visionary thinking and be able to delegate to others routine responsibilities commensurate with their available time and capabilities. As a matter of fact, much of the process of school administration is based on the premise of delegated authority and responsibility. Incidentally, assignments should not be confined to routine clerical tasks. Others should have opportunities to delve into creative, expressive activities as well. This is one of the best means for developing leadership within a department.

Music supervisors need to devote most of their energies, efforts, and time to work in the field. They should work directly with teachers and students to facilitate learning and improve instruction. However, to be truly effective, they must also learn to delegate responsibility and authority in certain areas of planning instruction. When teachers are permitted to make decisions or share with supervisors in planning and organizing activities, they grow and develop leadership capabilities.

To be effective, delegated responsibility must be clearly defined and be accompanied by the necessary authority and support to carry out the assigned tasks. When the authority is granted, however, the music administrator must not be punitive in reprisal for error. If this occurs, it will inhibit future decision making. When an error in judgment occurs, correction should be treated as a matter of education rather than something requiring penalty. So often administrators are reluctant to delegate authority for fear that it will undermine their own position or reflect incompetency. This is an immature posture and reflects certain basic insecurities. The moment more than one person is involved in an activity, it is imperative that the others know their duties and responsibilities. Administrators must make it clear to supervisors what is expected of them and how decision making is empowered to them. They, in turn, must delegate similar responsibilities to their teachers. Some of these questions may be answered by previous behavior or custom. On the other hand, it may be necessary for the music administrator and his supervisors to delineate these responsibilities clearly. In any case, the delegation of responsibility should be primarily based on departmental needs and potential for growth and development. Delegation of authority and work not only releases valuable energy within the department but also raises the esteem of those in responsible positions in the eyes of their colleagues and staff.

On the other hand, insufficient delegation retards growth within the music department. When all power and responsibility are retained in the hands of the administrator, the supervisors feel neglected. No individual, regardless of his position, should strive to make the music department completely dependent upon him.

To assign tasks without providing the necessary authority is to remove the force that makes it possible to fulfill the responsibility. This is a serious error most often typical of administrators in high positions of authority who are fearful of diluting their own power. On occasion, no suitable person is available to assume a particular task. In such an instance, it is incumbent on the individual in charge to develop the personnel necessary to implement such a responsibility.

TITLES AND POSITIONS

The music administrator may hold a variety of titles, but regardless of the official one given him by a school system, if he is held responsible for the final decision from the music department, he is its chief administrator. Titles are mainly for identification purposes and will vary according to community size and salary schedules, which are constructed on work loads. In some instances, the official title will reflect the emphasis and significance that a particular community may hold for its music program.

Director of Music. In large systems or even small communities where the music program is held in high regard, the title, "Director of Music" is utilized. It conveys the image of full responsibility for the school music program. There may or may not be supervisors on the staff, depending upon the size and scope of the music program. However, whether it be a large staff or a single individual, the director is responsible for directing curriculum planning and all tasks expected of the titular head of the school's music program. (See Appendix A)

Supervisor of Music. This title implies direct contact with teachers and the classroom. In many cases, it is assigned to a special curricular area or a particular level of instruction—vocal supervisor, elementary string supervisor, etc. In such cases, there is usually a director to coordinate the activities of the supervisors, and the role of the supervisor is of a different nature. However, there are many communities that use the nomenclature of "Supervisor of Music" to identify their chief administrator in music. Here he is considered the "Director." (See Appendix A. p. 147)

Coordinator of Music. This individual may have the responsibilities of a supervisor or a director, but as a coordinator, he may lack the authority for implementing his decisions. Under these conditions, he acts more as a resource person or in an advisory capacity. He assists in coordinating music activities throughout the school system as well as coordinating music with other areas of instruction.

Department Head or Senior Music Teacher. Within a building it is sometimes necessary to coordinate and administrate the music responsibilities of the staff members. Where this occurs, a department head or senior teacher may be designated as the individual responsible for administering the music curriculum within that specific building. He may be an expert teacher with the personal qualifications necessary for administrative leadership, and in a small school system he may be the sole spokesman or administrator for music education in that community.

Consultant. This individual serves in a resource capacity and functions primarily on a "call" basis. He may prepare bulletins and guides to assist teachers, but he lacks the authority to make decisions that affect policy.

PERSONAL CHARACTERISTICS

In our current atmosphere, it is essential that school music administrators and supervisors take a look at themselves as "human beings." No longer can they hide behind a baton or seek cover under the mantle of "Musicianship." It is true that this is an essential element in their equipment, but since they are responsible figures representing the board of education's public image in music, they must be concerned about personal traits and attitudes. If they are to be effective in changing curriculum and improving instruction, they must be able to work with people. In fact, their effectiveness is directly related to their ability to communicate with staff, administration, and public. They must be as effective in human relations as they are in music. No longer can music educators dismiss incompetence and ignorance in other pertinent fields as being inconsequential in relation to their "special" skill. By the same token, they cannot appropriately make decisions affecting music, if they are not musical persons—people who think as musicians.

Enthusiasm for the task and its inherent responsibilities is of utmost importance if administrators and supervisors are to provide the leadership necessary for success. This is a contagious trait that can pervade an entire staff. Other essential elements for effective music administration are *sincerity and integrity.* The nature of the job requires that the individuals in charge be dependable and responsible. Staff and public must have confidence in their judgment and reliability. In addition, they must possess the energy, vitality, and stamina necessary to pursue their objectives and overcome obstacles that normally exist in all climates. They should be able to remain calm under pressure and recognize the impersonal nature of attacks that may be leveled at schools during periods of stress.

Music administrators should be friendly and enjoy working with people—all people. There is no place for prejudice or discriminatory practices in a school program. As a matter of attitude, music administrators should convey a feeling of accessibility for the benefit of the community, school, teachers, and students by maintaining an "open-door" policy.

Changing neighborhoods and changing communities require changing programs. There is no excuse for anyone's deferring to his prejudices. Music administrators need to possess a sufficient measure of empathy that will enable them to see beyond the superficial emotional responses that cause so many personal and personnel problems. They should never be in competition with their staff members and should be more than willing to share the limelight with them whenever possible. Too many directors and supervisors feel that unless they appear on every program, their image will suffer. There are appropriate times to do this, but if the opportunity is better suited for someone else, then the music administrators should be wise enough to step aside and permit the appropriate person or situation to take precedence.

No one administrator can possess all of the qualifications and all of the skills identified in a text. Administrators are human beings with human frailties. It is the purpose of this portion of the book merely to identify these skills and hope that the conscientious individual will constantly strive to improve himself.

As musicians, the music administrators should have exhibited a degree of competency in a single area of instruction or on an instrument. As individuals who are responsible for general planning and interpreting the total music education program to professional educators as well as to the general public, they should be articulate and skilled as public speakers. They should be informed about current educational practices and techniques.

They need to be well organized and to be able to organize the work of others. They should exhibit those qualities that command respect, and equally important is their respect for the dignity inherent in all people—students, teachers, parents, and others. One cannot command respect by virtue of a title or through the authority vested in a position. It is a quality that is earned through proper processes and through individual behavior. Enlightened administrators in today's schools must possess greater executive skills in coordination, delegation, planning, and communication. They must possess the essential knowledge of the administrative process.

COMMUNITIES AND ADMINISTRATION

The role of the music administrator will vary with communities, the scope and size of his music staff, and the nature of the school music program (self-contained, departmentalized, etc.). It would be unusual for any two situations to be alike. No formula or panacea can be offered to apply to every situation. Potential music administrators must be flexible and be able to adapt according to the community and the school situation.

All communities have aspirations for their schools, and each envisions a particular music program for its school population. This is actually the point of departure. This is where the enlightened music administrator begins. It is not his responsibility to reject these aspirations but to accept them and, through educative processes, effect desirable change. This brings about one of the major dichotomies in education. It is an acknowledged principle that no program remains stationary. The "status quo" is impossible and undesirable and yet, one builds on it. If it is undesirable in the eyes of competent leaders, then one must educate for change so that ultimately the community rejects undesirable goals and selects aims more appropriate for improved education.

Music administrators must therefore continually evaluate objectives and quality in a program to determine whether or not the school music program is actually fulfilling the needs of the student body. They must constantly strive to develop programs that will bring greater literacy and understanding of all music as a communicating art form, as well as create the climate for the necessary exposures that guide students to the enjoyment of and love for the aesthetics of music. But above all, the music administrator must be devoted to music as an art form and devoted to teaching as a profession.

THE SCHOOL ADMINISTRATOR'S DILEMMA*

If he's friendly with the clerical staff, he's a politician.
If he keeps to himself, he's a snob.

If he makes decisions quickly, he's arbitrary.
If he doesn't have an immediate answer, he can't make up his mind.

If he works on a day-to-day basis, he lacks foresight.
If he has long-range plans, he's a daydreamer.

If his name appears in the newspapers, he's a publicity hound.
If no one has ever heard of him, he's a nonentity.

If he requests a large budget, he is against economy.
If he doesn't ask for more money, he's a timid soul (or stark mad).

If he tries to eliminate red tape, he has no regard for the system.
If he insists on going through channels, he's a bureaucrat.

If he speaks the language of education, he's a cliché expert.
If he doesn't use the jargon, he's illiterate.

* Permission granted by Phi Delta Kappa from *Catcher in the Wrong*, edited by Billy L. Turney, published by F. E. Peacock Publisher, Inc., Itasca, Illinois, 1968.

If he's late for work in the morning, he's taking advantage of his position.
If he gets to the office on time, he's an eager beaver.
If the office is running smoothly, he is a dictator.
If the office is a mess, he's a poor administrator.
If he holds weekly staff meetings, he's in desperate need of ideas.
If he doesn't hold staff meetings, he doesn't appreciate the value of teamwork.
If he spends a lot of time with the board, he's a backslapper.
If he's never with the board, he's on his way out.
If he goes to conventions, he's on the gravy train.
If he never makes a trip, he's not important.
If he tries to do all the work himself, he doesn't trust anybody.
If he delegates as much as possible, he's lazy.
If he tries to get additional personnel, he's an empire builder.
If he doesn't want more assistants, he's a slave driver.
If he takes his briefcase home, he's trying to impress the board.
If he leaves the office without any homework, he has a sinecure.
If he enjoys reading this description, he's facetious.
If he doesn't think it's clever, well, he's entitled to his own opinion.

Wallace B. Appelson

Selected Articles For Supplementary Reading

BRIGGS, PAUL, "Arts Can Shatter Urban Isolation," *Music Educators Journal* (January, 1970).

KAPLAN, MAX, "Music in American Society, Introduction to Issues," *Music Educators Journal* (April, 1967), 43.

MENC-NEA, "Music in the School Curriculum," *Music Educators Journal* (November–December, 1965), 37.

WEERTS, RICHARD, "The Role of the Music Supervisor," *Music Educators Journal* (March, 1967), 49.

WHITE, HOWARD G., "The Professional Role and Status of Music Educators in the United States," *Journal of Research in Music Education,* I (Spring, 1967), 3.

Chapter 3

TRADITIONAL PATTERNS OF
ORGANIZATIONAL STRUCTURE
AND BEHAVIORS

LINE AND STAFF RELATIONSHIP

In the United States a specific, basic structure that is fairly uniform throughout all communities has been organized for school operations. This may seem to be a surprising statement since there are so many variants. However, one should not confuse this with the practice of delegating responsibility or vesting authority in different offices. The basic structure may vary according to the size of the school system and the attitudes of its administrators, but the major premise for the functioning of this structure is fairly fixed.

The organization of the structure is based on the concept that the *local community is responsible for the education of its inhabitants.* There are a series of checks and balances to see that this is properly done. To educate its young, the citizenry elects a board of education, which may bear other titles in other communities, but still has the responsibility for carrying out the education of its children according to the ideals and mandates of that community. The "board" in turn selects a superintendent who, as a professional educator, is responsible for carrying out and enforcing the board's objectives and programs. He also serves as an advisor to the board and assumes the role of leadership for education in the community.

At this point the entire structure functions on a staff and line relationship, which is designed to expedite learning and implement instruction in the classroom in accordance with the Superintendent's and the board's mandates. The larger and more complex the system, the greater the number of individuals involved in these staff and line relationships and responsibilities. This, in turn, contributes to a more bureaucratic type of operation which can, on occasion, inhibit instruction and learning.

It is important that a creative, sensitive music administrator understand this structure so that he does not allow it to frustrate his efforts and those of his teachers. Instead, he will work within it to revise and change it when possible so that it does not impede education and learning. The line and staff relationships are arteries of communication, and administrators must be careful to see that these arteries do not harden or become inflexible. They will recognize that the arteries form a complex social system which is to be analyzed and studied in order to understand the individual behaviors that occur.

This does not imply that protocol is not observed or that it is ignored. It must be observed. What is implied is that a successful music administrator must assess the nature of the structure and determine its strengths and weaknesses. There are advantages and disadvantages to the staff and line organization. It does indicate where responsibility and authority lie. It shows at which level one is responsible for consultant status and to whom, and at which point the administrator has the authority for decision making. Needless to say, these decisions are always subject to review from line and staff relationships that exist above.

It is generally accepted in principle that staff members have expertise in special areas to assist and advise those on the line organization. A staff member's assignment is generally based on his expert knowledge in a special subject area or special field of the school operation. Though individuals on the line structure are empowered with varying degrees of decision making, they are dependent on staff individuals to assist in these decisions and to supply them with appropriate know-how and information.

On paper the line and staff type of organization appears to be rather rigid in its structure. One must remember that within each group there are sub-systems comprised of human beings and that when dealing with this structure, one is involved not only with the behavior of individuals but with the behavior of groups as well. With the stress on rapid change and technological advancement, it is of utmost importance that an internal environment be created in the total system that will enable the participants to grow according to their own unique capabilities and capacities and to prevent their feeling like pawns on a computer card. Unless this exists within the organization or music department, the organization itself cannot grow and deal effectively with the unpredictable changing environment outside it—the community. In addition, it is equally important that optimum cooperative relationships be developed between line and staff relationships as well as between the various subgroups that form within the individual departments. If a department of music or a total organization is to be effective, it is essential that competition between these groups become a matter of cooperation and collaboration rather than a source of anxiety.

On occasion "change" may be initiated by revising the line and staff

A TYPICAL LARGE CITY EDUCATIONAL STRUCTURE

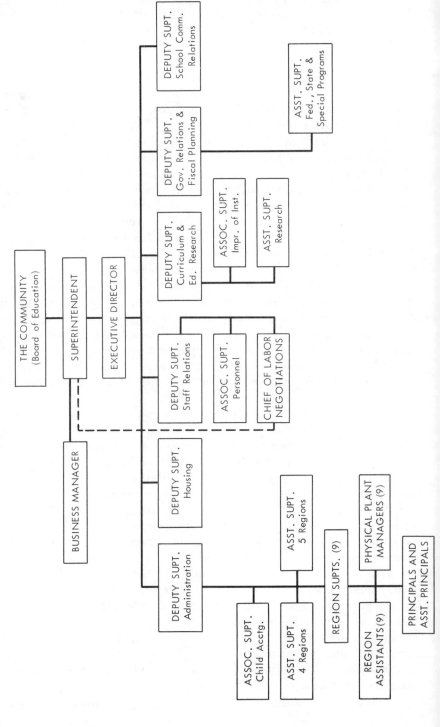

ORGANIZATION OF THE OFFICE
FOR IMPROVEMENT OF INSTRUCTION

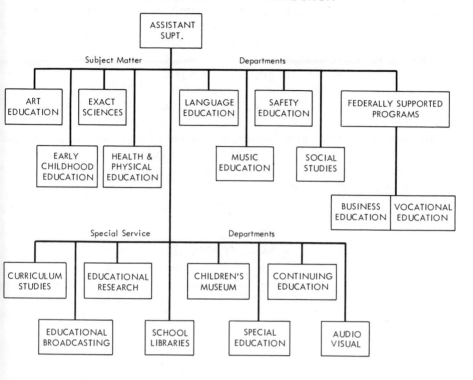

THE DEPARTMENT OF MUSIC EDUCATION

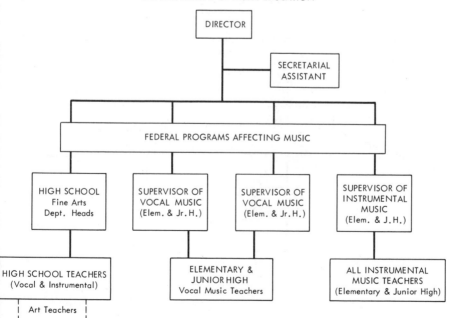

relationships under the euphemism of "reorganization." However, merely rearranging the boxes is meaningless unless responsibilities and roles are actually altered. Reorganization means utilizing an individual's competencies to better advantage or reeducating him for another task in which he may have a better potential for success.

Robert Roy in his book, *The Administrative Process*, identifies a third organizational relationship, "the functional executive." This individual is similar to a staff member in that he possesses special expertise, but he also functions as a line individual over his particular domain. Thus an assistant superintendent in charge of curriculum presides over all of the various subject areas which, in turn, function on a staff relationship with him. (See pages 26 and 27.)

A TYPICAL SMALL SCHOOL STRUCTURE

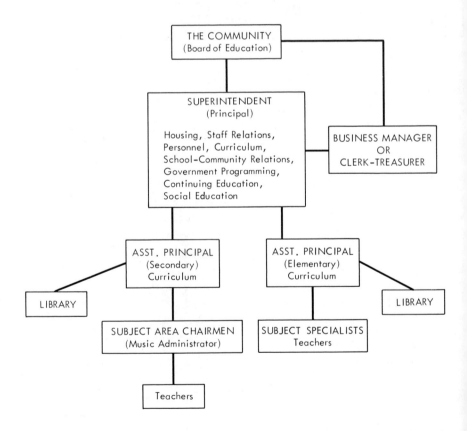

Most competent educators are sensitive to the needs of their school system. They will assist, when properly approached, in bending the structure where obstacles impede instruction and progress. For this reason alone, music administrators must be aware of the nature of the organizational structure and its function. Like all elements in education, this method of operation must be constantly evaluated and subjected to reorganization wherever it is in the interest of better education.

Today strict line and staff organization is being abandoned. Means are being devised to involve much more participation from those outside the line and staff structure. Programs of activity are being organized around those directly concerned with the activity. This includes parents, pupils, community and civic agencies, etc. The chart itself merely represents a hierarchy of authority.

In smaller communities, responsibilities will be combined and placed under the aegis of a single office. There may be fewer individuals involved, thus reducing the staff and line operation. However, someone must assume or be assigned the authority for each of the areas designated on the charts. They may be combined into departments or assigned to other areas of the operation, but the need for assuming responsibility for these duties exists in every school system. (See page 28.)

IDENTIFYING THE RESPONSIBILITIES OF THE CHIEF MUSIC ADMINISTRATOR: DIRECTOR OF MUSIC EDUCATION

The specific duties that a music administrator may assume will again vary according to communities and the significance they attach to their music program. However, if the music administrator is to assume a position of leadership and be effective in bringing about necessary changes that improve instruction, he will wish to assume responsibility for as many items listed as possible. His effectiveness may then be determined by the manner in which he arrives at his decisions as well as the degree of progress that he is able to attain in these areas:

1. Providing leadership and advice to the school system regarding the organization and content of the music education course offerings.

2. Developing and coordinating, under the appropriate assistant superintendent, the program of instruction designed to carry out the aims and objectives of the school music curriculum. (In smaller communities it might be a principal.)

3. Advising and assisting in the selection and placement of teachers of music in the schools.

4. Providing leadership in organizing and carrying out in-service training programs for the professional staff.

5. Recommending an appropriate budget for the total music program—equipment, supplies, all instruments, books, audio-visual materials, music, maintenance, etc.

6. Establishing the necessary liaison between the schools, the professional organizations, and the cultural agencies that exist in the community.

7. Maintaining proper evaluating procedures with the aim of improving and refining the school music program.

8. Serving as a central clearing house for concert dates; arrange schedule for in-school as well as out-of-school programs, community engagements, etc.

9. Assisting in planning for new buildings and future programs.

10. Organizing city-wide or county-wide programs.

The manner in which a music administrator pursues these responsibilities may have considerable bearing on how successful he is in accomplishing his goals. Success cannot be measured by how fast reforms are instituted, but rather by how long they remain in practice. Thus, if changes are to have a significant effect in school music programs, the process is as important as the idea itself.

IDENTIFYING THE RESPONSIBILITIES
OF THE MUSIC SUPERVISOR

As curriculum specialists, supervisors work more often in direct contact with teachers and students. The effectiveness of supervisors, like directors, is determined by their ability to work with people and instill confidence in their ability to assist. Although they are on a staff relationship with the director, they assume a line position with the teachers under their guidance and service.

Supervisors have the following responsibilities:

1. To assist the director in his role as an instructional leader by serving as a consultant to him and providing the necessary advice and guidance in their specific areas of competence.

2. To provide leadership for teachers in curricular matters.

3. To implement and improve instruction in the classroom.

4. To assume responsibility for coordinating specific areas of instruction, such as elementary instrumental music, general music in the junior high school, etc.

5. To assume leadership roles in developing guides and special programs under their jurisdiction.

6. To assume specific responsibilities identified by the director.

7. To assist in developing and maintaining an educational philosophy that aims to involve all segments of the community—teacher, pupils, parents, and school administrators.

TYPES OF ADMINISTRATORS

Administrators, both directors and supervisors, function in many ways to achieve their aims and goals. There is no one approach to deal with all problems. There are as many different ways to deal with them as there are individuals. These approaches will, of necessity, vary with the personality of the individual and the situation with which he is confronted. However, it is obvious that one cannot teach democratic attitudes with undemocratic procedures. On the other hand, music, by the very nature of the art form, is not always democratic. In classical forms and ensemble performances, someone has to determine musical interpretation and musical values. A conductor makes autocratic decisions on the podium, but matters change when he leaves his baton for an administrator's pen. This is the dilemma of music and ensemble performance. It often leads to misinterpretation on the part of music educators. However, we must not confuse lasting changes that affect long-range attitudes with those activities that demand immediate musical judgment. Change can only be realized through careful planning and by involving many people, even those with conflicting ideas.

Music administrators may be divided into four categories. First, there is the authoritarian who relies on his personal power and position. He justifies his actions by the speed in which decisions can be implemented and programs instituted. It matters not whether these ideas are generally accepted and will be continued after "the authority" is gone. The other extreme is the second type of administrator who is completely "permissive" in his approach to problem solving. Rather than make a decision for which he may be held responsible, he will form a *committee*. (This was typical of the attitude of administrators that prevailed in the 1950s.) Committees that are properly constituted with purposeful objectives are useful, but they cannot be substituted for decision-making responsibilities.

The third type of administrator is one who is complacent and happy, "having arrived." He may best be described as one who subscribes to a *laissez faire* policy. It isn't that he objects to change, but having achieved success in past programs, "why change?" This kind of administrator is impervious to the changing character of our society and the world around us.

The fourth type of administrator is the democratic administrator who consults and confers, yet is willing to accept responsibility for decisions. He believes in the democratic process and pursues it. He is one who is able to interpret and assess group response and is able to act accordingly. When change is necessary, he is willing to educate staff and citizenry so that there is a better climate for effective change and a measure of stability. He attempts to bring expertness, wherever it may be, to bear on the making of decisions in music that are crucial to the greatest number of people or the most needy.

Selected Articles For Supplementary Reading

BROUDY, HARRY S., "Educational Theory and the Music Curriculum," *Music Educators Journal* (November–December, 1964), 32.

CRONIN, JOSEPH M, "The Principal's Role in Change," *The Bulletin of the National Association of Secondary School Principals,* XLVII, No. 283 (May, 1963), 29.

GRIFFITH, FRANCES, "Six Mistaken Meanings of Democratic Administration," *Phi Delta Kappan* (October, 1966), 59.

PICERNO, CINVENT, "The Need for Elementary School Music Teachers in New York State," *Journal of Research in Music Education* (Fall, 1966), 21.

"School Administrators—Lip Service is Disservice Without Action," *Music Educators Journal* (January, 1970), 52.

STANTON, ROYAL, "A Look At The Forest," *Music Educators Journal,* (November, 1966), 37.

"Statements by City Superintendents," *Music Educators Journal* (January, 1970), 52.

Chapter 4

DESIGNING AND PLANNING CURRICULA

The primary function of the school music administration is to develop and improve instruction, and this can best be accomplished through the area of curriculum. One should not construe this to mean the guides or the courses of study that are published by a Board of Education, but rather the on-going experiences offered a child that enable him to grow and develop in a school environment. The guides or courses of study are merely intended as written guidelines which will assist the teacher in developing the experiences he offers in his classroom. With this in mind, curriculum planning is defined as organizing the content to be used purposefully by the school as a stimulus to learning. The guides then become means toward an end and not ends themselves.

In a broad sense, the term curriculum encompasses the instructional activities planned and offered to students which are based on "planned interaction of pupils with instructional *content,* instructional *resources,* and instructional *processes* for the attainment of educational objectives."[1] To further illustrate these relationships the U.S. Department of Health, Education and Welfare has prepared the design that appears on page 34.[2]

A curriculum that provides for all children must offer a variety of opportunities that enable each child to be selective. It must include experiences which will prepare students for the remaining years in this century as well as those of the next; yet at the same time, it cannot overlook the significant musical contributions that have preceded these years.

---

[1] Dale Chismore and John F. Putnam, eds., *Standard Terminology For Curriculum and Instruction in Local and State School Systems* (Washington, D.C., U.S. Department of Health, Education, and Welfare, 1970), p. 2.

[2] *Ibid.,* p. 2.

SOME ASPECTS OF CURRICULUM AND INSTRUCTION
AND THEIR INTERRELATIONSHIPS

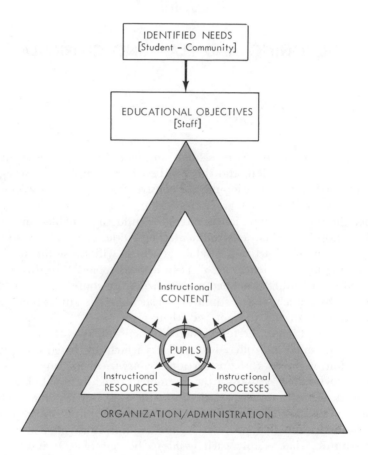

To introduce changes in the curriculum, the music administrators must structure a design based on the following five steps:

1. Determining the objectives for the new curriculum (based on student needs)
2. Developing a program of instruction
3. Implementing or developing instructional procedures and strategies for the new program
4. Preparing instructional materials
5. Evaluating both program and its instruction in keeping with its objectives

A DESIGN FOR CURRICULUM CHANGE

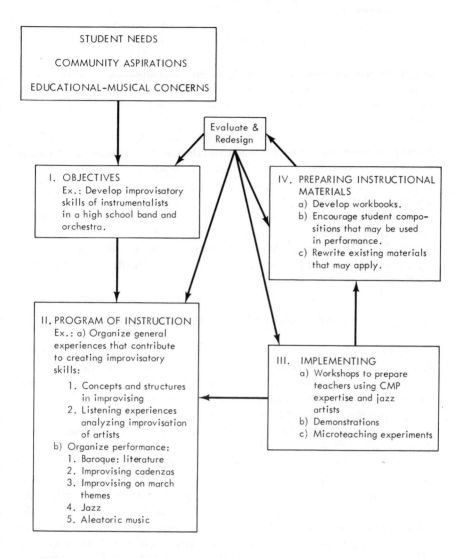

When a music administrator functions in this manner, he truly becomes an architect designing future music programs for the curriculum.

STANDARDIZING INFORMATION AND TERMINOLOGY REGARDING CURRICULUM AND INSTRUCTION

As it becomes more and more feasible for smaller districts and school systems to combine efforts to utilize modern technology—computers, systems, etc.—more economically, it is evident that some standardization in recording and reporting is necessary. The U.S. Department of Health, Education, and Welfare has published a handbook (referred to earlier), "The Standard Terminology for Curriculum and Instruction in Local and State School Systems," to facilitate this development. In addition, by standardizing terminology, the office hopes to improve decision-making capabilities in all areas of administration, guidance, curriculum, and instruction.

With standardization in terminology, researchers and others requiring information regarding curricular matters will be able to utilize automatic data systems for faster or more accurate service. Equally important is the need to convert many of our procedures from hand processing to automatic data processing, and it may be easier to convert if we can adopt a standard classification and terminology. To show how this might function, references in this chapter will include the classification number as it exists in the current "Standard Terminology" publication for music (12.00 00 00 00) issued by the U.S. Department of Health, Education, and Welfare.

FORCES INFLUENCING CURRICULAR CHANGE

Curricular concerns will vary from community to community. There is no set pattern. Chamberlain and Kindred in their textbook, *The Teacher and School Organizations,* identify the forces that shape these demands. They are as follows: 1) Custom and Tradition, 2) Textbooks, 3) Pressure Groups, 4) Philanthropic Foundations, 5) Colleges and Universities, 6) Mass Media, 7) Public Opinion, 8) Government Legal Requirements, 9) Professional Influences.[3]

It would be a comforting thought if music administrators could believe that "professional influences" were the dominating factor in shaping the curriculum. Unfortunately, the history of the schools has proven otherwise. Actually, no one single force is fully responsible for what is taught in a school. Rather than despair, the competent administrator will work directly and vigorously with all of these forces to bring about the changes necessary for an effective curriculum. His constant goal should be the ultimate achievement of music and music education as a part of the core curriculum. It must offer opportunities for musical experiences for all children based on their interest and ability.

In this period when segments of the public are concerned about whether or not education of uniform quality is being offered throughout a community, we cannot assure them of this as long as music is regarded

[3] Leo M. Chamberlain and Leslie W. Kindred, *The Teacher and School Organizations.* (4th Edition) (Englewood Cliffs: Prentice-Hall, Inc., 1966), p. 286–94.

as a "piecemeal elective." Until music, or at least a fine arts subject, is required for graduation, some students will have exposure to music throughout their school life and others will have virtually none. Until music is taught as a comprehensive art form, even those enrolled in music courses or organizations cannot be assured of uniform quality since, unfortunately, much instruction is mechanical—learning to perform in an orchestra, band or chorus. Our persistent focus in all music classes should be to develop a comprehensive knowledge of music. Students should learn to think and react musically in a musical situation. Every administrator must keep this goal foremost in planning curricula.

"Custom and Tradition" determine the conventional curricular offerings and are a reflection of past attitudes. According to some educators, it takes approximately fifty years for a new, worthwhile idea to permeate the entire educational system of this country. Its greatest deterrent or resistance may come from the forces of "Custom and Tradition." On the other hand, these forces have helped preserve some of the desirable aspects of a curriculum that might otherwise have been eliminated. (In Cleveland Heights they preserved a strong orchestra program. In Detroit special teachers were retained in music during the post-World War II period while the rest of the large cities moved to self-contained classrooms.) One has to distinguish between those attitudes that interfere with progress and those that protect desirable programs.

"Textbooks," by their content, can determine the direction that a curriculum may take. It is true that a textbook is only a resource tool or teaching aid in the hands of a teacher, but it does assist in providing the necessary content and information upon which instruction is so often structured. It can be an asset or a deterrent to good instruction. In this manner textbooks and textbook publishers too often play a major role in controlling the content of a course of study. A competent administrator will give appropriate direction to avoid this pitfall.

Today there are many books available on the market to meet the changing needs of most educational situations. However, Departments of Education are depending more and more on developing their own supplementary materials to provide immediate solutions to imminent crises. (For example, an "Afro-American Song Book" was prepared by the Detroit Board of Education because there was insufficient material in the current basic series. In San Antonio, units on Mexican-American music and art were prepared by enterprising teachers.)

Textbooks are improving and one can find ample, varied material in every series. Even the learning sequences are similarly structured so that it becomes a matter of individual taste regarding a particular feature of one book rather than that of another.

Too often a selected textbook determines the curriculum. In reality the reverse should be true. The educational philosophy of the community and the needs of the students should determine the choice of the textbook. It is the music administrator's responsibility to see that this occurs through democratic procedures. These procedures will be discussed in Chapter IV, "Improving Instruction."

"Pressure Groups" can be a positive as well as a negative force. Although they invariably represent a vociferous minority, they are effective because the majority of people are apathetic about curriculum and curricula reform. In the case of desirable change, they can help arouse the apathetic majority and their enthusiasm can be utilized, if done so judiciously.

One of the critical challenges of school administration is the manner in which it is able to deal with "pressure groups," both positive and negative. The perceptive administrator is able to distinguish between pressure and a genuine need which could be emanating from a basic community concern. The current emphasis in the school curriculum on Afro-American studies was a direct response to pressure, and the result of a long-neglected need. In this instance, needed curricular reform was actually initiated and supported by outside pressure groups in many of the nation's large cities.

Many school systems can point to cultural and community pressures as the source of their fine music programs, whereas others may have succumbed to pressures that have virtually eliminated basic music instruction because of short-sighted goals. Incidentally, it has usually been more difficult to eliminate a successful music program, based on substantial learning experiences, than one that has all the characteristics of a "frill."

There are over one hundred "philanthropic foundations" that are concerned with education. Almost all of them are non-profit, privately endowed organizations that are seriously committed to improving public welfare and education. They have stimulated a great deal of experimentation in new courses and developing new concepts.

The programs supported and developed by foundations have influenced many new directions and initiated curriculum reform. In Dearborn, Michigan, at the Edsel Ford High School, an entire humanities approach through the English curriculum was initiated as a result of a study funded by the Ford Foundation.

Published reports such as the Rockefeller Panel Report on *The Performing Arts; Problems and Prospects* have caused communities and school systems to appraise their own role in the arts. Other reports of a similar nature have forced schools to examine and revise their programs.

Through admission requirements "colleges and universities" have exerted considerable influence on the school curriculum—often at the expense of the arts. This is changing, and music educators need to keep informed regarding which college and universities seek students with a balanced education. Much of the confusion regarding entrance requirements is a result of misinformation and anxiety over admissions.

Most high schools belong to accrediting associations, which are administered by the colleges and universities in that region. In this manner the higher education institutions have played a significant role in determining class sizes, teacher qualifications, and materials utilized in instruction. Many outstanding high school programs are a direct result of institutional experiments by university scholars.

"Mass Media" has had a tremendous impact on influencing curricular change. Marshall McLuhan in his book, *Understanding Media: The Extensions of Man,* indicates that the whole nature of education is changing as a result of the tremendous developments in mass communication.

The arts have especially benefited from these developments. Artists and fine musical organizations can now be a part of one's evening at home and provide entertainment of the highest caliber. There is much more information and knowledge available to students today as a result of the accessibility of fine music through these media. Educators are still trying to determine how the media can be put to its most constructive use.

"Public Opinion" is probably the most potent force to offset undesirable pressure groups. In the final analysis, it is the public that has the last word in curricular reform. It controls the nature and content of the curriculum through its governing body, the Board of Education, and through its chief employee, the superintendent. Failure to comply or to understand the role of public opinion has led to many of the difficulties that schools find themselves in today. It is, therefore, essential that the public and the school administration educate themselves to properly interpret the weight and implications expressed by public opinion.

"Legal Requirements" generally stem from recommendations by State Boards of Education or State Legislatures. It is recognized that states have the right to legislate regarding content in certain areas of the curriculum. Unfortunately, they do not see the total responsibility and often act under the influence of "pressure groups" or vested interests. This militates against fine arts programs that may still be regarded as peripheral rather than as core subjects. On the other hand, state boards of education can be effective in retaining balanced programs by lobbying for legislation against such imbalances, if they recognize the values inherent in the humanities.

By far the most significant of the forces affecting changes can be the "professional influences." It is a truism that change in a school curriculum can be implemented only as far or as fast as the other eight forces, previously mentioned, will support this program. It is therefore, the professional educator's responsibility to assume leadership in working with all of these forces to bring about the desired changes.

There are other professionals in the school structure—superintendent, principals, etc.—who will also determine the nature and emphasis of music in a school program. If a superintendent or the curriculum director of a school system is interested in developing a music program, then the chances for success are far better than if they are opposed.

Other professional agencies, such as the Music Educators National Conference, the American String Teachers Association, American Bandmasters Association, etc., can also serve as pressure groups to bring about desirable changes where music programs are in difficulty. In addition, they help to call attention to and to support worthwhile projects which contribute to the improvements of curriculum. Wendell C. Allen, Assistant Superintendent for certification in the State of Washington, in his *Statement of Standards For Preparation of School Professional Personnel Teaching to Certification,* April 1968, Fourth Draft, advocates that professional organizations be involved in determining competencies for music teachers. It was coincidental that the release of this statement appeared at a time when the Music Educators National Conference's Commission on Teacher Education was preparing a competency statement for teachers of music. However, it is evidence of a trend which may or may not have been a direct result of activity initiated by the Conference. Full scores are now fairly standard with publications but they came only after a concerted effort on the part of the American String Teachers Association and the various band associations, who insisted that they be made available.

A successful music administrator will be sensitive and aware of all of these forces in working to bring about effective change. He will not rely solely on any one of them but utilize and fuse as many elements as the situation warrants.

An effective curriculum assists and somewhat assures the child of continuous, sequential musical growth through a comprehensive, balanced instructional program. The offerings should reflect the attitudes and philosophy of the music staff, the administration, and the community. The courses should include consideration for the interests as well as the needs of all of the students. To be so structured, it must be developed cooperatively, remain flexible, and be sufficiently open to invite scrutiny and study by all groups that influence change.

CHANGING THE CURRICULUM

Musical learnings are the responsibility of the whole school. They cannot be assigned to one teacher and forgotten by the others. Education in music begins in the pre-school years and continues until the student graduates from high school; it does not come about as the result of a course in the junior high school years. It is, rather, the product of everything musical that happens in twelve or thirteen years of schooling, indeed of everything musical that happens throughout a life-time.[4]

Only the administrator of the total school music program is in a position to see the complete continuum and plan for it. It is not something that just happens. It is a direct result of careful planning and direction.

To develop a curriculum with this concept requires the involvement of many people. Leadership roles need to be assigned at virtually every level of the sequence if a careful, well-conceived plan is to be developed.

J. Floyd Trump and Dorsey Baynham in their text, *Focus On Change,* indicate that *change* is now an accepted part of the school scene. If effective plans with appropriate objectives can be developed, enlightened administrators should be sympathetic to proposed, constructive revisions in the school curriculum and assist in the process. They need not fear change.

There are two types of change which concern the curriculum, *change in human behavior* and *instructional change* or *change* in content. Change in curriculum should not be confused with merely improving instruction. To some, curriculum improvement may mean merely changing certain subject emphasis without changing fundamental goals or course structure. To change the curriculum one must change the way one perceives the entire structure. It means changing the goals and even changing the processes.

The most difficult, yet the most effective, change occurs when a teacher, especially an experienced one, changes the way he has been conducting his music class for years. As indicated earlier, the Contemporary Music Project of the MENC-Ford Foundation has done much to effect both forms of change through its Composers-In-Residence program and its focus on Comprehensive Musicianship.

The curriculum should reflect contemporary knowledge of the subject area if it is to be regarded as both relevant and valid. Although there has been much abuse of the term "relevance," it can be generally applied to an idea that has widespread applicability and is in touch with the social and cultural realities of the community. This principle assists in establishing the relative importance of ideas in the study of music. One of the concerns that a music administrator is confronted with when determining the validity of the curricular offerings is the extent to which they reflect the music of all times, utilizing contemporary techniques and

---

[4] Karl Ernst and Charles Gary, eds., *Music In General Education* (Washington, D.C.: MENC, 1965), p. 9. Permission granted by the *Music Educators National Conference.*

knowledge. He must also ascertain what implications exist for learning values in a social and cultural setting. The emphasis, of course, is altered with the passing of time and changes in the social and cultural milieu.

MUSIC IN GENERAL EDUCATION (12.01 00 00 00)[5]

Music in general education, more commonly referred to as "general music" (12.01 00 00 00), is the core of the entire music program. It is the trunk of the tree with the various "special" organizations serving as branches. It should pervade the entire program. Because it does not receive the attention and acclaim afforded special groups, the general program in music is often slighted, but no concerned administrator will permit it to suffer. As the core offering in the entire program, it should provide for every child interested in music.

BALANCING THE "SPECIAL" PROGRAMS
TEACHING COMPREHENSIVELY

The vocal (12.04 00 00 00)[6] and instrumental (12.05 00 00 00)[7] organizations in a school system are the performance-oriented offerings in the music program. Although within the context of each one there should be appropriate allocations of time devoted to general music education, the motivating force of special groups culminates in a performance. This does not negate the teacher's responsibility to teach music in the comprehensive sense of developing musical understanding. Incidentally, one doesn't just teach comprehensive musicianship. It is a *way* of teaching that is reflected in musical response from the students. Too often music educators try to categorize comprehensive musicianship into specific activities and compartments such as composing (organizing sounds), analyzing, and performing. This compartmentalization is merely the means toward developing students who think and respond in musical situations as musicians. Comprehensive musicianship actually involves every musical activity. It is evident in the way students react in musical situations. The music administrator must be constantly alert to see that comprehensive musicianship is carried out in the schools under his jurisdiction, whether he works through his supervisors or in direct contact with the individual teachers.

To do this the music administrator must attend concerts in schools regularly. He must be firm in his conviction of the importance of this

---

[5] Dale Chismore and John F. Putnam, eds., p. 208.

[6] *Ibid.,* p. 208.

[7] *Ibid.,* p. 209.

task. Incidentally, this type of learning, "comprehensive musicianship," can be accomplished through a variety of music and under many different types of performances. As long as there is evidence, whether it be in performance or in a classroom of students being exposed to experiences that lead to comprehensive knowledge, the medium itself is not of prime importance.

In one school system it was the practice of the director of music education to review with the department heads and directors the contents of programs that were performed each year. A chart was prepared and the degree of representation from the various periods and styles performed was discussed to determine if the music was truly representative of all periods in music history. It proved to be a successful device for making teachers aware of historical imbalance in programming and focused on where they placed their musical emphasis or preferences. This is only one aspect of responsibility to the complete totality of music assumed by the music administrator. County school music administrators and supervisors —in fact, every teacher—should check their programming in a similar way.

If educators are to accommodate individual tastes and preferences, it is mandatory that schools maintain a variety of performing groups. Incidentally, to do this there must be some orderly procedure that provides information regarding students as they move from building to building, from grade level to grade level. Too often students are lost in transfer because no one has prepared the necessary organizational steps. This is really a clerical, administrative procedure, which, if not followed, can undermine a well-planned program. (See Appendix I.)

But even more significant is the responsibility that the chief administrator has to see that no one special area suffers because of a lack of interest or inertia on the part of the faculty. He must constantly strive to strengthen every facet of the special program where needed, whether it be orchestra (12.05 02 00 00),[8] band (12.05 01 00 00),[9] chorus (12.04 01 00 00),[10] or small ensemble (12.05 03 00 00).[11] Opportunities to participate in each of these musical organizations should be available at every grade level beyond the established starting point to accommodate a student's legitimate interests in performing music. The music administrator, from his position of authority, is in the best position to see that this is accomplished.

A balanced curriculum in the secondary schools includes special

[8] Chismore and Putnam, eds., p. 209.
[9] *Ibid.*, p. 209.
[10] *Ibid.*, p. 208.
[11] *Ibid.*, p. 209.

courses in music theory (12.03 00 00 00),[12] music literature and music history (12.02 00 00 00).[13] They need not be separate entities but may be combined under the aegis of one or two combinations of these titles. As indicated earlier, these elements are fundamental to "comprehensive musicianship" and are taught in all music offerings. However, I am referring to special offerings that place particular emphasis on these subjects. It is as much the administration's responsibility to see that provisions are made for these classes as for the others.

Related arts or humanities programs (12.07 00 00 00)[14] may not fall under the aegis of the music program, but if they do not exist in a community, the music administrator should assume leadership in initiating such programs. Where they exist he should maintain an active role in enriching them. He should work with the art department, the language arts department, the drama department, and the social studies department to see that music's role in the humanities is properly presented. But even more significant, he and his colleagues need to see that the humanities permeate the entire curriculum, grades one through twelve.

Any course that will add a new dimension to the school music program should be considered and investigated (12.99 00 00 00).[15] Creative thinking and imagination will vitalize the curriculum and stimulate enthusiasm. In Wichita, Kansas, it was a piano-mobile; in Philadelphia it was organs, percussion instruments in the elementary schools, and electronic synthesizers in the junior high schools; in Cleveland a supplementary education center for the arts was developed. Detroit began preschool violin programs, elementary troubador harp programs, and electronic organ programs in junior high schools in inner-city areas of the city. Arkansas was able to send professional ensembles all over the state, particularly through rural areas by means of a trailer equipped for such presentations. All of these programs were the creations of imaginative teachers and administrators, who were willing to be embarrassed by an occasional failure rather than be so careful that they failed to introduce or permit any innovation at all.

Selected Articles For Supplementary Reading

BABCOCK, CHESTER D., "The Emerging Role of the Curriculum Leader" in *ASCD 1965 Yearbook,* ed. Evelyn F. Carlson.

---

[12] *Ibid.,* p. 208.
[13] *Ibid.,* p. 208.
[14] *Ibid.,* p. 209.
[15] *Ibid.,* p. 209.

EISMAN, LAWRENCE, "Teaching The Difficult General Music Class," *Music Educators Journal* (November, 1966), 51.

FROUDE, VELMA, "Not Only Little Angels Play the Harp," *Music Educators Journal* (October, 1969), 37.

GARY, CHARLES, "Curriculum Handbook for School Administrators." Ch. 9 (Reprint) *Music Educators National Conference,* Washington, D.C.

HAGEMANN, VIRGINIA S., "Are Junior High Students Ready for Electronic Music?" *Music Educators Journal* (December, 1969), 35.

JIPSON, WAYNE R., "The Other Eighty-Five Percent," *Music Educators Journal* (January, 1969), 35.

Music Educators Journal (November, 1968) entire issue on Electronic Music.

Music Educators Journal (November, 1969) entire issue on "Rock" Music.

ROSENBLOOM, PAUL, ed., *Modern Viewpoints in the Curriculum,* New York: McGraw-Hill Book Company, 1964, 103.

SAND, OLE, "Bases for Decision" in *ASCD 1965 Yearbook,* ed. Evelyn F. Carlson.

SANIFORD, CLARENCE, "Music In General Education: Are High Schools Doing Their Part?" *Music Educators Journal* (April, 1969), 83.

SHEDD, MARK, "The Beat of American Youth," *Music Educators Journal* (September, 1968), 30.

THOMPSON, WILLIAM, "New Math, New Science, New Music," *Music Educators Journal* (February–March, 1967), 30.

WAGNER, GUY, "What Schools are Doing: Developing Elementary School Curriculum Guides," *Education,* LXXXVIII (April, 1968), 376.

WALLIS, JAMES, "Cleveland-Supplementary Center; It adds to the Arts *Music Educators Journal* (November, 1969), 41.

WENDRICH, KENNETH, "Music Literature in High School: The Yale Curriculum Development Project," *Music Educators Journal* (March, 1967), 35.

WOODWORTH, G. WALLACE, "Place of Music in the Curriculum," *Music Educators Journal* (February–March, 1965), 48.

Chapter 5

THE IMPROVEMENT OF
INSTRUCTION FOR CHANGE

There are many avenues available to a music administrator for improving instruction. In the previous chapter the curriculum was examined for this purpose. Another major area is the one dealing with personnel matters. It will be dealt with separately and in depth in Chapter 6. Other means for improving instruction are as follows:

1. In-Service training: workshops
2. Guides
3. Observing demonstration lessons
4. Textbook adoptions
5. Research and advanced study
6. Curriculum centers
7. Attending professional meetings
8. Microteaching

WORKSHOPS

No teacher training program can possibly prepare a teacher for every emergency or for every situation. In-service workshops serve two functions: 1) to inspire and challenge in the broad sense, 2) to deal with a specific problem.

Workshops should emanate out of the needs of teachers to improve instruction for pupils. They may be directed toward providing basic information that may or may not be readily available, or they may be organized to offer a fresh approach for a stagnant program. This principle applies even to those workshops that introduce new concepts, new materials, or new media. However, once it has been decided for whom the workshop is intended—a grade level, a special area, a system, or a single school—it then becomes the administrator and his staff's responsibility to set the machinery in motion. They need to organize committees, disseminate information publicizing the workshop, and notify those affected whether attendance is required or optional. Certain social amenities need to be observed if a guest is presenting the workshop, or even if it is entirely a local meeting. These little amenities are designed to set people at ease and may enhance the general atmosphere of the workshop.

Regardless of the nature of the workshop or institute, it is intended to change the behavior of the teacher in the classroom. The need may not originate with the music administrator or from his supervisors; it may come from a teacher's request or a pupil's concern. It may stem from a change in the nature of the school. It is the administration's responsibility, however, to be sufficiently sensitive to recognize the concern when it manifests itself and then proceed to act upon it.

How the workshop is organized will vary. Democratic procedures are generally the most acceptable. No single administrator should feel automatically compelled to assume full responsibility. Whether he is selecting a speaker or a clinician, others involved in the workshop should be consulted. Occasionally one sees or hears a speaker or a performance that is so compelling he must have it for his staff. This is the exception. Even under these circumstances, however, it helps to consult with those for whom the workshop is intended.

GUIDES OR COURSES OF STUDY

A music guide or course of study as defined here is a compilation of recommended music materials, methods, and experiences with suggestions which will aid the teacher in organizing and presenting them. Actually, the chief function of this printed material is to help teachers provide better learning experiences for children. In addition, however, guides are most helpful in providing printed information for new teachers or lay people who want to know about the school music program. Although the ones who learn most from a guide are those who prepare it, it is useful as a means of providing some assistance not only to all teachers but to administrators such as principals, curriculum coordinators, etc. All guides should contain the aims and objectives of the specific area for which they are prepared. They should reflect the current philosophy of the total school music program and should serve as guidelines and not directives. They are intended to free the teacher rather than impose uniformity. If a teacher is to plan musical, educational experiences for the needs of individual learners, he needs optimum freedom and flexibility to function within the governing principles dictated by the educational-musical philosophy of the school.

Guides and courses of study are intended to be informative and help-ful. They should be developed cooperatively and primarily by the people who will be using them. Often outside professional assistance may be required. Although the actual productive work will take place among the local personnel, committees are stimulated by the ideas of others. When this is done, the consultants should be informed as to their functions and specific purposes in appearing before a group so they may prepare the appropriate materials and ideas. When experts are given responsibility for directing the development in certain areas of the music guide, they should also be given the status of regular committee members; however, they should not be allowed to use their status of authority to dictate the program. In fact, a guide should never be dictated by the people in authority and handed down as "words from above."

The organization for developing the course of study will depend on the local situation. If the staff is small, it may operate largely as a com-mittee of the whole. If the teaching group is sizable, a division of labor may be effected through creation of subcommittees. Those in charge of recommending members for committees should be familiar with their personal characteristics, backgrounds, reactions to pupils, and educational ideals. A cooperative and open-minded attitude is a most desirable quality. The influence of members on the other personnel in the system is another important consideration since committees must have sufficient prestige among the faculty so that their work might be acceptable.

The music administrator should take the initiative in organizing committees and assist them in their preparation. The people who make up the study committee should represent as many points of view within the system as possible. However, they must be the kind of people who are not obstructionists and can resolve differences. There should be both men and women on the committees as well as representatives from various ethnic and religious groups. Administrators and curriculum specialists in the system should be included.

The committees may be organized several ways—by grade or school levels; by subject areas such as instrumental, general, vocal; or by specific types of activities within a subject area. It is desirable, however, that there be articulation of the work of all areas. In initiating a committee for a guide or course of study, the director must give each committee an adequate perception of its role in the total plan as well as a clear sense of direction and purpose.

All teachers should in some way be involved in the study. Although it is usually physically impossible as well as undesirable to assign all teachers to committees, there are activities to keep them aware of the need for continuous growth. Occasional group meetings can bring everyone together to hear important presentations, progress reports, and evaluation of accomplishments. A very large number of teachers can be used in experimental programs. All teachers can be urged to send in written comments and evaluations of the methods with which they are working, descriptions of their most successful activities and programs, and suggestions for new methods. Their reactions to grade placement of instructional units and their needs for textbooks, audio-visual aids, and creative materials can be quite valuable.

It is desirable that participation on these committees be rotated among the staff members, but continuity should be retained by overlapping some committee members. Some experts may be invited for one particular meeting, while others will be retained throughout the study.

The administrator or the supervisor concerned should help the committee by arranging for a suitable working environment and seeing that appropriate procedures for democratic interaction prevail. A member of the music administration usually serves as chairman but need not always do so. Because of the facilities available to him, it is helpful if a supervisor serves as chairman. However, he may offer the use of these facilities as a committee member even if a teacher acts as chairman. All guides should be considered tentative and be reviewed at least every five years.

Although they will vary in format, guides should include, in addition to the statement of philosophy, aims and objectives, a plan outlining the "scope and sequence" for the music course or the area being covered. Aims which are intended for the total program may be stated in broad, general terms. Objectives deal with specific programs and should be constructed so that they are established in terms of "behaviors" that can be identified and measured.

Specific suggestions and procedures for teaching activities are particularly useful for new teachers. Lists of resource materials, including supplementary song material, records, films, and other pertinent information should be included. Philip T. McClintock, in his unpublished dissertation,[1] prepared a "check list for the examination of curriculum guides in music" that may provide some direction when preparing or examining other guides in music. (See Appendix B.) All guides should be used at least one year experimentally before being put into their final publication form. In smaller communities, it is usually desirable to have a special committee just to edit the materials and supervise their publication. The editing committee is mainly concerned with achieving uniformity in the publication so that all teachers in the community may use

[1] Philip McClintock, *An Examination of Curriculum Guides in Music With Reference to Principles of Curriculum Planning,* unpublished dissertation (Bloomington: Indiana University, 1970), p. 99.

it easily. In larger school systems there is a publications department to oversee this final production.

When planning a guide, one should not overlook the possibility of its being used by school administrators and school officials. The guide can be an excellent aid in supplementing the efforts of the music administration in providing school principals with the information that they need to determine the scope of their school music offerings.

Improvement in instruction will not result automatically from the mere issuance of a new guide or course of study. Improvement occurs only as teachers develop better learning experiences for children. However, teachers who are genuinely interested in providing better experiences for their children can receive immeasurable assistance from well designed courses of study or guides.

OBSERVING DEMONSTRATION LESSONS

A most effective method for improving instruction is to have a teacher who might be having difficulty visit a classroom being taught by a successful music teacher in an analogous situation. The key word is *analogous*. Do not have the teacher observe a situation that is completely antithetical and expect a positive reaction. Visiting classes of successful teachers is especially useful to new teachers.

Since the visiting teacher may observe methods and techniques for teaching under actual "combat" conditions, it is much more convincing. It is helpful if the demonstrating teacher or supervisor is aware of the specific problem that concerns the visiting teacher. This will enable the demonstrator to focus on this problem when preparing his lesson. If there is no specific concern, the observing teacher should be given some background on what to expect and the nature of the lesson. Following the demonstration it is desirable to plan a conference between the teachers. This will give the observing teacher an opportunity to ask questions and gather additional information that might be of assistance.

Another type of demonstration lesson is one that is planned by the administration to introduce new procedures, new equipment, new materials, or new guides. These lessons are given to large groups of teachers and may be presented by an outstanding teacher, a visiting clinician, or a member of the supervising staff. A guide may be introduced at several buildings by members of the workshop who helped develop it. (Video tapes and specially prepared "microteaching" excerpts are also of immeasurable value in this type of situation. They will be discussed as a separate item later in this chapter.)

It is more effective if the need for the latter type of demonstration emanates from the teachers. However, it may be incumbent upon the administrator to initiate such a program because of changes and developments occurring through action taken by the administrative authorities in a school system. (When the Detroit Board of Education decided to change to non-graded primary units in the elementary schools, not only was it necessary to retrain the elementary classroom teachers but in addition music specialists needed to readjust to teaching music to this type of school grouping. Numerous demonstration lessons were given by supervisory personnel and outstanding teachers in the specific buildings where this change was introduced.)

Observation visits need not be confined to the local school system. Teachers should be encouraged to visit neighboring school systems where outstanding teaching is also occurring. No opportunity to observe a demonstration that will contribute to a better lesson in the classroom should be overlooked.

TEXTBOOK ADOPTIONS

Textbooks are merely tools and resources utilized by teachers and students to facilitate learning. They are not the curriculum nor should they determine the direction a course should take. Too often basal series are selected on the basis of being the best one available after comparisons are made. Before examining any books, the committee should determine the objectives, the scope, and the sequences of its school program. They then search for books that best fit this scheme, even if books from several different series must be adopted. (In this computer age, textbooks will ultimately be a composite of pages selected by each individual school system from several publishers.) It is advisable that a school system set up a schedule for textbook adoptions on a regular basis. In most school systems it will vary from six to eight years. When one knows well in advance of an impending adoption, it then becomes possible to experiment in advance with all of the new series music texts under consideration.

When the appropriate time arrives, it may be necessary to submit a workshop budget, depending upon the school system. If teachers are paid to participate in this kind of workshop—the practice in most large cities —then one must determine the number of meetings and the expenses involved. It may include consultants from outside the school system, secretarial expenses, use of buildings, and numerous other small items for which a board requires budgeting if it is to provide those services.

Just as writing a new guide can be a valuable experience for those participating, so is serving on a textbook selection committee. The committee should consist of men and women, classroom teachers, and special music teachers. There should be representatives from a variety of ethnic

groups to see that different views and prevailing attitudes are represented. The committee should include a member of the principal's group
and, if possible, a general curriculum specialist. In some communities,
committees are encouraged to utilize an outside consultant from a local
or neighboring university's music education faculty to participate. As
indicated earlier, the committee chairman is usually a member of the
supervisory staff. He may be the music administrator, depending on the
available staff or how he envisions his role in relation to the task. If he
has shown expertise as a junior high school general music teacher, he
would certainly be chairman of a committee selecting a basic junior high
text book for general music classes. However, if the committee were selecting a series for string instruction, an outstanding string teacher in the
system would be appropriately appointed chairman of that group, if there
were none in the administration.

The director or chairman of the selection committee with the aid of
the music administrator then prepares a "Preliminary Philosophy and
Pertinent Information Bulletin." This bulletin should contain the prevailing statement of aims and objectives for the area of music for which
this series is being selected. It should review the purpose of the committee: 1) to formulate criteria for the new music text or series; 2) to
examine and evaluate available texts; 3) to recommend a text or series
for grades or a course; 4) to establish procedures and responsibilities of
the committee.

Another section in the bulletin should include certain evaluative
features to look for when examining texts. They may be 1) physical
characteristics of the book; 2) authors; 3) organization, content, and style;
4) publication data; 5) teacher's manuals; 6) student's editions; 7) supplementary materials, and 8) prices. Above all, do not forget to include a
tentative work schedule.

All publishers being considered should be notified about the adoption.
This notification usually comes from the particular assistant superintendent's office in charge of curriculum and instruction. The information
bulletin should be sent to the publishers, and each member of the committee should receive copies of the books being considered.

The early meetings should be devoted to establishing evaluative
criteria, reviewing reports from teachers who used the books experimentally, setting up a schedule of time allotments for presentations by
textbook publishers, and determining what the basis will be for the final
selection. The music publishers involved are then notified and invited to
make individual presentations at specific dates and times. Avoid having
overlapping presentations and be certain to provide time for a lengthy
question and answer period. Not only should evaluation criteria include

the concern for musical content, but some consideration should be given to the text's treatment of the various groups that make up the plurality of our nation. (See Appendix C.)

RESEARCH AND ADVANCED STUDY

Essential for the continued growth of any school music program in a school system is a concerted effort on behalf of research and development in music. The research may be an opportunity for a staff member to secure a meaningful project in advanced studies or it may be in the nature of personal investigation. If it reflects creative thought and sound processes, it should be explored. One must remember that if it is an experimental program there must be a time limitation followed by a period of assessment. Incidentally, it is not necessary that every research project be successful. We often learn as much from negative findings as we do from successful experiments.

Under the aegis of research, music departments are often able to secure needed equipment. Some of this equipment will have lasting value long after the research has been concluded.

Assisting individuals outside the school system in the conduct of research programs may become burdensome and time-consuming. However, if it is a valid, bona fide piece of work, one must contribute when possible. It indicates a positive attitude toward the benefits that the entire profession derives from these efforts, and as the music administrator in your community, you should encourage other music teachers to involve themselves in these activities.

Most school systems construct into their salary schedules financial incentives for advanced study. The music administrator should encourage music teachers to pursue advanced degrees to keep the program from stagnating. Appropriate recognition should be given these individuals, and if they are working on a project that has a definite effect or has ramifications for a school music program, they should be given time and facilities to explore and develop these projects. This attitude helps keep a music program dynamic and alive.

MUSIC CURRICULUM CENTERS

It is not always economically feasible that every classroom have every piece of desirable equipment or materials in it. Modal centers placed at strategic points can serve as warehouses to circulate the material based on need and demand. They may also provide demonstrations and instruction on how to use the equipment and generally contribute to the overall in-service program.

Usually the music center is equipped with professional books and a variety of basic music series. Kits such as those containing instruments of the orchestra, related art material, and visual aids should be available for circulation. The center should contain equipment such as Autoharps, resonator bells, sets of percussion instruments, and ethnic instruments. Each center should house a recording library with listening stations for teachers and students. The center should contain duplicating equipment and other equipment essential to provide music for teachers and the classroom.

One should regard the center as the model for equipment of any kind that contributes to better instruction. Experimental equipment, such as Orff instruments, may be distributed through this facility. One advantage of this kind of loan system is that teachers and schools may borrow equipment and material for an extended period of time, and should it prove sufficiently useful, they may decide to purchase it through their own school funds.

Each center should be staffed with a music consultant, a director and a secretary-librarian. The music center staff is responsible to the music administrator for planning and presenting workshops for individuals as well as for entire schools. This center can be a dynamic influence in keeping a school system well equipped and up to date and is especially useful in rural areas where a county system can provide this service throughout its district.

ATTENDANCE AT PROFESSIONAL MEETINGS

In many large school systems attendance at professional meetings is unfortunately reserved for the administration because of the economics involved. This practice is most regrettable since teachers benefit from these meetings in many ways. Such meetings are not only inspirational but offer opportunities to exchange views with colleagues in the field on a vis-à-vis basis. Latest materials and equipment are exhibited, and the many demonstrations and clinics not only help keep the profession current but often lead to generating other creative ideas for use in the classroom by those in attendance. Music administrators, directors, and supervisors should work with principals in arranging to cover classes as much as possible, thereby enabling teachers to get to meetings in the vicinity. It might even be to the administrator's advantage to take the classes himself for a day. Unfortunately, in many large systems the administrator avoids making a decision about who should or should not go.

Regardless of who attends a professional meeting, there should be some form of report and review for all teachers and staff following the meeting. Not only is this an obligation to the school system that has given those in attendance released time and possibly some financial assistance, but it can be utilized as another opportunity for in-service education. When this is done it tends to mitigate somewhat the resentment that those who were unable to attend might feel.

A good music administrator will not only encourage but try to make it possible for his teachers to take advantage of these meetings to improve themselves. He will exert every effort to see that the budget does consider and provide for this need. Since there will be limitations, the music administrator should develop an equitable arrangement that rotates this opportunity so that the benefits are offered to as many as possible.

Attendance at professional meetings should not be confined to national and state meetings. There are many local and university workshops that offer similar opportunities for improving instruction.

It is especially important that members of the school music administration be active in other professional organizations that service the total field of education as well as music. It is not enough just to belong! They must participate and accept responsibility in these organizations so that music may be represented appropriately. In addition, they will grow and better understand the role of music in the totality of education.

MICROTEACHING

The most recent vehicle for improving instruction is the development of the concept of microteaching. However, one must be fully informed of its use and abuse before utilizing it. Microteaching is basically a technique evolved out of an idea. It is not a panacea. It can be either helpful or destructive, depending on how it is applied.

Essentially, microteaching is based on the principle that by isolating a single concept or skill to be learned and examining it in a miniature practice setting, one can learn as much about instruction as one might learn in an actual classroom, since microteaching is actual teaching under specific conditions. Its advantage is that although it is a practice session, it is real teaching. It enables the teacher to tryout, strengthen, and improve his teaching behavior during the course of several brief, simulated teaching situations.

It is of utmost importance that when microteaching is used for in-service analysis it be conducted in such a manner that it is absolutely clear to the teacher he is not being evaluated. The entire emphasis must be placed on instructional assistance and not on rating. Although it is important that the microteaching session be videotaped, it is not an essential part of the process. When a video tape machine is not available, a tape recorder may serve the same purpose even though the visual aspect of the teaching is omitted.

Essentially, microteaching is selecting a single special technique, skill, or lesson and teaching it to a small group of children in a short, specified amount of time. The process is built around the sequence of teach—analyze—reteach. Its purpose is to focus the teacher's attention on teaching behaviors and provide an opportunity for controlled "practice" teaching. Teachers are actually given an opportunity to see what they do when they teach a single aspect of a music lesson.

For taping to be an effective in-service vehicle, every effort must be made to reassure the teacher of his security. First, the taping is done with a small, limited group of children (four to eight) who are not regular members of the teacher's class. Second, the taping is usually done in a room other than the teacher's regular classroom. And third, the objective for microteaching, as well as the problem to be analyzed, is clearly defined before the teacher begins taping or recording. The entire filmed presentation should not take more than five to eight minutes.

As soon as the lesson is completed, the students fill out prepared forms indicating what they learned and how they perceived what the teacher was attempting to do. The supervisor then reviews his notes with the teacher and the teacher reviews the tape. Incidentally, it is not necessary that the entire tape be replayed. Once the appropriate point is made or observed, the rest of the tape may be set aside. In addition it can be disconcerting and defeating if the supervisor speaks excessively or gets involved with matters that were not agreed upon initially. When the analysis part of the process is completed, the teacher again teaches the lesson to a different group of students.

"If teachers had a microteaching clinic as a part of the professional resources—like workshops and professional libraries—available to them, they could use it to systematically improve their instructional skills and to try out new curricular materials."[2] In addition, a microteaching lab could be utilized by supervisors and teachers to serve as a model for demonstrating or introducing new materials or new techniques to other teachers. "In a sense, it could be the setting for the professional dialogue among teachers that is frequently absent from our schools."[3]

A model for a micro-teaching experience might be structured as follows:

[2] Kevin Ryan and Dwight Allen, *Microteaching* (Reading, Mass.: Addison-Wesley Publishing Co., Inc.), p. 6.
[3] *Ibid.*, p. 6.

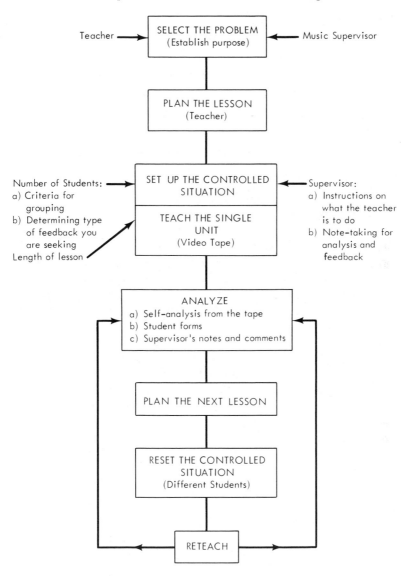

Teacher ——▶ SELECT THE PROBLEM (Establish purpose) ◀—— Music Supervisor

PLAN THE LESSON (Teacher)

Number of Students:
a) Criteria for grouping
b) Determining type of feedback you are seeking
Length of lesson

SET UP THE CONTROLLED SITUATION

TEACH THE SINGLE UNIT (Video Tape)

Supervisor:
a) Instructions on what the teacher is to do
b) Note-taking for analysis and feedback

ANALYZE
a) Self-analysis from the tape
b) Student forms
c) Supervisor's notes and comments

PLAN THE NEXT LESSON

RESET THE CONTROLLED SITUATION (Different Students)

RETEACH

For example, if the selected problem is to introduce the concept of rondo form to a group of fourth-grade students, the teacher would then plan a series of short lessons. He would then focus on the first step, which would be to introduce the concept in a microteaching laboratory. In setting up the controlled situation, it would be determined that x small number of fourth-grade students, whom he did not know, would be invited to serve as participants. It would have to be determined whether or not they should be selected at random out of a general music class or from a special class such as band or orchestra. The length of the lesson might be arbitrarily fixed at seven minutes. The supervisor would then instruct the teacher as to procedures to facilitate taping and specifics regarding the lesson. (It might be predetermined that the rondo form would be introduced via the Orff method, whereby the teacher presents a rhythmic theme A and each child responds with a contrasting theme B, C, etc. However, after each child presents his theme, the class responds with A—result, a rondo.)

The presentation is then made and analyzed as indicated on the chart on page 57. The feedback is real and immediate. A record is then kept of the original teaching performance for comparison with subsequent reteaching. At the reteaching stage, it is often more interesting and beneficial to focus on the same technique with new students and a fresh start than to redo under the same conditions. However, after a series of lessons it may even be determined that the Orff approach does not lend itself to the purpose of the lesson and a new or alternate approach might be considered for teaching the rondo.

It is imperative for music supervisors to understand that microteaching does not apply to every situation. To be effective, it must focus on a single idea; it must fit a specified lesson. It might be appropriate for teaching how to hold a violin bow but not necessarily for an orchestra rehearsal. The example of the microteaching lesson introducing the rondo form in a listening lesson within a given, limited amount of time would be valid; however, microteaching could not be used for an entire listening lesson. To develop an entire lesson, the various components would have to be broken down and each one studied independently:

a) Introducing the concept of rondo
b) Developing the ability to recognize a rondo in a simple song
c) Developing the ability to recognize a rondo in more complex forms
d) Writing an original rondo

From each of the four items above, a separate microteaching lesson could be developed.

Best of all, microteaching can be used as a device by supervisors to show teachers opportunities where they may involve students that are usually overlooked. Its use applies to experienced teachers as well as to new teachers. Many of the constraints of the normal classroom may be eliminated and controlled conditions can be developed. By reducing the complexities of the typical classroom, the teaching-learning environment can be manipulated to direct attention to a limited number of specific techniques.

Supervisors and administrators are constantly searching for ways to improve instruction. Microteaching offers an opportunity for teachers to become involved in the process through self-analysis. In a microteaching clinic supervisors can assist teachers in a brief concentrated way that may eliminate time-consuming hours of sitting in the back of a classroom to the discomfort of teacher, students, and supervisor. However, as a word of caution, microteaching is not to be construed as a device to eliminate the important need for visitation and interest in what the teacher is doing in his own classroom. It merely eliminates some of the anxiety and tension that occurs when retraining is done in the teacher's classroom with his own students. In a sense, it is artificial in that no regular classroom resembles the microteaching model. The success of microteaching will depend on its judicious use for the appropriate situation. Its potential for the improvement of instruction is unlimited.

Selected Articles For Supplementary Reading

ADLER, SAMUEL, "CMP Institutes and Curriculum Change," *"Music Educators Journal* (September, 1968), 36.

BALL, CHARLES H., "The Answer Lies in Improved Teaching," *Music Educators Journal* (October, 1969), 58.

COAKLEY, MARJORIE, "Music Curriculum Guides: Their Development and Use," *Music Educators Journal* (November, 1966), 51.

GOODLAD, JOHN I., "Our Education System Corrupts the Human Spirit," *Music Educators Journal* (December, 1968), 28.

KLOTMAN, ROBERT H., "The Supervisor Must Know the City Score," *Music Educators Journal* (January, 1970), 58.

MILLER, RICHARD I., "Regional Educational Laboratories," *Phi Delta Kappa* (December, 1966), 144.

TIPTON, GLADYS, "The Changing Emphasis in Music Materials," *The Instructor* (March, 1964), 63.

Chapter 6

PERSONNEL PRACTICES

CLASSROOM VISITATION

The functions of classroom visitations are varied. In some cases the number and timing are dictated by edict. A board of education or a state tenure law may make a certain number of classroom visits within a designated period of time mandatory for a new teacher. (See Appendix D.) Unfortunately, this type of visit is primarily for the purpose of participating in evaluative procedures to determine the desirability of the teacher. If possible, this type of observation should be left under the aegis of the supervisory department, and only when extreme circumstances dictate should the director of music become involved with it. This statement should not be misconstrued to imply that the music administrator does not visit or observe in the classroom. On the contrary, this is his most effective way of dealing with the individual teacher. It is merely that it is easier to help people if they are not always working under the threat of being rated. This applies to supervisory visits as well.

Classroom visits open up communications on a face-to-face basis. One teacher greeted her new supervisor in a large city in tears. She had been in the system seventeen years and had never had a visit from "downtown." She thought that they had forgotten her and didn't even know she existed. She was overjoyed to know that someone was interested.

Visiting a school can also supply the administration with information about the school, its pupils, and its administrators that does not always appear in written reports. All of this information is of the utmost importance when making decisions that affect curriculum and programs in a building.

Essentially, classroom visitation should be thought of in a positive sense. Its purpose is to assist in instruction. It may be to help an inexperienced teacher or to assist an experienced one. It may be to assist some non-certified individual or it may be to implement a group project. At times it may be to help a principal who needs assistance in dealing with a specific problem in his building.

CONDUCTING AN OBSERVATION

When observing a class, be certain to remain long enough to assure the teacher that he has been given ample opportunity to display his ability. However, stay only long enough to ascertain the quality of instruction. It is better to observe for something specific. Plan the visit so that it is systematic and determine beforehand the specifics that need be observed. Of course, be flexible enough to shift focus as the situation demands. Do not be hasty in forming conclusions and reserve judgment on techniques or materials until you have had a chance to see the whole lesson and discuss it with the teacher.

No one likes criticism. Some can handle it better than others, but no one enjoys it, no matter how sincerely it is offered. It is, therefore, imperative that those supervisors or directors understand the nature of the individual with whom they are dealing and be aware of his needs as they offer help. This requires tact and diplomacy. However, the music administrator need not avoid the issue or abrogate his responsibility. Concern for the student and instruction is always the prime consideration and an administrator must weigh in his mind the best way to achieve his goal of improving teaching.

When discussing the lesson, provide the teacher with alternatives. Try to get him out of lock-step patterns. Remember that a good music administrator releases a teacher's potential; he does not restrain him. If you see something that is effective, encourage it, even if it doesn't always comply with traditional methods or established procedures.

The question of note taking during an observation is questionable. Avoid profuse writing but jot down a few comments unobstrusively to remind yourself of something, positive or negative, that you want to call to the teacher's attention. Whatever is written should be shown to the teacher so that he doesn't think that you are preparing a secret "dossier."

The music administrative staff should prepare an observation form to be filled out and given to the teacher after each visit. This not only informs the teacher of specifics referred to in the discussion but also serves as a reminder for follow-up visits. Some school systems are now using portable tape recorders and cassettes when observing a class. Later the tape is given to the teacher so that he has chance to hear himself teach. It becomes a form of self-criticism and evaluation. The observer may or may not add comments to the tapes. However, it can also be unnerving to a teacher. Let each one decide if he prefers the tape and/or written comments.

When talking to a teacher, avoid using the same phrases or terminology that is characterized by cliches. When making constructive criticism, conflict may be created. At all costs avoid polarization. Generally, direct comments to what occurred or what needs to be done *to improve learning for students.* If there are personal matters involved, be concerned only with their effect on the learning situation. The best type of criticism is that which engenders self-analysis. Remember you are not there to establish your authority. Be considerate. From the moment an administrator or supervisor walks into the room it is no longer a normal situation!

Some supervisors and administrators have attempted to video tape classes and use them for evaluative purposes. This is totally unfair and should not be done. First, the moment a camera is introduced into a classroom, no matter how unobtrusively, it alters the atmosphere to such an extent that much of what occurs is artificial and inordinately overt. Secondly, videotaping is an effective in-service device, as in microteaching; using it in classes would undermine its positive values. Finally, to obviate the first two objections would require such extensive preparation and expense that the information gained in return for evaluation is completely out of proportion with the results. Reserve videotaping for the functions that it can serve best—instruction and training.

Under no circumstances should any observer undermine the teacher's authority in the classroom. When the observer leaves, he must remember that the teacher remains to face the class.

As indicated earlier, most evaluative visits are left to supervisors. However, the music director is always on call to assist in the process. As a matter of fact, administrators should always respond to any call in some fashion.

Above all, administrators must realize that all teachers are individuals requiring individual approaches and attention. Not every problem can be solved, and some may resolve themselves. A sensitive administrator will establish priorities in dealing with staff. He must decide where he can achieve the most progress in the least amount of time when assisting a teacher.

TEACHER SELECTION PROCEDURES

The quality of experiences offered in a school classroom is directly related to the quality of a teacher in that particular situation. There may be other factors involving personnel that impinge upon these learning experiences, such as internal conflicts within a school, but essentially a creative, competent teacher will manage almost any situation with varying degrees of success. It is, therefore, incumbent upon a music administrator to pursue every means to secure the most able teachers for his school system. Many school systems have prepared printed materials describing and publicizing the advantages of teaching in their school system. (See Appendix E.)

Procedures for selecting teachers will differ with school systems. In larger, urban communities the office of personnel may be the sole agency for selecting, appointing, and assigning staff. It selects the teacher and then notifies the director or the music department of the appointments. It is then the administration's responsibility to assimilate, orient, and develop those individuals into the practices and curricular concepts of the school system. Incidentally, regardless of the size of the community, if possible, it is desirable that the building principal meet the new teacher before the assignment is finalized. Leaving the sole responsibility for selection to a personnel office, unfortunately, has too many negative aspects for music teaching. Rather than emphasizing the quality of the teacher secured, such a plan operates on the basis that once a so-called qualified person is found, the system will educate and develop him. In some cases this practice was established to eliminate the abuses of prejudice and discrimination in selection procedures. In some instances, it was a more expeditious way of dealing with the problems of school staffing.

This method may be adequate in certain areas of instruction. Music, however, is an art form that deals with organized sound involving aesthetic judgment and musical communication. As such, it must be taught by teachers who possess, in addition to educational skills, certain artistic skills that can be measured only by an audition. Arguments by school officials against the audition type of selection are based on the idea that by virtue of a certificate and a college degree, candidates have exhibited proper training that merits at least an opportunity to prove themselves in a classroom. Intellectually this may be true, but what a transcript primarily reveals is the number of courses taken and the academic success in those courses. It does not measure musicality. It is true that a skilled administrator can find subtleties in a transcript that are clues in these areas. However, in such cases it is even more to the advantage of the candidate to be auditioned. Any misconceptions regarding his musicality may then be dispelled. "The Interim Report of the Music Educators National Conference Commission on Teacher Education" has identified the competencies desirable for teaching music in today's classrooms.[1] It may be used as a basis for criteria in discussions with school personnel departments.

Furthermore, the audition should not be just a performance test per se. It should consist of two parts, an interview and a performance, includ-

[1] "Interim Report of the Commission on Teacher Education." *Music Educators Journal* (October, 1970), p. 33.

ing some conducting. Teachers cannot be expected to maintain the same proficiency on their instrument—voice, piano, trumpet, etc.—as a professional. They should, however, be rhythmically accurate and be able to distinguish intervals properly. They should also be able to hear discrepancies in intonation. Regardless of the level, the performance should be musical. They should be able to discuss their philosophy of music education and its application in a classroom situation.

Elementary vocal music teachers should be able to read at sight from the average fourth- or fifth-grade text. They should be able to improvise and perform simple accompaniments to these songs. (This might be on the piano or a guitar.) The degree of piano skill expected will vary according to the attitude of the music administrator and the curricular objectives for music in that school system. Musical examinations need not be complex or technically demanding to be revealing.

The interview should be conducted in such a manner that the candidate is comfortable and reassured that the director is genuinely interested in his ability and potential. There should be ample preparation before the candidate arrives. His transcript and credentials, including his recommendations, should be fully examined so that when he appears, the interviewer is already aware of his background and can direct the interview accordingly. It is important that the applicant be given every opportunity to express himself rather than be the object of an administrator's frustration in monologue in the form of an interview. Specific answers are not nearly so important as thought processes, and questions should be aimed toward revealing these processes. It is important that the potential teacher be able to explain *why* he prefers a particular series or text rather than the specific one chosen. Opinions may change and one's ability to think and communicate is far more significant for growth and development than precise, expected responses. A teacher's potential is as important as his existing knowledge and that can best be revealed by the candidate's expressing himself at length.

It is important to remember that interviews and auditions, by their very nature, are periods of stress and anxiety for the applicant. Empathy and sympathy are important. A sensitive interviewer does not allow the nervous pressure of the moment to influence his judgment. And under no circumstances should race, color, or creed be a factor! If a rejected candidate wishes to reapply he should be given every opportunity to do so. Every effort should be made to guarantee the applicant a fair and equitable hearing. Otherwise, the entire audition privilege for the department may be revoked.*

---

* In the Detroit public schools the director or his designated supervisor conducts the audition to determine the candidate's musicality and interviews the prospective teacher to ascertain his knowledge of materials, technique, and procedures. If there are

Finally, one of the most important services that the interview-audition renders is diagnostic. It not only gives the candidate an opportunity to analyze his own capabilities under pressure but it may also serve as the initial step toward in-service education for a probationary teacher. He becomes aware of his weakness and his strength before even entering the classroom. The supervisor assigned to him can anticipate some of the problems and obviate difficulties with preliminary assistance and training.

Under no circumstances should the interview-audition be regarded as a means of eliminating candidates. It should be regarded only as a means of finding desirable, competent teachers. Successful interviewing is a matter of attitude.

RECRUITING TEACHERS

Since a music program is no better than the teacher in the class-room, everyone in the music department is involved in securing competent personnel. The music administration is especially concerned that the supervisors and music administrators should pursue every avenue and source for both experienced and inexperienced personnel with potential. Since some of the most competent teachers have come directly from campuses, an active recruiting program should be maintained there.

Visits to select institutions should be conducted on a regularly scheduled basis. If a music supervisor or director conducts the interview, it may be handled on the scene, with advance notification. This saves considerable time and expense and indicates an interest in the university's graduates on the part of the school system. This interest builds rapport with the institution and aids in procuring the better graduates.

In addition to the recruiting done by the music department, practically all school systems, large and small, maintain an active office or department that develops and conducts a recruiting program. To assist these departments as well as serve its own purpose, the music department will prepare materials and brochures describing the local program and highlighting its advantages (See Appendix E, p. 157). These materials should be brief and direct with sufficient eye appeal to attract attention when posted on bulletin boards. They not only serve as aids to recruiters but help build a public-professional image for the music education department.

---

any questions beyond these factors, the candidate is then referred to a representative committee made up of administrators, teachers, and personnel. They make the final decision regarding the candidate's desirability. This procedure eliminates most prejudicial practices.

Without a definite recruiting plan, one has to rely too much on those who may submit an application for employment to a school system. With an active recruiting program, the music administration can exercise more quality control.

DEALING WITH INCOMPETENCIES

No teacher should be considered incompetent until there have been several observations by at least the principal or his assistant, a music department head or a music supervisor, and the music director. A teacher should be given every opportunity and ample assistance to prove his competency (see Improving Instruction), and only when all efforts have failed should any action be taken.

Throughout these proceedings, visitation records should be kept. As indicated earlier, these should be given to the teacher as well as to the chief personnel officer for the school system. Contrary to popular opinion, tenure laws do not protect incompetent teachers. If enough proper evidence is available, even tenured teachers may be dismissed. Too often administrators lack administrative courage and find the due process of law too troublesome. It is easier to avoid the issue. Under these circumstances the fault lies with the administration. Too many individuals are content to rely on the cliché that tenure protects the incompetent teacher. Tenure laws were established to guarantee academic freedom and in a democratic society it is essential that a teacher, who is a public servant, be protected. For example, without tenure laws, one might hesitate to play music by Russian composers or even fear the use of religious music under certain conditions. Tenure guarantees a music teacher's freedom to be artistically honest and should be protected. Unfortunately, without administrative courage, its purpose is lost under the guise of protecting the incompetent.

Proper evidence in incompetency cases should be based on learning experiences in the classroom and children's growth and not on personal appearance or personality conflicts. These latter factors are considered important only when they interfere with learning in the classroom. When teachers are confronted with bona fide evidence, they usually do not wish to jeopardize their careers. They should be given the opportunity to resign. No matter how much the observing supervisory individual may feel threatened, he must remain detached, objective, and impersonal.

At no time should any one music administrator undertake the responsibility of dealing with this type of incompetency alone. He should enlist the aid of all personnel involved in such matters when dealing with the problem.

OUTSIDE WORK

It is not uncommon for people in music to "moonlight." This is of no concern to the music administration unless it interferes with teaching. Teachers need to be reminded that teaching is their chosen profession and that class schedules or concert schedules cannot be constantly adjusted to accommodate "gigs." One needs to be sympathetic to the financial plight of the staff and an occasional adjustment might even be in the best interest of musical growth for the staff member, but prolonged engagements interfering with class activities must be avoided.

INTER-STAFF RELATIONSHIPS

Anyone employed by the Board of Education is a part of a family. In fact, anyone interested in the education of the children in that community is a member of that group. It is extremely important that the music administration build an "esprit" within the department that will contribute to the "team" effort and not to the aggrandizement of any individual.

Each member of the music department should be given proper recognition for his achievements and ample opportunities to display his talents. The music administrator should not compete with his supervisors nor they with their teachers. It is wholly unnecessary and only reflects insecurity on the part of the individual.

Teachers, supervisors, and even directors are human beings. Personality conflicts cannot help but arise. Music administrators must remain impersonal in these matters and not become involved. They should be aware of these conflicts and try to avoid them by making assignments carefully.

This kind of situation is usually more difficult for someone who "has risen through the ranks" in the system where he is the administrator. Years of work have established personal ties and loyalties that cannot be disregarded. Being friendly, outgoing and open-minded does not mean that one must always be "buddies" with everyone. It all becomes a matter of personal judgment and judicious application.

ORGANIZATIONAL DEVELOPMENT

The term "organizational development" is derived from a technique devised by the business world as a way of looking at the human aspects of its various organizations. It concerns itself with developing the natural potential that exists within the individual resources of an organization, particularly at the leadership level. Often music administration departments are so involved in developing programs in schools and with faculties that they tend to overlook the potential and need for development and growth of individuals in their own departments. As John Gardiner's article so aptly described the need, "Organizational Development" is a way of avoiding "organizational dry-rot."[2] Unless there is concern for this aspect—the human aspect of administration—music departments tend to stagnate at the leadership level and limit the growth of those on the administrative and supervisory lines.

To avoid stagnation a music department must not only have an active recruiting program outside the school system, but it must provide ample opportunity for those working in the system to grow and advance. It cannot permit highly motivated music teachers to feel that there is no opportunity for advancement or that their talent has insufficient outlet. Every effort must be made by the music administration to provide such opportunities.

Furthermore, if creative music teachers and supervisors have creative ideas and they are stifled by not having an appropriate outlet, the students as well as these teachers suffer. They feel as though they are being confined to routine traditional procedures and methods with little opportunity to experiment and be imaginative. Under such conditions, they cannot produce ideas that will institute change and they may even resist ideas of change when produced by other members of the department.

The third rule in Mr. Gardiner's article is based on the principle that "organizations must have built-in provisions for self-criticism. It [the music department] must have an atmosphere in which uncomfortable questions can be asked."[3] Much of this freedom to question will depend on the personality of those in charge of the music department. Some people feel threatened by challenging questions. Enlightened music administrators do not.

"Organizational development" utilizes the knowledge and technique developed from the behavorial sciences. It attempts to integrate the need for growth and development of the individuals with the goals and objectives that the music department establishes for itself. In a sense it is a state of mind, an attitude, an approach that enables the supervisory staff to participate in self-examination and seek ways to improve its mode of operation.

[2] John W. Gardiner, "How to Prevent Organizational Dry-Rot," *Harper's Magazine* (October, 1965), 20.

[3] Gardiner, "How to Prevent Organizational Dry-Rot," p. 20.

In a music department regular staff meetings may be held not just for taking care of housekeeping chores but also to determine how the school music administrator and the supervisors can most effectively achieve their objectives for the school music program. In addition, planning time needs to be devoted to giving those individuals responsible for the development of the goals and objectives the optimum personal satisfaction if maximum results are to be obtained. The behavorial sciences have long acknowledged that secure individuals whose personal needs are satisfied do not avoid challenge and responsibility. They usually are the ones most interested in work and they expect full recognition when a performance is well done. It is this kind of concern that produces satisfying interpersonal relationships within a department and helps a music department grow at the supervisory and administrative level.

The behavioral scientists have emphasized people's basic drive toward self-realization and growth. When the school music administrator provides an atmosphere in his department that conveys a genuine honest interest in the individual's development at the staff level, more productive results will be realized.

As the members of the staff realize that they are not being manipulated and that there is ample opportunity for open, frank discussion where they may express both positive and negative feelings, they will develop stronger identification and a sense of loyalty which will enable them to deal more effectively and more constructively with some of the disruptive issues occurring in today's schools. Furthermore, when positive changes of this nature occur in the administrative office, they have a better chance to occur in a classroom that identifies with the goals and objectives of the total program. In this way the administrative staff can exert more influence in the schools and is more effective in influencing change in the classroom.

A music department undertaking an "organizational development" program would follow the following process:

1. Identify the behavioral objective or problem with which the project is going to concern itself.
2. Establish priorities within the objectives.
3. Share all data regarding the objective or problem under study. This data will include technical information as well as personal and interpersonal factors. It will include total staff expertise.
4. Develop a plan of action, including alternatives should the plan encounter obstacles or unforeseen variables that might impede progress.
5. Implement the plan, including some testing and examining of the alternatives.
6. Review results and pursue additional action plans.
7. Recognize the individuals involved in the entire process.

As the plan is implemented, other alternatives and modes of operation will become apparent and the benefits derived from a successful operation will tend to compound themselves. Basic to the technology of "operational development" is the utilization and development of the human resources within the *staff* and *organization* of the total music department. Outside consultants may participate and assist in planning, but their primary function will be to stimulate the capacity for growth for those within the department. To illustrate how "organizational development" might function in a music department, let us refer to the earlier example regarding the introduction of electronic organs into a junior high school in Detroit.

When the superintendent of schools announced to the community and staff that he had established a target area in a school constellation to see if basic skills as measured by national norms could be improved with the aid of special services obtained through a federal grant, it became incumbent upon all departments to focus most of their activities in their classrooms on basic skills in support of the superintendent's commitment. It was obvious that departments that could not contribute to the basic program would suffer in these schools, at least temporarily.

At a meeting of all the music supervisors, including the one responsible for the target junior high school, the director of music identified the problem as being the improvement of basic skills—particularly reading—through music. There were several ways that this activity could have been approached but it was agreed that if every student could be involved in playing some musical instrument, he would of necessity develop some reading skills. It was then determined that the electronic piano might be the best device for a junior high general music class since it offered such a variety of musical exposures and experiences.

The fine arts department head in that junior high school, the general music teacher, and the school music accompanist (a professional employee in the Detroit system) were then consulted. They were interested. Bids and programs were solicited from the various piano companies. The teacher was sent to Michigan State University to observe piano class instruction with electronic keyboards to see how its program might be adjusted to accommodate urban, inner-city junior high school classes. The Wichita piano-mobile program was studied and every effort made to obtain appropriate information and data from a variety of resources.

The entire school music team with the supervisor then met to plan an approach and method for the class. They were literally pioneering in a sense that this was a domain never attempted before in Detroit under these conditions. It was suggested that alternate plans might include recorders, or a traditional reading program based on the singing or vocal program should the electronic piano not be forthcoming. Initially, two groups were established, one following the usual general music pattern with emphasis on reading in the singing activity and one using the keyboard program. The success of the electronic keyboard was so evident and so marked in the early stages that by November, three months later, electronic keyboards were placed in the second classroom.

Review of the program revealed that existing materials were inadequate and new, original materials had to be developed. There was no question about the improvement of reading, at least in music. This was born out by periodic tests.

Throughout the entire process, the supervisor, the department head, the teacher, and the accompanist were given full recognition and prestigious publicity. They received much attention for developing their own materials and contriving a special language based on the type of communication that was carried on by the astronauts and men in space. This was done to stimulate the students' imagination and it was so effective that they talked about it even in their homes.

Whenever visitors came to observe the program, those involved acted as hosts and informants. Although the entire idea had originated with the director, he removed himself from the forefront and made certain that those involved in implementing the program and developing the materials received all the recognition and attention they so well deserved. A first-year teacher and an accompanist who had been in and about Detroit for years became consultants and clinicians helping others develop similar programs. Their own personal satisfaction and growth were assured.

THE MANAGERIAL GRID:
THE MUSIC ADMINISTRATIVE GRID

Both industry and government, as a result of their involvement in the technique of "organizational development," have utilized "managerial grids," and although the grid has not appeared to any extent in education, its application for programs and teachers makes its utilization inevitable. By substituting "programs" for production or output, "staff and teachers" for employees, and the word "administrative" for "managerial," a grid would function as follows in a school music department. There are two key variables found in every music department. They are existing programs and members of the staff. An administrative grid concerns itself with the relationship between these programs and its concern for people. In this particular case the word "concern" applies not simply to meeting human needs or devising programs as such but to measuring how program development and meeting human needs influence and interact with each other.

The various combinations are shown on the "grid" diagram. The horizontal line represents programs and the vertical line measures the concern for individuals. The scale is from 1 to 9 and is based on 1 being the lowest or least concerned, and 9, the highest or most concerned.

The 1, 1 in the lower left-hand corner indicates a minimal concern or interest in members of staff and a minimal music program. The upper left corner, which reads 1, 9, indicates the maximum concern for total staff but a minimal concern for music experience and programming. The 9, 1 reading in the lower right-hand part of the "grid" exhibits the maximum concern for programs with little concern for human relationships and staff needs. The ideal, of course, is the 9, 9 found in the upper right-hand corner, which reveals concern for optional programs with maximum concern for staff. In the center of the diagram we find the middle-of-the-road 5, 5 which indicates a 50 percent concern in both areas.

Once the music administrator and/or his supervisors have studied and reviewed the "grid," they may wish to revise priorities and practices. The "grid" should force them to assess their procedures and adjust them as they work toward the 9, 9 maximum goal on the grid.

Steps taken in the process are as follows:

1. Each music administrator and music supervisor examines his own style or approach utilizing "administrative grid" procedures. It should include a self-analysis instrument, self-administered testing based on current practices in behavioral objectives, and other pertinent evaluative educational devices.
2. The members of the staff then involve themselves in a group evaluation in order to determine the "team" effectiveness.
3. The entire staff of music administrators, supervisors, department heads, or whoever else is included in the administrative design for music then review, diagnose, and determine the major areas needed for improvement.

The entire approach is self-administered by the administration. A consultant may be involved, however, only at the instigation of the group doing the self-evaluation. Once all factors have been determined, then a program of in-service education for the administrative staff may be instituted to improve the weak areas so that the ultimate 9, 9 on the "grid" may be achieved.

Actually, both "organizational development" and administrative or "managerial grids" are based on common-sense procedures. However, unless a definite program is designed or structured, like so many obvious common sense procedures, they may be overlooked or never used.

A MUSIC ADMINISTRATIVE (MANAGERIAL) GRID

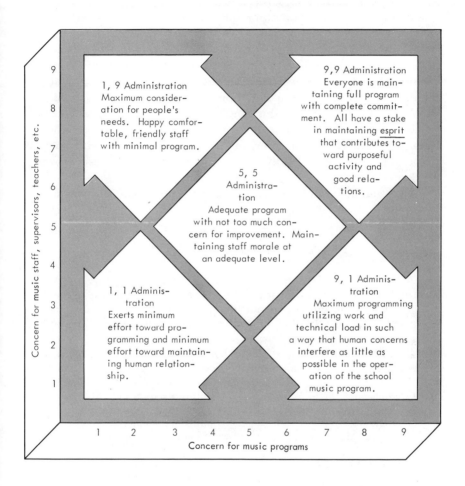

Concern for music staff, supervisors, teachers, etc.

1, 9 Administration
Maximum consider-
ation for people's
needs. Happy comfor-
table, friendly staff
with minimal program.

9,9 Administration
Everyone is main-
taining full program
with complete commit-
ment. All have a stake
in maintaining <u>esprit</u>
that contributes to-
ward purposeful
activity and
good rela-
tions.

5, 5
Administra-
tion
Adequate program
with not too much con-
cern for improvement. Maintaining staff morale at
an adequate level.

1, 1 Adminis-
tration
Exerts minimum
effort toward pro-
gramming and minimum
effort toward maintain-
ing human relation-
ship.

9, 1 Adminis-
tration
Maximum programming
utilizing work and
technical load in such
a way that human concerns
interfere as little as
possible in the oper-
ation of the school
music program.

Concern for music programs

PUPIL-TEACHER LOADS

There are many factors and various formulas to determine the teacher's pupil and class load. Sometimes this is a negotiable item in salary
talks between the board of education and the teachers' bargaining agent.
Where this is rigidly interpreted, it often creates problems, particularly
if the issue is a minimum class load or hours in a work day. In the state

of Michigan, the Michigan Music Educators Association and the various affiliates under the leadership of Elizabeth Hays White, President of MMEA, became sufficiently concerned in October, 1970, to ask the Michigan Education Association's Office of Professional Negotiations to issue a statement expressing its position on the matter of contract negotiations and its effect on music programs. Not only were the music teachers concerned about abuses in teaching loads but the prospect also existed that programs might be inadvertently phased out. To protect music instruction in the schools, the Assistant Executive Secretary of the Office of Professional Negotiations, Tom Patterson, issued a statement of guidelines which might be used where this concern became an issue. (See Appendix J.) He urged bargaining units in communities to utilize the specific guidelines prepared by the music organizations when dealing with contract negotiators who were not fully cognizant of the needs for music programs in their schools.

The sample schedule of conditions drawn up at that time was according to the following format:

SPECIAL PROGRAM CONDITIONS*

A. Vocal and Instrumental music shall remain as an integral part of the total school curriculum throughout the duration of this agreement. Budgetary and personnel expenditures in the area of music shall not be decreased below the level of expenditure reflecting a budgetary percent during the 1970–71 school year.

B. Secondary class size shall be determined by the nature and scope of the activity reflecting the following maximum and/or minimum norms.

1.	Bands	_____pupils (maximum)
2.	Choirs	_____pupils (maximum)
3.	Orchestra	_____pupils (maximum)
4.	General Music	(Shall conform to academic class load maximums.)
5.	Beginning Instruments	_____pupils (minimum)
6.	Theory	_____pupils (minimum)
7.	Voice Class	_____pupils (minimum)
8.	Music Literature	_____pupils (minimum)
9.	Ensembles	_____pupils (minimum)

C. The Elementary Vocal Music Program (K-6) shall meet in a normal classroom situation and be conducted by music specialists no less than two (2) separate days each week for periods of time no less than twenty-five (25) minutes each. The maximum teaching load shall be eight (8)

---

* Prepared by the Michigan Music Educators Association, Michigan School Vocal Association, Michigan School Band and Orchestra Association, November 10, 1970.

periods per day. Music class size maximums shall not exceed the number of pupils assigned each elementary classroom.

The District shall provide time to take care of exceptionally talented pupils, i.e., Select Choir, opportunity for General Chorus, i.e., one chorus per grade level.

D. The Elementary Instrumental Music Program shall be conducted by instrumental specialists and will require the meeting of classes for periods of time no less than forty (40) minutes each. There will be maximums of _____ pupils in elementary instrumental classes and _____ pupils in elementary string classes.

E. Where music instruction and responsibility which must of necessity fall outside the regular school day is an added assignment and/or expectation and is not covered in Salary Schedule "B" attached, the following teaching load adjustments shall be in effect:

F. Further concerns in the area of music that become evident during the duration of this agreement will be referred, with accompanying rationale, to the "Instructional Policies Council" for consideration, study, and subsequent recommendation for implementation following the expiration of this agreement.

Music is an activity that accommodates small ensembles, large performing groups, and normal classroom sizes for general instruction. Therefore, in determining a music teacher's class load, one cannot assess each class individually. Administrators should compute the pupil-teacher ratio on an average per-class basis. Otherwise, small group instruction will be eliminated.*

Budget is the most critical factor in determining class size for a school administration. It is regrettable that educational philosophy is often dictated by available funds. When making recommendations for staffing, the music administrator must be extremely sensitive to the budgetary demands involved and their effect on the total school budget. He cannot ignore this item, for if he does, his requests are not even considered and his effectiveness as an administrator diminishes. The subject of budget will be discussed in full detail in Chapter 9.

Selected Articles For Supplementary Reading

Administrators Forum Problem: "Board Member Wants Measurable Standards, Standards Set-up for All Employees," *School Management*, II (October, 1967), 39.

---

* This can be justified further on the basis that larger music classes reduce the overall pupil-teacher ratio in a building, thus allowing the school to have more teachers in other subject areas.

BOARDMAN, EUNICE, "New Sounds In the Classroom," *Music Educators Journal* (November, 1968), 62.

DAVIS, SHELDON A., "An Organic Problem-Solving Method of Organizational Change," *The Journal of Applied Behaviorial Science,* III, No. 1, (1967), 42.

GARDINER, JOHN W., "How to Prevent Organizational Dry-Rot," *Harper's Magazine,* CCXXXI 231, (October, 1965), 20.

HACKEL, M.D., and C.H. MANNEL, "Problems in the Recruiting Interview," *Journal of College Placement,* XXIX (October, 1968), 38–42.

HUNT, R. G. and C. M. LICHTMAN, "Counseling of Employees by Work Supervisors: Concepts, Attitudes, and Practices in a White Collar Organization," *Journal of Counseling Psychology,* XVI (January, 1969), 81–86.

MCKEOWN, L. W., "On Merit Rating," *Phi Delta Kappan* (October, 1966), 77.

"Stop Sending Innocents Into Battle Unarmed," *Music Educators Journal* (January, 1970), 102.

TONNE, HAROLD A., "Personality Versus Skill," *Journal of Business Education,* XLIV (January, 1969), 142–43.

WERNER, ROBERT, "The Individual Teacher and CMP," *Music Educators Journal* (January, 1969), 47.

Chapter 7

EVALUATION AND THE
PROCESS OF CHANGE

As society and music increase in complexity and change becomes even more accelerated, it is essential for music education, if it is to remain an efficacious force in the schools, that music educators become more specific about what they hope to accomplish, how they intend to achieve their goals, and how they will know if they have accomplished these goals:

> ". . . Where am I going
> How shall I get there, and
> How will I know I've arrived?"[1]

These questions need to be answered in such a way that ambiguities and clichés are dispelled. They must contain demonstrable, well-defined behaviors that can be evaluated within a given time as well as those long range aims that can be measured only in terms of the future and maturation. However, even long-range goals need to be stated in such a way that anyone conducting long-term research may measure or evaluate them in a specific identifiable manner at the end of a reasonably specific time, no matter how distant that may be.

On the other hand, music administrators must not be caught up in rejecting certain aspects of music as art forms that defy measurement. Aesthetics and attitudes or the affective domain are equally important in music, and it is a misguided idea that some of these areas are universals that can be measured only as fixed behaviors. Opinions and judgments change as one matures, and provisions for this growth must also be considered.

One must not confuse measurement with evaluation. They are completely different and serve different functions. Evaluation implies determining the quality of an offering, while measurement is determining the

---

[1] Robert F. Mayer, *Developing Attitude Toward Learning* (Belmont, Calif.: Fearon Publishers, 1968), p. vii.

amount or extent of the offering. Often under Title I "evaluation procedures" schools were merely required to list the number of students attending the program. The students were then asked a perfunctory "did you like it?" This was a form of measurement. The real impact would be to determine the effect that the program has on a child's attendance at programs fifteen years later. This would be "evaluation."

EVALUATION IN PERSONNEL

Discrepancies of opinion occur when in evaluating the work of an individual music teacher or staff member, the teacher perceives his role or the objectives of the music program as different from those perceived by the evaluator. Under the circumstances, one can see why it is extremely important that the function, goals, and objectives for the music program be defined as clearly as possible. Even where clarity exists, individuals will still disagree as to what is expected of them. These disagreements may or may not be serious, depending on the extent and importance of the area of disagreement. Not every discrepancy that may exist between what a music supervisor or director expects of his teachers and what the teacher is doing is serious enough for drastic action or polarization. However, if the discrepancy or deficiency is sufficiently serious, then the music supervisor needs to determine a course of action. Often it is merely a matter of supplying the teacher with some pertinent information or providing him with some in-service training.

If it is a matter of inability, a lack of a particular skill, musical or educational, every opportunity should be given the individual to develop that skill. Where talent or ability is completely lacking to such an extent that even training cannot remedy the situation, it than becomes the supervisor's or director's responsibility to consider changing the assignment so that the skill in which the individual is deficient is not utilized to the same degree or with the same importance.

Occasionally, individuals may possess the skill necessary to achieve the goal, but they are completely uninterested in using it. If it interferes with instruction, drastic courses of action may be considered to motivate the individual. Although this implies a threatening tone, it is not intended. The course of action will depend on the individual, the skill involved, and the situation. Often it is due to improper feedback or communication from either the students, the administration, or the community. Failure to utilize a skill may be merely an attention-getting device. Supervisors need to make frequent visits in this kind of situation to give appropriate attention and even to supply the necessary feedback or information regarding the quality of the individual's teaching performance.

For example, one of the reasons many teachers avoid teaching twentieth-century music and twentieth century devices is because their own education did not prepare them for current musical exigencies. They may have the musical ability to teach these subjects but lack the incentive to do so. Encouragement and on-the-job demonstrations can help the teacher become more comfortable and perhaps even adventuresome in pursuit and presentation of "new" music. In spite of the fact that they have the essential talent, they may not have the knowledge for such instruction. In the matter of recognition, it may be that insufficient recognition or approval is given to individuals who pursue these areas of music.

Transfer of assignment or termination of employment is not always the solution, particularly when a teacher possesses the potential for success in his present assignment. Actually, as indicated earlier, transfer or termination should be considered only after all other courses of action have failed. The key to successful personnel procedures is matching an individual and his musical skills to the classroom situation that ideally fits his capabilities. This will obviate much of the difficulty that occurs when discrepancies in skill and teaching assignments arise.

In music it is not unusual to find some outstanding teacher not performing as expected because he may be punished for doing so. He may even be rewarded for performing at a substandard level. For example, when attending a concert, the music supervisor may find that the entire time is being devoted to "pop" music of an ephemeral nature. Apparently it makes the "kids" happy and provides the teacher with gratification in knowing that the students "love his class—he's really with it!" The parents extoll his praises because his classes and concerts are always "so much fun."

By the same token, this could be a teacher who is perfectly capable of making music of greater depth and significance equally exciting but is afraid of being "turned off" by the students or even the parents. The music administrator or supervisor's challenge is to see that similar gratification and approbation is given this teacher for providing a balanced program that includes all facets of music and music education. He will have to convince the teacher that, in the long run, his career will not suffer and that such performances can be equally rewarding in terms of the acclaim and recognition that he will receive from the more musically knowledgeable members of the community. He can still teach from a student's point of view without sacrificing his musical principles.

When desired behavioral change occurs, it is of critical importance that such change be acknowledged and rewarded. Too often individuals in responsible positions fail to respond regardless of what occurs. If the members of the music administration never attended the concerts given by schools under their jurisdiction, the implication is that they don't care how well the school and its music director is performing. If the administration gives attention only to problem situations, those who need attention may create problems to obtain the necessary gratification.

The evaluative process in personnel matters is essentially to identify the problem and then analyze the cause. Once this has been accomplished, the evaluator should select a course of action for solving the problem. Finally, the entire process remains incomplete until the supervisor or director evaluates the results of his action. Evaluation basically is controlling quality and determining courses of action to solve problems that improve the quality of musical offerings in a school. Not all problems, however, have solutions. At times, a music administrator will have to be content with a partial solution because it will result in a sufficient amount of progress and change that will make the situation more tolerable. To demand or seek a full solution in some instances may undermine the measure of success achieved and destroy a program that may bear fruition over a period of time. It is much like the anecdote, "The operation was successful but the patient died." In the case of the teacher who performed only "pop" music, if he introduces one or two pieces of significant literature in his next concert, it is a step. Rather than condemn him for still having a limited diet, compliment his progress and encourage him to attempt more.

EVALUATING CURRICULA

The evaluative process is governed by the established objectives as they relate to growth and development of the student. However, they must not be so restricted as to materials and procedures that they obviate flexibility. Objectives are not arbitrary products of a music department's staff. In developing them, one has to consider many factors. First and foremost, objectives should relate to the art of music and what it does for and to people. In addition, the needs and aspirations of a community and society as a whole must also be considered when establishing goals. This includes the student's needs, his interests, and his degree of maturity. This information is then absorbed, evaluated, and organized into a statement of goals.

Once a music department has some idea of where it is going, it must then determine how it shall get there. Instructional patterns are developed and a series of musical experiences are then constructed to assist the student in reaching his destination—an education that will aid and guide him in a changing society. To provide for these experiences, one has to allocate space, resources, personnel and students. Budget must be provided and all facets that contribute to a desirable learning situation must be taken into consideration. An appropriate faculty needs to be secured to implement instruction, and a climate conducive to learning must be created.

When this has all been accomplished, one needs to measure the success of the program to see if it has arrived. In order that the evaluation be reasonably valid, the program has to be measured in terms of whether or not the student truly reflects the objectives initially stated. If one were to diagram the entire process, it might appear as follows:

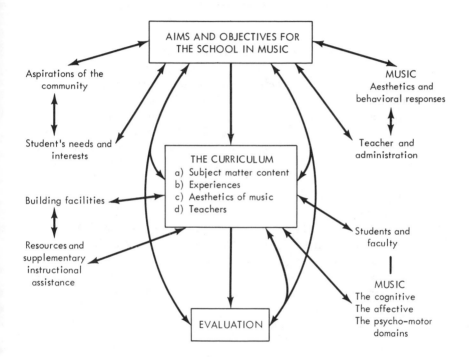

The entire system is dependent upon open lines of communication and feedback moving in either direction. It is bound together by a complete loop evolving from the evaluative process.

A small community, for example, might be concerned with becoming more culturally self-sufficient. It has no string program in the school and no civic orchestra to stimulate and encourage orchestral performances. Many students who don't want to play in the band but who are interested in playing string instruments have no outlet. Informed persons are sufficiently concerned that their children are not being exposed to the great cultural heritage that reposes in orchestral literature and that their aesthetic development is being restricted.

The individual in the position of leadership in music education is equally concerned and with his staff sets up a five-year plan to develop a school string program that will fulfill the need expressed by the community. A string staff needs to be employed, facilities need to be provided, and equipment must be secured. In the meantime as the staff is being assembled, incipient stages of "the curriculum" are being planned. Appropriate experience in a well-designed sequence will be organized by the music teachers and music administrators and to be certain that the program be more than just performance-oriented, specific goals in aesthetics and the affective domain will be identified.

At the end of the year, the entire program should be evaluated. This evaluation should be based on the criteria established when developing the overall aims. When the program does not meet its criteria for a successful experience, adjustments should be made. It might be that the students are not developing a particular skill that was a goal for the first year or it might even be that there has been insufficient sustained interest. At any rate, the chief bases for the evaluation should stem from examination of student growth, student development, and student response. Objectives may be revised and changes could be made in the curriculum sequence after each evaluation. At the end of five years, the entire program should be given an overall evaluation, and as a result the string plan might take a new direction or be continued as it exists. On the other hand, if evaluation reveals that the program does not meet the criteria as reflected in the aims and objectives, there may be other ways of achieving the original goals so that the project may be abandoned in favor of another approach. This is merely a broad description of a new program and how a music department would evaluate its success and progress. In an actual situation, each item would be specified and evaluated on its own merits as reflected in its criteria for success.

ACCOUNTABILITY

As indicated earlier, the citizenry is becoming increasingly concerned with "accountability." Basically, this implies holding educators responsible for what children actually learn in a classroom or, more specifically, for achieving their educational goals. This can best be ascertained by following the evaluative process. If outside agencies determine goals and objectives which are to be measured, they will select objectives that suit their vested interest. Unless educators are prepared to abdicate this responsibility, they must be willing to be held accountable to insure properly balanced programs that meet the needs of the whole child. Otherwise, programs will be constructed on purely functional goals that can be easily measured by arbitrary tests such as reading levels, math, grammar, etc.

To avoid this type of direction, the music directors and supervisors will have to assume a more aggressive role in identifying goals that can be measured behaviorally so that specific outcomes in music may be demonstrated and accounted for. They will have to improve the efficiency of their own operation to be certain that it can be upheld under close scrutiny and public debate. They can no longer rely on euphemisms, platitudes, and clichés to describe the inherent value of their programs.

The concept of accountability can be traced to four developments that were initiated in the sixties:

1) Federally initiated programs requiring evaluation as a part of the commitment when receiving federal funds
2) The increasing concern about the cost of education in the late '60s and early '70s.
3) Reassessing of educational priorities resulting in increased concern for the economically and educationally "disadvantaged"
4) Decentralization and its efforts to make the schools more responsible to the community and the people who are directly affected by its presence

All of these forces were instrumental in awakening the educational establishment to its responsibility in justifying its results with children.

These concerns also raise other issues. Who should be held responsible for musical outcomes and behaviors, and how much responsibility should rest with whom? Stephen M. Barro suggests, "Each participant in the educational process should be held responsible only for those educational outcomes that he can affect by his actions or decisions and only to the extent that he can affect them."[2] Music educators, through proper procedures, need to determine these outcomes, identify and define them so that they may direct the experiences essential for a developmental program.

One of the first performance contracts ever issued to a private corporation to manage an entire program was contracted by the Gary, Indiana Board of Education with Behavioral Research Laboratories of Palo Alto, California in 1971. One of the reasons the state of Indiana rejected the original contract was that there was little reference to being accountable for the fine arts and other enrichment areas. The entire commitment initially was merely to raise the testing level in reading, math, and language. It was quite obvious that under this type of commitment the

[2] Stephen M. Barro, "An Approach to Developing Accountability Measures for the Public Schools," *Phi Delta Kappan*, LII, No. 4 (Dec., 1970), 196.

entire school program would be focused on fulfilling the contract at the expense of all other facets of the school curriculum—particularly the arts. Only when the state intervened was some commitment made to the enrichment areas, and this was only with certain perfunctory activities.

The best defense against such an occurrence is to make music and the other fine arts so responsible that there can be little question regarding their contributions to learning and to developing aesthetic judgment. There must be a commitment and a willingness on the part of the music staff to state music's function and purpose—its goals and objectives—in measured terms. It must be able to identify and prove conclusively that it has achieved its goals or at least achieved them with a measure of success. This is what "accountability" implies and when music educators accept it as such, there will be no need for outside agencies to dictate the nature and direction for school music programs.

EVALUATING PERFORMANCES

Aesthetic judgment is a difficult area to evaluate. One cannot apply a simple rule to every aesthetic decision. There are many variables that one must consider. As a music supervisor or music administrator, one needs to take into consideration the nature of the situation as well as the values of the community and those who comprise it.

There are technical aspects of a performance that are fairly fixed. Such universals as tone quality, phrasing, etc. are fairly standard, but the more subtle aesthetic values are not as easily identified, particularly when one is concerned with raising musical standards. This standard, incidentally, is not to be confused with recognizing that when one assesses the performance, it should be considered in the context of that idiom and not evaluated in terms of another genre.

To help resolve this dilemma, a good rule to apply is that it is far better to aspire for a musical performance higher on the aesthetic scale and fall slightly short of it than to set your goals on music at an extremely low end of the aesthetic scale and achieve it. For example, a musical performance that is attempting to realize a performance of music that might have a standard of 80 on our imaginative aesthetic scale of 100, and achieve only 70 percent of its goal is far more commendable than that of a performance of music that rates 25 on the same musical scale and realizes 100 percent in terms of the performance standard. If one is interested only in music of low aesthetic value, the students cannot grow in aesthetic perception and value judgment. On the other hand, one should be equally critical of a performance that is so far beyond the technical and aesthetic level of the students that it doesn't achieve even a 50 percent rating in accomplishing a performance standard.

As long as they are responsible for standards and aesthetic values, music administrators must determine some criteria for evaluation. Without them, they are unable to enforce or justify their position regarding aesthetic standards. However, one should not interpret this to mean that any supervisor or director, whose cultural background may be different from that of the music being performed, should arbitrarily impose his values on the situation being evaluated. These judgments must be made in the context of the society and social milieu from which they originate and are being performed. One does not pass judgment as to whether or not a gospel song is more or less significant than a Lutheran hymn. If it is a gospel song, it must be performed in the best tradition of gospel singing. If it is a Lutheran hymn, the standard for that musical form prevails. Each idiom must be examined in terms of its significance for the performer and its contribution to the growth, development, and understanding of the people involved.

Respect for the performance styles of ethnic groups other than Westerners is extremely important, and music administrators need to be better informed about them. When dealing with the traditional Western-Germanic music, aesthetic values that apply to this tradition need to be enforced. One enforces standards for each milieu but does not assess one in comparison with the other.

EVALUATING FOR CHANGE

It is possible to develop a structure based on evaluative processes to attempt to produce desirable change. Such a design is essentially a systems approach and has proven most effective in industry. Whether consciously or not, this was basically the same approach utilized by the Music Educators National Conference in its Goals and Objectives Project (1968–1970) under the leadership of Frances M. Andrews and by the subsequent Action Plans that emerged from it.

The initial step in any systems approach is the formulation of specific statements of what needs to be done and what the department or profession as a whole is able to do. As a word of caution, these goals or objectives should be stated as precisely as possible, but they should not be governed by restrictions of materials or procedures that would limit the program. Such factors are introduced later, once the objectives have been determined. If a department decides that its chief objective is to increase the use of contemporary music in concert programming, it will not specify initially which songs (for chorus, orchestra, or band) until the objective priority has been established. It may then focus on one particular type of organization or on all three or even on a particular level of instruction before it even considers implementation.

The next step might be to establish precisely what is defined as "contemporary music" and the staff may then discover a need for improving specific musical skills if the objective is to be achieved in a qualitative manner. Before embarking on a total program it would be further desirable to set up some model programs in a specific school that might be interested in utilizing more contemporary ideas. If it proves successful, this school's program would serve as an example for other schools to imitate. Many innovative musical programs were introduced in the Detroit Public Schools by using Cass Technical High School as just such an example.

Michael Caldwell, Associate Director of the Evaluation Center at Ohio State University, has diagrammed an Educational Improvement Cycle that is based on four interacting major steps for action.

EDUCATIONAL IMPROVEMENT CYCLE*

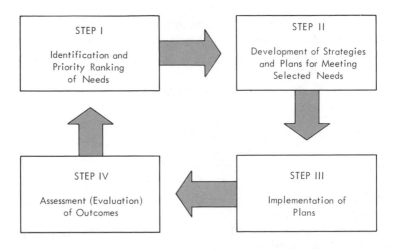

CONTEXT EVALUATION AND CIPP

Under traditional evaluation procedures one would look at the concert programs and determine whether or not the goals had been achieved without consideration of the quality of the performance, the nature of it, and its effect on the total music program and the community. A more recent design developed by Stufflebram at the Ohio State University

* Shelley Umans, *The Management of Education* (Garden City: Doubleday & Company, Inc., 1970), p. 40.

Evaluation Center would concern itself with these other factors. The design referred to as "Context Evaluation" includes four types of evaluation: context, input, process and product (CIPP). It was developed for specific application to education and is essentially based on a systems concept since all four factors are interrelated and part of an accepted systems approach. The CIPP design or model can be applied to evaluating a new curriculum, teaching methods, and even assessing community-school involvement. It may be applied by administrators without the assistance of computers or technical experts.

Context evaluation, the first step in CIPP, refers to the environment where the desired change will occur. It determines its unmet needs and the problems inherent in meeting these needs. If the community is a part of an inner-city and there is need for Black identification, the focus for a contemporary project would involve Black composers and Black music. The problem might be in selecting the music and bringing some of the Black idioms to the music class. It is therefore through "context evaluation" that the individual making the decisions can determine how to serve the objectives as they relate to the environmental needs.

"Input evaluation" is designed to assist the music administration in utilizing the available resources that will enable it to meet its goals. It begins by studying the available designs, systems, and planning strategies from existing programs or designs, and investigates which composers are available in the community, among the students, on the staff, or through the CMP project. As a result of the information from "input evaluation," decisions are made involving operational procedures and schedule for the plan, budget, and staff requirements. If additional input or data is required, it will be determined at this stage of development, especially if a model is designed and information is gained from it.

Once the action plan has been designed and approved and is under way, it then becomes necessary to begin "process evaluation." During this stage, administrators will, at regular established intervals, receive feedback regarding the success of the plan or where failures and weaknesses will appear. It might be in skills or attitudes of the personnel involved, or it may even be a procedural matter in dealing with staff. It may even be a matter involving facilities necessary to perform the music especially composed for the situation. This is an extremely important phase, since it will provide not only information for future operational patterns but also a record or report of the experimental model, which in turn will provide additional data when assessing the value and outcome of the entire project.

The final step in the CIPP system is "product evaluation," which relates outcome to objectives and to context and input. Its objective is to measure and interpret the final results or to what extent the plan

actually succeeded. Based on the information gained from "product evaluation," if we may refer to a student as a product, the administrator will
then determine whether to pursue the plan or discard it. His staff may
decide to modify or redirect the activity and involve it in another phase
of the process of change or merely emulate the model in another setting.

Regardless of the design used in evaluating for change—and industry,
the military, and education are constantly seeking new ones—the systems
must be designed to provide the person in a position of leadership, the
director of music, with effective means for arriving at his decision. Robert
Hammond of the OPIC Evaluation Center at the University of Arizona
has identified the following six criteria as essential factors in assisting an
administrator in the decision-making process. They are 1) relevance, 2)
significance, 3) scope, 4) credibility, 5) timeliness, and 6) pervasiveness.

To be useful, data and information must be pertinent, *relevant*, to
the objective. Although a great deal of information may be available, one
has to determine what is *significant* and just what its *significance* implies.
Even though the data may be relevant and significant, unless it is of
sufficient scope, it is limited; if it lacks *credibility*, it is suspect, especially
if the administrator is dealing with an unfamiliar phase or technique of
the operation. The information must be in the hands of the individual
making the decision within an appropriate amount of time (it must have
timeliness) to be useful. Often individuals providing data or information
are so inordinately concerned with perfect information that they neglect
to submit the necessary data within the designated time and the final
budget date may have expired! And finally, *pervasiveness* implies that the
data involves and provides for all individuals or groups involved in the
objective or plan when the data is being disseminated. It would be ridic-
ulous to bring a contemporary composer to a community or school for
the purpose of introducing contemporary music without consulting with
the teachers and building administrators where he may be assigned to
introduce a model or initiate the project.

The first composition that Richard Felciano wrote for the Detroit
Public Schools was composed for an inner-city high school and was based
on a Shelley Hischier poem dealing with the ghetto and its oppressive
walls. This was *relevant*. Another factor in evaluating the program was
that many individuals did not approve of the avant-garde style of the
composer's work, and many did. The director needed to weigh the significance and representation from both sides before determining his own
course of action and support. One teacher complained that the time
students spent preparing a four-minute piece by the composer-in-residence
was greater than all of the rehearsal time combined for the rest of the
program. An examination of the program revealed that there was more
significant learning to be obtained from that one four-minute piece than

from all of the other pieces of "instant" music combined. The time spent was well justified!

Change, even in music and music education, is inevitable. It is better to plan and attempt to guide it rather than have it sweep over us like a tidal wave and leave us inundated. Too many music programs in communities have been eliminated because no one anticipated change and planned for it.

Selected Articles For Supplementary Reading

ANDREWS, FRANCES M., "Music Education: Responsibility for Change, Accountability for Progress," *Music Educators Journal* (May, 1971), 26.

COLWELL, RICHARD J., "Musical Achievement: Difficulties and Directions in Evaluation," *Music Educators Journal* (April, 1971), 41.

CRAM, DAVID D., "Let's Be Objective About Music," *Music Educators Journal* (January, 1971), 48.

DIAMOND, ROBERT M., "The Systems Approach: Teaching Full Circle," *Music Educators Journal* (January, 1971), 37.

GORDON, EDWIN, "The Source of Musical Aptitude," *Music Educators Journal* (April, 1971), 35.

GREER, R. DOUGLASS, "Introduction: The Researcher's Role," *Music Educators Journal* (April, 1971), 34.

MADSEN, CLIFFORD K., "How Reinforcement Techniques Work," *Music Educators Journal* (April, 1971), 38.

STUFFELBEAM, DANIEL L., "Toward a Science of Educational Evaluation," *Educational Technology*, VIII, No. 14 (July, 1968), 5–12.

KLOTMAN, ROBERT H., Chairman, "Teacher Education in Music," *Music Educators Journal* (October, 1970), 33.

Doctoral Dissertations

OWENS, THOMAS R., *The Roles of Evaluation Specialists in Title I and Title III Elementary and Secondary Education Act Projects.* Ph.D. dissertation, Ohio State University, 1968.

TAYLOR, HUGH., *A Comparison Between Two Methods for Developing Attitudes Toward Evaluation.* Ed.D. dissertation, Washington State University, 1968.

Chapter 8

SCHEDULING AND ITS IMPLICATIONS

The function of a schedule is twofold: first, it represents an effort to organize someone's time, and second, it is a way of establishing priorities whether this be intentional or not. One usually plans a schedule, whether it be his personal one or for a student body, on the basis of what is most important.

There are three areas of scheduling that we need to deal with in this text: the administrator's or supervisor's schedule, teacher's schedules, and scheduling for students. The first is particularly important as a way of functioning for music administrators. It assists them in predicting their commitments and work loads and helps anticipate certain demands. It is quite easy to become so involved with "house-keeping" chores that school visitations, individual teacher's conferences, and other essential duties are neglected. A concerned music administrator, however, needs to plan his weekly, monthly, and yearly schedule well in advance so that what is most important to him in his role as a music supervisor or director is accommodated and ultimately accomplished. When this is done, other matters of secondary concern may then be built around these obligations. This planning, incidentally, includes attendance at concerts and programs.

Unfortunately, one cannot anticipate emergencies, special meetings, and special performances called by those higher on the line organization or even by those who need assistance on a lower line or staff level. Of course, adjustments will be made, but if there is definite planning and commitment, those special calls or meetings may sometimes be adjusted for a previous obligation. However, one must be realistic, flexible, and judicious regarding such emergencies. An administrator or supervisor should never schedule his work to complete capacity, as this eliminates desired flexibility and opportunities to adjust. He should keep some reserve time to handle items not accomplished or postponed because of other priorities.

Some individuals will hasten to point out that the so-called "house-keeping" chores can be important, and when set aside, the work still remains on the desk. This is true. As indicated earlier, if these are routine matters, they may be handled by non-specialized personnel. In addition, such chores are usually the kinds of activities or paper work that can be handled outside of school hours. One may not like the thought of additional hours of work, but unfortunately, the higher one climbs on the line or staff structures, the greater the demand for his time. The busiest man in the school system and the one who usually puts in the most hours is the school superintendent.

TEACHER SCHEDULES

Special music teachers or music coordinators who actually teach music in the elementary classroom will be governed by the school's schedule and prevailing attitudes toward music. I will not attempt to discuss the merits of the length of different music periods or whether skills of music should be introduced by the special music teacher or the regular classroom teacher. As a generalization, one may assume that the younger the children, the shorter the periods should be. Forty-minute or one-hour music periods are too long for elementary children, especially primary children. When scheduling a music teacher's program, be certain that travel time is built into the schedule. It is unrealistic to plan a schedule that doesn't allow time to move between classes, whether it be the teacher or the students who do the moving. Allow appropriate time to travel between buildings. Without these considerations, music teachers cannot do an efficient job of teaching music.

Where classroom teachers possess the essential skills and are interested in teaching their own music, they should be encouraged to do so. This will free the music specialist to devote more time to classes where his or her services are more necessary. The specialist can always be on call to assist or conduct demonstration lessons for the more competent classroom teacher as the need arises. Incidentally, having the music specialist available for call from any classroom teacher applies to all school situations. However, the music specialist should be able to reserve more time to assist those teachers who are less able to present effective music programs, and this can be done only when schedules are kept flexible.

It is especially important that elementary schedules for music specialists be organized in such a manner as to permit considerable flexibility. It is unrealistic to have the elementary music specialist visit every classroom in a building for the same amount of time. This might be appropriate if the music specialist taught all the music to all the children in a particular building. However, even where special music teachers are employed for each elementary school in a system, such a practice is rare.

In Akron, Ohio, a formula had been worked out to determine how much of the special music teacher's time would be allocated to each elementary building. For every two hundred (200) children, the building was provided with a full day's services. Thus, a building with an enrollment of eight hundred to one thousand (800–1000) students would normally have a full-time music teacher, whereas a building with an enrollment of seven hundred to eight hundred (700–800) students might have four days of service. The figures themselves served merely as guide lines. Where a building might have eight hundred (800) students but an interested principal who maintained an active, dynamic music program, rather than trying to find a one-day spot to fill a teacher's load, the school could conceivably have a full time music teacher.

In Columbus, Indiana, in 1968, a committee of elementary music teachers under the direction of Marjorie Fritz, acting music coordinator, made a study of class schedules and teaching loads and proposed the following schedule for music teachers:

Each music teacher to be given a load of approximately eighteen classes in order to provide the following services:

1. Grades one through three to be provided with two twenty-five-minute periods

2. Grade four to be provided three music periods, the extra period to make possible:

   a. One period per week to be devoted to some sort of melody instrument instruction and/or

   b. An exploratory instrument class

3. Grades five and six to be provided with three periods, the extra period to make possible:

   a. One regularly scheduled choir of the gifted students

   b. One period for remedial singing study for the students who need it

   c. One group sing for the students who are not selected for choir, but do not need remedial work

4. Five periods weekly during which the music teacher is on call. Suggested uses of the flexible periods would be:

   a. The classroom teacher could request:

      1. An extra period when she desired special correlation with some subject area

      2. An extra period when her class might be preparing some sort of sharing program

3. A period of rhythmic activities when children could not get outdoors
4. Extra music in general if she thought it would benefit the children
b. The music teacher could request:
1. Combined group sing of any grade level
2. Combined group sing of different grades
3. Small group instruction where not disruptive
4. Work with the problem singer
5. Helping individual children learn to play the Orff or rhythm instrument accompaniments that can enrich the full class when it meets
6. Working out dramatizations, reports, etc. that could be shared with the whole class
7. An extra class session with children who are preparing a musical program

This proposal was an attempt to introduce some flexibility into the special music teachers' schedules to enable them to implement their basic goals for music education. Their justification for the schedule was expressed in a supporting statement of philosophy and objectives that accompanied the proposal. In addition, they cited the recommendations from the state guide, *Music Education in Indiana,* as further support of their position.[1]

A. Elementary General Education in Music

1. Primary Grades: Classes should meet *daily* for at least *twenty minutes.*
2. Intermediate Grades: Classes should meet a minimum of *three times per week* for at least *thirty minutes* per session.
3. It is recommended that each elementary school encourage *choral activity* as an outlet for the children who are both interested and talented in vocal music (to be *scheduled in addition to the above*).

B. Elementary Instrumental Music

1. An exploratory program as a forerunner to formal instrumental study should be conducted in the fourth grade.
2. Class instruction for students in instrumental music can generally begin at the fifth-grade level.
3. It is recommended that instrumental music classes meet a minimum of two thirty-minute class periods per week.
4. When possible, homogeneous grouping of instruments is preferable.
5. In addition to elementary music classes, it is further recommended that an informal elementary band and/or orchestra be offered as the students are musically ready for this experience.

Although the proposal was approved and accepted by the administration, it was not implemented because to do so required additional staffing

---

[1] *Music Education in Indiana* (State of Indiana: Department of Public Instruction, 1963) Bulletin No. 370, pp. 71–72.

and no funds were available at that time. Individual music teachers, however, used the recommendations as a means of injecting some flexibility into their own building schedules. Thus, the proposal indirectly served as a catalyst for revising some of the traditional barriers that had been imposed on special music teachers' schedules preventing needed flexibility that would enable them time to work with classroom teachers.

Incidentally, these examples apply only to situations where elementary music is taught primarily by a special music teacher. Where the classroom teacher does her own music instruction, supervisors or music specialists need blocks of time when they can be available to assist these classroom teachers in the conduct of their music programs. The chief advantage to a program where the classroom teacher conducts her own music is that she can adjust her music schedule to accommodate the needs of her children as they arise. Where this kind of situation exists, it requires close supervision and assistance in organizing musical activities and seeing that they are carried out. Like all general statements, this concern does not apply as stringently to an elementary classroom teacher who has the necessary skill, interest, and capability to organize and conduct her own music program.

Instrumental schedules in an elementary school will depend on the attitude of the principal and the teacher in that particular school. Some teachers prefer that all the instrumental students leave the class at the same time. Under these conditions, instrumental music classes will be taught in heterogeneous groupings. If the prevailing attitude is that the students leave the class a few at a time, the music class will be conducted in a homogeneous manner. Some systems stagger the instrumental teachers' schedules so that students do not always miss the same period.

It is the director's responsibility through his supervisors to see that the services in each of these buildings are properly utilized. Occasionally, some building principal might underestimate his need because of his own disinterest in maintaining an adequate music program. It then becomes incumbent upon the music administration to call this to the attention of the principal and take the necessary steps to ameliorate the situation.

STUDENT SCHEDULING

Because of the nature of the music program, particularly in the secondary schools, it is almost impossible to avoid schedule conflicts unless provisions are made for special music classes (floating period, a zero period that does not have academic classes, special modules, etc.).

Although scheduling appears to be a mechanical, administrative function, it remains a very important factor affecting instruction. Interestingly enough, one can almost ascertain a community's interest or an administrator's educational philosophy by examining a school's schedule. Where genuine concern for the fine arts exists, schedules are made to include them, even under the most adverse conditions. It is essential that the music administrator develop skills in constructing schedules so that he can aid concerned building administrators who wish to provide time for the arts.

Obstacles that occur in scheduling usually fall in the following categories:

Block scheduling
Tract scheduling (reading ability, I.Q., etc.)
Core programs
Limited periods in the day
Conflicting philosophies between principal, staff, community and others
Lack of communication between levels (elementary and secondary)
Personality conflicts and conflicts of interest involving counselors and teachers
Physical facilities
Academic emphasis and the "college obsession"
Activity periods substituting for regular in-school scheduling

Schedules are the products of much planning and should reflect the changing aims of the total school program. They should never be regarded as permanent or fixed, but rather as being open and subject to continual review. A schedule design should be based on considerations involving students, staff time, curricula, and facilities. The design structure, in turn, is governed by factors that may be rigid or those that may be flexible. For example, the division or allocation of time is flexible, whereas the plant facilities are fairly fixed. The number of students will vary from year to year but when schedule planning occurs, the administrator is then governed by fairly fixed numbers. However, depending on one's philosophy, even an imaginative administrator can make a plant reasonably flexible to adjust to the number of students.

Charles Gary in *Scheduling Music Classes* states:

Schedules are impartial, they do not deny a student the chances to participate in orchestra, band or chorus because they dislike music or twelfth grade oboists, but only because they are designed to do something else that educators considered more important.[2]

[2] Robert H. Klotman, *Scheduling Music Classes* (Washington, D.C.: Music Educators National Conference, 1968), p. 1. Permission granted by the *Music Educators National Conference*.

Solutions to the problems may be found in a variety of ways. Some schools have resolved their difficulties and expanded their offerings by utilizing elements of modular scheduling. Others have devised rotating schedules with a movable period that occurs in a different position each day. Still others have adjusted traditional schedules by reducing the length of each period so that there are more periods in the school day. Examples of all these types of schedules may be found in the book, *Scheduling Music Classes*, published by the Music Educators National Conference.

An excellent example of the utilization of modular scheduling is one described by David Amos at Patrick Henry High School in San Diego, California.

MODULAR SCHEDULING OF MUSIC PROGRAM AT PATRIC HENRY HIGH SCHOOL, SAN DIEGO, CALIFORNIA, FROM 1969–1971. DEPARTMENT CHAIRMAN AND INSTRUMENTAL DIRECTOR: DAVID AMOS; CHORAL DIRECTOR: ROBERT KELLER

Patrick Henry High School is in San Diego, California and is one of twelve high schools in the San Diego Unified School District.

The experimental scheduling and teaching methods were jointly sponsored by the District, and the Model Schools Project of the National Association of Secondary School Principals.

During 1969–70, the school day was divided into twenty-minute modules. (See sample schedule.) During 1970–71, a forty-minute mod daily schedule was adopted. Unless the same class meets for two consecutive mods, there is a five-minute break between each mod.

Students are scheduled to attend classes during specified mods. During the mods where there are no regularly scheduled classes, a student has the option to schedule himself into various resource centers, discussion groups, teacher conferences, tutor assistance, library, music practice, test makeup, intramural sports, or various other learning centers where a faculty member or a teacher assistant is present to help the student with a particular subject area. The student schedules his daily open mods during the Guidance, or Administration period (mod 3). The Guidance teacher is the one who "guides" and assists the student in making his choice for the day's schedule; furthermore, the Guidance teacher acts as a counselor for the entire three years of his student's high school career. Through this form of modular scheduling, student and teacher time, as well as the physical plant, are used to fullest advantage.

Teacher assistants, certified college students with training in a specific subject, are allocated to each department according to the number of students enrolled in the subject area.

Extensive use of educational TV is made. All rooms are wired for closed-circuit TV. In this manner a single teacher could lecture to hundreds of students, if desirable.

The music department has a Listening Center, which is a practice room that had been converted to a resource room. It is equipped with record players, tape recorders, a full reference library, a piano, music paper, and study scores. A teacher assistant is in full charge of this room. Students may schedule themselves into the room to complete music assignments, study a musical composition which is to be performed by a school ensemble, receive assistance in Music Theory or Literature, compose, or simply enjoy some good music. An electronic music center is also being planned for the near future.

Class Offerings for 1970–71 school year were as follows:

Beginning Class Piano
Bands (Concert, Symphonic and Marching)
Harmony-Theory (A class in Comprehensive Musicianship)
Mixed Choir
String Orchestra (Full orchestra met in the evenings)
Jazz Ensemble
Madrigal Ensemble
Girls' Chorus
Music Appreciation

Performing Organizations for 1970–71 were:

CURRICULAR:	EXTRACURRICULAR: (meeting regularly)
Marching Band	Pep Band
String Orchestra	Improvisation Chamber Ensemble
Stage Band I	Stage Band II
Concert Band	Full Orchestra
Symphonic Band	German Band
Madrigal Ensemble	Various small ensembles
Girls' Chorus	
Mixed Chorus	

DAILY SCHEDULE OF CLASSES FOR PATRICK HENRY HIGH SCHOOL

Mod	Time	Instrumental Teacher	Choral Teacher
1	7:20	Band	Band
2	7:45	Band	Band
3	8:10	Guidance	Guidance
4	8:35	Harmony-Theory	Girls' Chorus
5	9:00	Harmony-Theory	Girls' Chorus
6	9:25	String Orchestra	Madrigal Ens.
7	9:50	String Orchestra	Madrigal Ens.
8	10:15		
9	10:40	(Lunch, sectionals, extracurricular	
10	11:05	ensembles, individual conferences,	
11	11:30	and listening center).	Mixed Chorus
12	11:55		Mixed Chorus
13	12:20		
14	12:45	Stage Band I	Music Appreciation
15	1:10	Stage Band I	Music Appreciation
16	1:35	Beginning Piano	

(Continued)

Mod	Time	Instrumental Teacher	Choral Teacher
17	2:00		
18	2:25		
19	2:50		
20	3:15		

This schedule seemed to have the least number of conflicts for the music students, both from within the department and the entire school master schedule. The horizontal pairings as well as open mods allowed the greatest flexibility for combining classes on occasion and for faculty meetings and student and parent conferences.

The Eckstein Junior High School in Seattle, Washington had an unusual schedule that permitted it to involve almost one half of its student body in music classes. Each day contained a daily activity period that occurred at a different time. This activity period was in addition to classes that met before school and to other classes that alternated music with other subjects. (See *Scheduling Music Classes,* p. 12.)

The Dade County Schools in Florida have introduced a new concept in school schedules, referred to as the Quinmester Project—an effort to schedule a year-round program. The schedule calls for five, nine-week sessions. Programs are designed so that "all courses will be based on identified levels of musicianship as well as unique performance skills."[3] Attempts are made to design courses that are nonsequential. However, entrance in a course is based on minimum competencies. Students are grouped according to achievement necessary to assume success. There is a sufficiently diversified number of offerings in music to accommodate any pupil's ability. This includes making available a large number of alternatives in addition to performance organizations.

Under this program pupils choose to go in or out of a "quin" (a nine-week unit) within a shorter period of time. Students may then have opportunities for broader and more different types of musical experiences. Since this program was introduced in 1971, it is too early at this time to determine its effectiveness. It certainly is an experiment worth observing.

Music educators also need to reconsider their inflexible attitude toward performing groups which require daily rehearsals of equal length of time. Perhaps they could use the time to better advantage if they met less often for a longer period.

Total staff meetings held to discuss schedules before they are constructed often help resolve personality conflicts and power struggles over the use of student time. If a schedule is to be accepted, everyone affected

[3] Howard A. Doolin, Personal correspondence (February 26, 1971).

by it needs to be given an opportunity to express himself, including teachers, students, and parents. The music administrator can often alleviate much teacher anxiety involving schedules by working with the building principal to see that this is done.

COMPUTER SCHEDULING

Many schools rely on computers for class schedules. Contrary to a popular misconception, computers are not responsible for scheduling students out of music. Computers merely facilitate assigning students in compliance with a schedule developed by people—teachers and/or administrators. If schedules are designed to accommodate music students and music students are scheduled first, they will be in the appropriate class. And even when conflicts occur, the computer is capable of printing a list of these conflicts, and those students listed may be individually hand-scheduled by a counselor or another designated individual.

Computers can be most useful in sorting and identifying groups and names. Because of their speed in operation, they can introduce much flexibility by setting up new schedules quickly and frequently. (This is especially useful in modular scheduling.) Furthermore, computers can be programmed to accommodate individual school needs and certain unique qualities that need to be identified in each program.

Rather than fear computers, music educators should study their uses and their abuses so that they may utilize them to improve and facilitate instruction. They can be tremendous timesavers as well as a means for improving efficiency in instruction. However, educators must never lose sight of the need for human control and human judgment in the final decision that affects a student's education and needs. These functions the computer is unable to perform.

In the final analysis, schedules are effective only if they accommodate the individual student. Where the pupil is the major consideration, principals and teachers will cooperate to see that each child participates in a music program according to his needs and interests.

Selected Articles For Supplementary Reading

Benson, Earl C., "Modular Scheduling in Music," *Music Educators Journal* (December, 1969), 55.

Thompson, Scott D., "Beyond Modular Scheduling," *Phi Delta Kappan,* LII, No. 8 (April, 1971), 484.

Chapter 9

BUDGET AND BUSINESS

There are probably no more frustrating responsibilities confronting a music administrator than matters dealing with budget and finance. However, one can neither ignore nor dismiss them. Virtually every decision under consideration affects budget directly or indirectly, and if one is to be an effective administrator, he must learn to deal with budgetary matters in a responsible way.

Practices regarding budgets are as varied as are communities and no attempt will be made to set up model budgets. What is important is that there be some basic understanding of the structure of a budget and that the design should reflect some underlying philosophy that can be interpreted in educational terms. It should reflect short-range as well as long-range planning.

Budgets should be designed out of educational needs and not just from expediency. After all, educational needs should determine priorities within a school system, within a department, and even within an individual building in order to determine the kind of education children receive.

PLANNING A BUDGET FOR CHANGE

In an effort to improve its operation, education has increasingly imitated industry, the government, and the military in planning procedures. There can be little argument that efficiency and economy are desirable. However, before one bows to the double "E," one has to know the advantages and disadvantages to determine the point of diminishing return involved in economy and efficiency. Saving is too often achieved at the expense of accomplishment. One violin amplified might be more efficient than twelve violins playing the same melody, but in a symphony, the desired effect suffers with such amplification. On the other hand, in a rock group the desired effect might be enhanced. Therefore, a budget planner has to determine what he is trying to accomplish and what sacrifices need to be made to reach these goals. Systems and computers do not take these matters into consideration. These decisions are made by individuals—human beings—and before one engages in systems budget planning, one has to be aware of its limitations as well as its advantages.

Modern managers and planners in industry and government are depending more and more on systems analysis for problem solving and long-range planning. The theory behind this approach is that virtually all problems are based on a series of interrelated parts which, when assembled, comprise an orderly structure. Although the human anatomy may be so structured, anyone who has functioned in a classroom made up of individual human beings with unique personalities is acutely aware of the fallacy of this theory. This is not intended as an argument against systems and their avowed purpose of Efficiency and Economy, but rather as an attempt to show some of the inherent weaknesses in a systems approach to educational planning. I fully advocate its use if handled judiciously. Although one can plan a production line systematically, one cannot always account for human variables, and the success of the system will depend upon the manner and understanding which the user applies to this type of planning.

Change, as we know, is usually not accidental. It is a result of careful planning. A systems approach can aid in the process if appropriately directed, since it is dependent on a clear definition of objectives. Consequently, if a new direction in music is the objective, then the music director is in a position to plan a series of organized steps with the appropriate budget to accomplish this change. If his plan is accepted and is then built into the appropriate computerized system, the possibilities for its being realized are much better.

PLANNING-PROGRAMMING-BUDGET SYSTEM (PPBS)

As a result of experiments conducted by the Pentagon and more recently by the government, a different, "more scientific" approach to efficiency and planning, referred to as Planning-Programming-Budget System (PPBS), has been designed by these agencies. On the surface the plan seems scientific, logical, and organized. However, as we shall see, it does not accommodate solutions for all educational problems. First and foremost, the entire plan is based on primary, identifiable objectives. One can anticipate a scene of great confusion in a discussion of objectives among educators. However, even if this concern were resolved—and it could be since each community determines the objectives for its own system—there are other pitfalls. Harry J. Hartley identifies twenty-five major limitations of the various systems approaches as they are applied to education. They are:[1]

1. Confusion over terminology
2. Problems in adapting models
3. A wisdom lag
4. Illusions of adequacy by model builders
5. Inadequate impetus from states
6. Centralizing bias
7. Unanticipated increased costs
8. Goal distortion
9. Measuring the unmeasurable
10. Cult of testing
11. Cult of efficiency
12. Spread of institutional racism
13. Political barriers
14. Conventional collective negotiations procedures
15. Lack of orderliness for data processing
16. Monumental computer errors
17. Shortage of trained personnel
18. Invasion of individual privacy
19. Organizational strains
20. Resistance to planned change
21. Antiquated legislation
22. Doomed to success
23. Imagery problems
24. Defects in analysis
25. Accelerating social change rate

An analysis of these limitations reveals the following:

1. There are so many acronyms for systems approaches that the word "systems" itself is confusing. Too often the implication is that PPBS or systems planning is merely another computer-based technique. This is a complete misconception. Computers are merely tools in systems planning and not the system itself. PPBS deals with the area of formulating a policy based on strategic planning. As indicated earlier, the term "system" implies that the character of the organization being analyzed consists of two or more interrelated parts and the relationship between these two or more parts forms an entity which can be identified and defined, such as the components that comprise the regular budget of a music education department or the components utilized when planning a new music room in a humanities wing of a building.

2. When adopting models from other areas, it is imperative for planners to understand that the models must be adjusted to fit specific situations. This procedure does not apply as much to the practice of borrowing one model in music education for another music education situation which may be similar, as it does to utilizing models in business or the military for educational purposes. The basic concepts and objectives in business differ greatly from those in education. Schools are much more complex and deal with people in a different context. One might imitate

---

[1] Harry Hartley, "Limitations of Systems Analysis," *Phi Delta Kappan* (May, 1969), 515. Permission granted by *Phi Delta Kappan*.

a model for developing a long-range plan for purchasing instruments or textbooks for one city from another of comparable size. But one would certainly not borrow the plan for the purchase of tanks for a military operation when considering educational items.

3. Mr. Hartley in his reference to the "wisdom lag" points out that though it is possible to analyze educational lags and problems with computers, we are unable to deal with our information in terms of relevance to human values. "The tragedy of our era is that human intellectual capacity, as addressed to problems of human relationships, seems, if anything, regressive."[2] The challenge of educational leadership is to reverse this trend.

4. Too often model builders become enamored of their labor and create "illusions of adequacy" by not questioning or interpreting their data or premises properly. This is a poor research practice, and music educators, who are often overwhelmed by the plethora of statistics sometimes demonstrate this failing.

5. Smaller schools will be unable to acquire facilities for appropriate "systems analysis." Only when state departments set up regional, cooperative centers will it be financially feasible for smaller communities to utilize a systems analysis approach to problem solving. Mr. Hartley feels that there is at present "inadequate impetus from states" to increase timesaving support for necessary equipment for systems operations. This lack of state support may change as the national government moves toward more financial support for the schools.

6. Today's schools are confronted with an interesting dilemma. Large communities are decentralizing while small communities are consolidating. As more and more schools rely on centralized equipment, decision making becomes more centralized. On the other hand, this raises the issue of an individual's rights to participate in determining the direction, goals, and aspirations as it affects his situation. A balance needs to be found between the advantages of efficient procedures in planning and preserving the individual's involvement and the right to deviate from the "centralizing bias." Those at the local level or those individuals in direct contact with the problems are often in a better position to determine what is needed to solve the problem, whether it is musical or educational.

7. Contrary to much of the current publicity, PPBS is not a move toward greater economy. When properly applied, PPBS has no position in matters pertaining to economy or cost reduction. Objectives and planning may even lead to a cost increase, especially if one is concerned about building music programs rather than about items to be purchased. (See Item 11.) If the systems objectives indicate a need to build instrumental

---

[2] Hartley, "Limitations of Systems Analysis," p. 516.

programs in the elementary school to achieve a result aimed at the high school, it could be very expensive. Purpose, not economy per se, determines the expenditure.

8. There has been considerable emphasis on goals and objectives as they relate to systems planning. Mr. Hartley hastens to point out in his list that too much emphasis on this aspect may lead to "goal distortion" or placing greater emphasis on those goals that are most easily mastered, such as cognitive mastery, and neglecting some of the more important concerns that cannot always be quantified and measured.

9. In music there are many areas that involve aesthetic judgment and they cannot always be measured in accurate, specific terms. It is true that there must be some measurable form or standard of performance when utilizing systems approaches if they are to function properly. However, systems planners must also be careful not to set up a system that is "measuring the immeasurable."

10. There are many educators who place unequivocal faith in testing as a means of measuring results. Tests must consider all variables that exist in every situation. For example, a variable could be an improper instrument that is designed for a situation that would not apply to the area in music being tested. This in turn would lead to improper interpretation of the information gathered. Earlier, a reference was made to the matter of aesthetic judgment in the selection of literature. Although one can count the number of pieces from the various historic periods, it is far more difficult to establish a measuring device for the quality of each performance. Furthermore, data may be manipulated by bias and this, of course, destroys the effectiveness of systems planning.

11. Too often, departments enter systems analysis with the predetermined notion that it will improve efficiency and result in a savings. As indicated earlier, this preconceived position undermines the entire approach to systems planning. Under these conditions the planners have already determined that priorities will be given to matters that will result in a savings rather than what can be accomplished in terms of goals. Such bias would dictate that it is better to buy fifty of the cheapest violins regardless of their tonal properties or construction rather than purchase ten violins that will be used for ten years in an all-county orchestra.

12. Systems are planned and prepared by human minds. They are merely means to an end and not the ends in themselves. Under no circumstances should they be designed to promote personal bias. Individuals planning and preparing systems analysis must eliminate any racist feelings. This has become an issue not only in major cities but in suburban areas as well. An administrator may point out that he has allocated $2000 for an inner-city school as well as for a suburban school. But if he has decided that in the inner-city there exists a specific culture, which,

incidentally, he may know little about, he might spend the entire money on metal clarinets, trumpets, and saxophones. On the other hand, if those involved in the school were permitted to help develop objectives for purchase based on community-school-student needs, such purchases might take a completely different direction.

13. Program budgeting could be used as a political football. Under a systems plan, an individual is required to express his priorities and this in turn exposes his sense of values. Whenever one places himself in such a position, he is subject to criticism. Budgets are not secret. They are published and discussed in open forum. This leaves one open to criticism both from within the educational structure and from outside it, and he should not permit himself to be swayed by pressure outside of those premises and needs that are educationally valid.

14. In a system that utilizes PPBS for planning salaries, this function could be either a serious limitation or a means for enhancing programs. Allocations may be maneuvered so that salaries are victimized and the blame placed on the system, just as teachers blame computers for poorly organized schedules.

15. Many institutions and school systems, in an effort to update their programs in educational administration, have attempted to develop elaborate data bases. The primary difficulty in adapting an information storage and retrieval model in educational administration, as in the behavioral sciences, is one of the orderliness of content.[3] Since there is no fixed comprehensive theory of educational administration, it is extremely difficult to establish an orderly system for storage and retrieval of information. Some form of taxonomy in educational administration will have to be developed before an accurate data base can be established.

16. Computers have been represented as being infallible and impartial. Computers are machines and as such subject to mechanical failures and malfunctions. They are extremely expensive pieces of equipment, and their errors can be very costly because of the high rate of speed at which they function. Students have been scheduled out of music classes in large numbers even when the schedule has been properly designed. A constant vigilance must be maintained to see that these errors do not occur.

17. With current inadequate funding for schools, it is difficult to train present school administrators in the function and operation of facilities needed for systems planning.

18. The use of computers in a systems design could serve as a bank to accumulate a dossier on individuals. This could be a dangerous practice and certainly an "invasion of individual privacy." Computers are not intended as repositories for such information. Centers should be used

---

[3] Hartley, "Limitations of Systems Analysis," p. 518.

for planning and design and not for the purpose of gathering minutia and statistics that do not relate to educational concerns.

19. When designers utilizing systems begin measuring performance quantitively, it may place stress on those who are concerned only with values and aesthetics. This may cause some conflict that may only be resolved by fully understanding the objectives that underlie the gathering of information and treating the information from an objective viewpoint.

20. There are those who will always object to change or innovation under the best of conditions. Furthermore, there exists in all people the fear that change or analysis may reveal a weakness that might be threatening to one's position.

21. Legislatures generally are oriented toward appropriations based on cost per item or cost per student rather than on the needs of programs.

22. Whenever an evaluation is conducted by the individual who has introduced a piece of new equipment or a new program, it is most likely that he will do everything possible to have the program or modern device appear in a positive light. This can interfere with the future revision and reorganization that might be necessary. As a result, there is often confusion over the potential value of a new concept and appropriate validation of its use.

23. Administrators who are misinformed about the machinery utilized in systems planning often regard the equipment as being highly involved and overly sophisticated. They feel that only a staff of experts and highly trained personnel can function with such modern devices and that if a systems approach is to work, it requires an expensive computer installation. This of course is not always true. Much depends on the nature of the operation, its scope and purpose.

24. As indicated earlier, data is often misinterpreted because of human error. Some errors occur in incorrect choices because of complex issues. A systems objective that arbitrarily establishes acceptance of a behavioral objective in a musical performance as requiring the performance to be 85 percent accurate, may be setting a standard that is too low if it is "The Star Spangled Banner," or too high if it is a complex étude being sight read.

25. There are many who feel that because of the rate of change presently occurring in our social system, tomorrow's schools are already passé. Today in large cities there are elements of society trying to eliminate schools as we know them. Under those conditions, schools today are hardly an organization of harmonious, interrelated parts, which is essential for systems planning. It makes one wonder just what is needed to solve the complex problems of educational planning if schools are to survive in this present atmosphere of change.

In his conclusion, Mr. Hartley points out that "systems procedures are a means, not an end, for achieving educational equality and excellence."[4] Although a considerable amount of space has been devoted to its limitations, the potential advantages in systems planning far outweigh the limitations.

PPBS does provide a basis for checking and comparing costs as they relate to deferred goals. In addition, it can provide an analysis of costs compared to benefits based on similar objectives from alternative programs and projects. Its major advantage in budgetary planning is its focus on the objectives and purposes for programs rather than items and objectives for purchase. It is a way of thinking that permits the judgment of many experts to participate in decision making. It applies not only to budget but to such matters as curriculum design, facilities, instructional media, personnel, and general long-range planning.

According to Robert J. Parden, there are ten distinct steps in planning a programming budgeting system. They are as follows:[5]

1. The objectives of the institution must be identified and goals established which would satisfy these objectives. [Goals must be quantified.]

2. All of the programs which might reasonably accomplish these goals are then developed. This accommodates and encourages all of the innovation the viable institution is seeking.

3. The costs, or resource requirements—money, people, facilities—for each of the alternative programs are assigned.

4. The benefits, or goal-satisfying potential, of each of the alternative programs are identified. This is a new dimension required by program budgeting and also one of the most difficult to accomplish. It is intrinsic to developing *priorities*.

5. To quantifiable costs and benefits, the decision maker must add his own assessment of the difficult or impossible to quantify—quality, personnel, potential, political expedience—and select those alternatives which appear to best satisfy the objectives and goals of the institution.

6. The long-range fiscal implications of those decisions are tested by projecting their impact over the next five to ten years.

7. The annual budget is developed from the data for the current year of the long-range fiscal projections.

8. The program alternatives which were selected, budgeted, and implemented are evaluated to see if the anticipated benefits were actually realized.

[4] Hartley, "Limitations of Systems Analysis," p. 520.

[5] Robert H. Parden, *An Introduction to Program Planning, Budgeting and Evaluation for Colleges and Universities*, The Proceedings of a Conference, July, 1970 (University of Santa Clara: Office of Institutional Planning).

9. The costs of the selected alternatives are reviewed to develop new standards to be used in assigning resource requirements to new program proposals and other alternatives.

10. The cycle is repeated on a continuous basis to allow for changes in objectives and goals, for new program innovations, for changes in available resources, and for changes in the environment in which the institution operates.

Actually there is little new in the idea of PPBS. Comprehensive advanced planning and anticipating budgetary needs based on programs have been with us for a considerable time. What is a new direction is identifying "organizational objectives and what should be done about them, the use of a multi-year program arranged to show how resources are being used to obtain organizational goals and objectives over an extended time (typically five years), consideration of alternative courses of action, the extensive use of quantitative analysis, and the integration of all these to achieve the best choice of decisions for the system as a whole."[6]

About twenty-five school systems in the United States were experimenting with PPBS at the time of this writing. The success of their programs will not be based on how efficiently they operate, but whether or not each unit or department within the total plan achieves its goals and whether or not the subject area departments interrelate with each other so that they all function as a unified system whose focus is improving the student's instruction in keeping with a rapidly changing society and changing times.

A detailed budget outline, based on PPBS, from Columbus, Indiana, may be found in Appendix N. page 208.

SOURCE OF FUNDS

The chief source of funds for a school system is *local* taxes. This is the crux of financial responsibility. It is even the practice in many states to limit state aid to the local per pupil expenditure or the local tax base rate. The second major source of income is the state. Unlike the local board, the state is much more susceptible to political maneuvering because policies are determined by elected state officials with party affiliations. Since they are somewhat removed from the local situation, they are, however, not as sensitive nor as accessible as the members of the local board of education. Making financial decisions removed from the con-

[6] Hartley, "Limitations of Systems Analysis," p. 519.

cerned area does have the advantage of minimizing sustained local pressures by vested interests. On the other hand, state legislatures, under these circumstances, may not always understand the needs and imminent pressures of a critical local situation.

The last major source of revenue available to a board of education is the national government. In recent years, it has assumed a larger role in funding local schools in an effort to equalize educational opportunities and raise the level of education in economically "depressed" or "deprived" areas. This has raised some interesting controversy. For years conservative educators have been concerned that "federal aid" would mean "federal control," despite the fact that for years the government has subsidized construction in education and aid to states for school food programs, vocational training, etc., with a minimum of interference.

In 1965, The Elementary-Secondary Education Act was enacted and large sums were given to the music education department in Detroit as a part of cultural enrichment programs. At no time was the Detroit music education department told *how* they were to teach or *what!* Implementation of the program was restricted to the guidelines established by the act and in the context of the Detroit board of education's *own proposal.* In addition, they were required to evaluate the program and account for the money spent; however, this is a good business practice and cannot be construed as interference.

By contrast, the Detroit Public Schools were approached by a commercial organ company and asked to conduct an experiment on the use of the organ as a classroom instrument. All procedures were agreed upon and the structure and basic utilization of materials was approved. Shortly after the organs were placed in the classrooms, representatives from the company wanted to come to classes and push the "easy availability of these instruments for purchase." They also wanted to see that more time was devoted to organ instruction. This was in direct violation of the agreement and obviously a sales-oriented "experimental program." The organs were removed. A school system need not subscribe to dictation or control from any outside source; nor does the desire to control school policies always stem from the federal government.

In essence these three governments—local, state and federal—are the sources of income available to public schools and budgets are determined by them. Occasionally, grants from foundations or private contributions may be made but they cannot be considered in overall budget planning. These contributions become the property of the board of education and do not belong to a single individual or, in the final analysis, even to a school building. It is the board's prerogative to distribute these funds in what they consider to be in the best interest of education. Their only restrictions are the guidelines of the contribution as agreed upon.

Often departments of music feel compelled to raise funds through special fund-raising activities such as candy sales, tag days, etc. Although the motivation for such projects may be justified on a special occasion, the practice itself can be somewhat degrading. Fund-raising has become such a big business that one can find almost as many exhibits at professional meetings promoting fund-raising gimmicks as displays of professional materials. The administrators in music should discourage such practices and generally avoid departmental involvement in them. Departments of music are the bona fide responsibility of the board of education and fiscal responsibility belongs to the tax payers through the board and not by means of gimmicks. The only possible exception to this position might be an activity sanctioned, approved, and supported by the board of education with a direct stipulation that funds for a project need to be raised from outside sources.

RESPONSIBILITIES FOR BUDGET

The total budget for the school system is the responsibility of the superintendent. It is the usual practice for him to submit the budget after consulting with the business department or chief financial officer and other administrators. Any anticipated expenditures from the music department that may require adjusting or reorganizing within the budget structure should be submitted to the responsible person in advance or during the budget preparation period.

One practice in some communities is to assign a lump sum to departments, and they, in turn, divide it within the department according to educational considerations. Another practice—one that is more prevalant —is to assign amounts to various expenditures according to the overall structure, and in accordance with previously planned considerations. Some of the items are then subject only to authorization by the music administrator. Other items, depending upon the limit set by the board, would then require consultation with and approval by others higher in the line and staff organization.

In most school systems one cannot transfer funds from one category to another without approval from the appropriate office. This creates some confusion in the minds of some administrators and even teachers because they assume that when a sum of money has been assigned to a music department, it doesn't matter from which category it is utilized. One needs to know existing practices within his own system before making these assumptions. It is advisable that every embryonic music director and supervisor acquaint himself with the financial structure and the rules that govern administering it within his school system.

BUDGET CATEGORIES AND PLANNING

Budgets are usually divided into several categories: *supplies* (office and classroom), *equipment* (musical instruments, office equipment, classroom instruments), *textbooks and supplementary book material,* pianos (they may be part of equipment), and *maintenance* (piano tuning, repairs, etc.). Instructional salaries are usually considered as part of the personnel department's budget. However, they are considered a cost item when determining per pupil expenditures for a department.

When preparing budgets for projects or other educational activities that require the submission of a budget, all of the above should be considered. In addition, remember to include ancillary services and other supplemental service, such as secretarial help and staff assistants who will be used in the project.

One way to remind oneself of the various budgetary items that keep coming up throughout the year is to maintain a file of folders for each of the different categories. This file would serve as a repository for notes and requests and, at the appropriate time, would help the music administrator remember his commitments, consensus, and ideas.

In addition, the individual responsible for submitting the budget from the music department to the superintendent should prepare an "action" calendar. Beginning with the date that the budget is due, he should work back and establish key dates for information needed from other sources that would affect his overall recommendation. Time should also be allowed in this schedule that will enable others on the staff to secure their information from their resources. By careful planning, one can avoid some of the frantic scurrying to secure information that accompanies so many of these "crises." When spending public funds, it is better to give evidence of carefully thought-out decisions rather than appear to be making hasty judgments. Under these conditions, one is less inclined to be critical of such decisions regardless of their outcome.

Most school systems distribute budget planning forms. These are in the form of work sheets and assist the music director in organizing his budget report.

BUDGETS FOR NEW BUILDINGS

There are two types of budgets functioning in a school system that are the concern of a music administrator. The first, which we have been discussing, is the annual budget. The second is ad hoc in nature and deals with specific buildings or programs. It is generally referred to as "capital outlay."

Each time a new school is planned, the music administrators should be certain that sufficient funds are allocated in the proposed expenditure to see to it that the students in that building are provided with a minimum amount of equipment and supplies that will permit them to function in an educationally desirable environment. This budget should be a part of standard, existing policies.

Most school systems, both large and small, maintain a "table of allowance" that indicates the minimum number of instruments that the board of education assures the school of having. (See Appendix M.) This table is usually the basis upon which purchases are made to equip a new building or in some cases to upgrade an old one where the instrumentation may be below the standard allotted by the table. The list should be reviewed periodically by a committee of administrators and teachers and should be adjusted according to current trends in music as well as to accommodate growth or decline in population within the school community.

PLANNING FOR NEW BUILDINGS

When determining housing needs for a new building, one must first consider the nature and philosophy of the program being planned for that community. Once this has been determined, some responsible official must then ascertain the anticipated enrollment and the percentage of the student body that will be served in the various music classes and activities. Based on these anticipated needs, decisions are then made for housing in that building. It is too limiting to rely entirely on past building plans designed for outmoded or past philosophies. (For ideas about new buildings see *Music Rooms and Equipment,* published by Music Educators National Conference.)

Teaching is affected by the physical environment. It can greatly influence the degree of success or failure achieved in a new unit. Music administrators need to be alert and even aggressive in seeing to it that the music department is given an opportunity to voice its concern for housing, storing, and maintaining the facilities provided in its unit, and for securing appropriate equipment.

PLANNING A NEW UNIT

When planning the new unit the director should be certain to involve and consult with those who will occupy the new building. This includes not only the music staff but also the building administration and the various building committees. At these meetings the basic philosophy governing music education in that community should be clearly stated and reviewed. Decisions affecting the following list of items that will be under consideration will be determined by this philosophical position:

1. Musical activities
2. Classroom floor space
3. Practice rooms
4. Musical equipment
5. Instrument storage space
6. Chalk and tack boards
7. Audiovisual aids
8. Storage compartments
9. Cabinet storage
10. Room acoustics
11. Strategic placing of electrical outlets
12. Music library
13. Sinks
14. Office space
15. Security

The director or his designated supervisor should make preliminary sketches of the unit and check the sketches in relation to the remainder of the building. He should keep a detailed check list of miscellaneous items such as chalk and tack boards, audio-visual aids and installations, bookcases, and closets. He should examine the latest classroom equipment to determine the type of chairs, instrument storage racks, and all movable furniture that will be needed. All these items should be selected on the basis of the prevailing educational philosophy, aims, and objectives as they relate to that specific program or school. If there is to be a great deal of emphasis on related arts programs, rooms must be designed for this purpose.

It is advisable and desirable to meet with the school architect and the building architect, if they are different individuals, to discuss the materials being utilized and acoustical planning; do not minimize the importance of soundproofing. It can interfere with the effectiveness of any music unit in relation to other classes as well as within its own confines. Instruments and electronic equipment storage areas will require a humidity control apparatus. Rooms should be well ventilated and protected against extreme heat and excessive moisture, since those conditions affect glued joints and wood parts. (Review *Music Buildings, Rooms and Equipment* published by the Music Educators National Conference.) Concern for ventilation and humidity, incidentally, is equally important for rehearsal rooms, since pitch is affected by temperature change and humidity and students need to rehearse under conditions that will promote musicality rather than inhibit it. Check the location of the music unit in relation to other instructional areas. It should be segregated as much as possible from other sources of sound. The music suite should have easy access to the auditorium stage. Although the music administrator must accept the architect's concept in terms of the total building plan, he should be responsible for applying and checking its relationship to the music unit's use.

Finally, all music administrators should take pride in the new construction. They should watch the building grow; follow reports on its construction. The director should get to know the superintendent in charge of construction for this building. If one discovers accidental omissions or other problems, he should report them immediately to the proper authority. Don't wait until the building is completed! All school systems may not permit their director or his supervisor to take such an active role in new building construction, but all directors of music should seek these responsibilities if they want to assume an active role in decision making for the future of their program.

PURCHASING EQUIPMENT

Procedures for purchasing equipment vary with boards of education but certain practices are consistent. Boards or states usually set a maximum figure for the purchase of equipment without submitting formal bids. Purchases made below this figure present little problem. However, if it is necessary to submit a bid, the variance in quality in construction and manufacture is so great that it is virtually impossible to assure a school system of appropriate equipment, unless a specific, uniform program is established.

Like every other decision, selection and purchase of equipment should be based on established educational philosophy. Is the emphasis to be centered on building a program for the future or is it to reinforce an established one? Will the budget seek to provide quality or quantity? This, incidentally, introduces another consideration. There is a point of diminishing return when selecting only the lowest bid for the purchase of equipment. In some cases the repair costs of a "cheaper" piece of equipment over a period of years would have enabled the music department to have purchased several items of far superior equipment during the same period. In addition, an instrument that does not produce a desirable sound even under the best of conditions is a liability throughout the life of that instrument. Over a period of years, inadequate instruments that have been purchased in large numbers to fill only *numerical* requirements for classes provide inadequate tonal properties and become a constant source of irritation.

To assure schools of proper music equipment, stringent specifications should be developed by those who ultimately use this equipment. This involves them in decision making and helps obviate future resentment regarding the material received. The instrument specifications, for example, should be designed for three categories: first line instruments, second line instruments, and third line instruments. When selecting a standard for purchase, be certain that all dealers are bidding on the same appropriate category, first line, etc. This helps obviate some of the current practices of bidding a third line instrument against one in the first line and thus securing the bid because of lower cost. The same principle applies when purchasing equipment for the "general music" class or the *choral* department. Administrators must be alert and vigilant to see that all specifications are adhered to when making their decision regarding choice. It is the students who ultimately suffer when inferior equipment is substituted, and the board is actually being defrauded. Teachers using the equipment or a selected administrator should also inspect the equipment before final approval for purchase is given.

Many boards have permitted their music department to include "acceptable tone" as a specification. This is usually handled by a committee or team of experts from the total staff under the aegis of the supervisory department. They will hear questionable instruments and their decision to accept or reject them will be based on a group decision so that it is not a matter of personal opinion. (See Appendix K.)

Not all business departments are sensitive to these complexities. It is the responsibility of the music administration to work with business agents and try to educate them when necessary. This requires patience and understanding on the part of the music administration, who should also try to understand the complexities of the job of these representatives from the business office. They are also there to facilitate instruction and anything that can be done to make their job easier will be appreciated. As indicated earlier, the teacher is the key to quality instruction, but even good teachers can do better if provided with appropriate equipment.

MAINTENANCE

There is no more severe drain on a music budget than the item listed as "maintenance." In large urban areas where theft and vandalism represent major outlays, it is advisable to have all equipment visibly marked, identifying it as the "property of" and in such a way that to remove it would deface the instrument sufficiently to destroy its market value. This may add slightly to the cost of the instrument, particularly if it is done at the factory, but the savings in discouraging theft more than offset this outlay.

Pianos should be inspected and tuned on a regularly scheduled basis. It is impossible to develop good musical ears if they are constantly adjusting to poorly tuned instruments. In addition, it is better for the instruments and helps prolong their life.

In Akron, Ohio a regular piano tuning form is filled after each tuning so that an active record is kept on each instrument. This record reflects the condition of the piano and accounts for repairs on it.

PIANO TUNING FORM

SCHOOL_____ ROOM_____

PIANO (Brand)_____ Make_____ Ser. No._____ Age___

Tune_____   Condition: (check one)

Repair_____   Good___ Fair___ Poor___

COMMENTS:

Tuned by_____   Signature:_____
                                         (Music Teacher or Principal)
Date_____

(Please return form immediately to the Office of Music Education)

Piano tuners, like potential teachers, should be auditioned and interviewed to determine their competency. This can be done by giving them one or two pianos to tune. Depending on the size of the community, they may then be placed under contract or assignment to see that the regularly scheduled tuning is assured.

Moving a piano can be dangerous and there have been actual instances where students and teachers have been injured in the process. To safeguard against legal action for injury, only authorized individuals should move a piano. To assure the school of proper protection, the following form is utilized in the Akron Public Schools for piano moves:

MOVING PIANOS IN SCHOOL BUILDING

Date ....

Name of school applying ....

Day, or days, weekly, or monthly, (be specific) ....

....

From .... to room .... and return ....

....

Purpose of moving. . . . .

. . . .

The undersigned is to take all responsibility for moving the piano. This application is to be made out and signed in duplicate and returned to the office of the Music Department for approval.

Principal's signature . . . .

Address. . . . .

Permission is given for the above.

Signed. . . . .

Supervisor of Music

Some urban communities maintain their own repair shops with the repair man being a staff member. He usually makes regular visits to the buildings for routine maintenance with some special provision being made for emergency repairs. Other communities may specify certain shops that have the necessary qualifications to handle appropriate repairs. Teachers or students may take or send the instruments directly to them.

Regardless of who does the repairing and maintenance, some procedure should be established to see that it does not interfere with instruction. A student sitting in a classroom, biding his time until his instrument returns from the shop, represents wasted money in lost learning time. It is poor economy regardless of the pennies saved by so-called good business procedures. Every effort must be made to find ways to minimize red tape that prolongs repairs and maintenance. In addition, it is advisable to maintain some record of the repair costs. When an official record is kept, it is much easier to approach a business department or superintendent for an instrument replacement. The statistics and not opinion are concrete evidence of cost factors, and the argument for a point of diminishing return in so called "austerity" or "economy" programs can be better substantiated.

Some schools systems will assign a budgeted amount for maintenance to each building, which the teachers may spend at their own discretion. Another method is to have a maximum figure for repair that does not require official approval. Unfortunately, there have been too many abuses of this practice and although it expedites matters, it has proven excessively costly. One way of dealing with this approach is to have each approved repairman submit a cost list to the department which automatically would cover almost every expediency. It is also information that teachers should have when advising students regarding repair shops.

It has proven to be worthwhile to establish specifications even for repairs, especially when large quantities of work are being submitted for bids, as is done in the summer. These are difficult to enforce, but they provide a basis for demanding quality service.

Certain pieces of equipment, like bows and mouthpieces, should be kept on hand as supply items to avoid lost instruction time. (Incidentally, fiberglass bows for beginners have proven to be excellent substitutes for wood bows that break easily, and as a result, good fiberglass bows are more economical over an extended period of time.) Strings, tail gut, valve buttons, and other small items that affect maintenance should be easily available so that instruments are not incapacitated for extended periods by such easily repaired items.

Many systems rent the smaller, more popular school-owned instruments for a designated period of time, usually one or two years. The money derived from rentals is used to replace worn-out equipment and provide funds for repair and maintenance. To protect the school system, contracts are issued to the parents. These contracts serve as a means of assuring some responsibility for the instrument as well as obtaining a commitment from the parents and students for the school's musical instrument and the program.

The Akron Public Schools require that their form, shown below, be made out in triplicate, one for the central music office, one for the principal's office at the school, and one to be retained by the parent.

INSTRUMENT RENTAL AGREEMENT

_____School

I desire to rent the_____ Make_____

Number_____ Value at $_____ for one semester, beginning

_____ 19_____ for which I agree to pay, in advance $_____
During the period in which this instrument is in my possession I agree to take full responsibility for its safety and proper use, keep it in playing condition, pay for any damage done to it and return it in good condition to the Music Department. I further agree to use it in some school activity, lessons, orchestra or band.

Signed:
Telephone_____ Pupil_____

Address_____ Parent_____

THIS COPY TO BE RETURNED TO MUSIC OFFICE
IF PAID BY CHECK, PAYABLE TO THE
AKRON SCHOOL MUSIC FUND

For the purpose of inventory control, the Warren Consolidated School District utilizes the following form. The explanatory material is separate from the form and sent out by the business department to the coordinator, teachers, and schools. (See Appendix O, p. 216, p. 205 in the Procedure Manual).

INSTRUMENT RECEIPT

Recipient:	Use this column if applicable			
	Student's Name:			
Address:	School:			
Date:_____Phone:_____	Expected Date of Graduation			
	Month: Year:			
(Signature of Recipient)	Date Equipment to be Returned			
Lender:	Month: Day: Year:			
Location:	Rental Fee: $			
CASE NO.	ITEM	SERIAL NO.	CONTROL NO.	COMMENTS

White Copy: Lender
Yellow Copy: Recipient
Pink Copy: Music Office

Consolidated Instrument Receipt is the term used for the complete listing of equipment a person has signed and is accountable for. These are brought up to date every six months (for our purposes, October and June seem more practical) and are done in duplicate. One copy goes to the file of the person receiving equipment and one to the file of the person to whom he is accountable. CIR is prepared by Central Office according to their records and is sent to the person receiving the equipment. One copy is to be signed and returned. Signature acknowledges accountability and/or responsibility for all items on the list. Accountability is the key word. If a teacher is well organized he will be able to account for a piece of equipment at any time. Naturally to protect himself as well as his equipment, the teacher will accomplish an inventory before he affixes his signature to the CIR.

Individual Instrument Receipts are used for a variety of purposes. They are printed in duplicate or triplicate on carbon packs or self-carboning paper. The original (white) copy is kept by the person lending equipment to someone. Second (green) copy is kept by the receiver of the

equipment. Third (pink) copy is not absolutely necessary but it might be good practice to keep a file of third copies at another location in case of loss or destruction of the other IIR's. Some of the uses are as follows:

a) Supply coordinator signing out a new piece of equipment to a teacher. When the new CIR's are made up these items will be added to it and the IIR's destroyed.

b) Teacher signing equipment over to parents for use by students. Our present procedures for this may be used but it need not be called a Parent Loan Form as one form of the IIR will serve a multiplicity of purposes.

c) One teacher signing something over to another teacher (an area that needs much improvement.)

Organization: A teacher's file may look something like this:

OPENED MANILA FOLDER

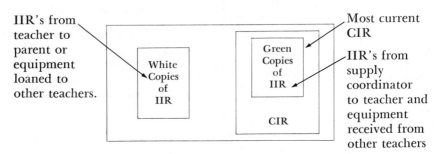

IIR's from teacher to parent or equipment loaned to other teachers.

White Copies of IIR

Green Copies of IIR

CIR

Most current CIR

IIR's from supply coordinator to teacher and equipment received from other teachers

This side represents all items for which the teacher is accountable but does not have under *lock and key*. In instances when a storage security in a certain school is weak and the teacher is there only three hours a week it may be wise to sign some items out to school administrator.

This side represents every piece of equipment for which the teacher is accountable.

The supply coordinator's file would be similar to this but much larger because he would have on the left side of his folder the original copy of the CIR signed out to each teacher.

Control Numbers: In the past this school system has utilized three different sets of numbers: the case number, the serial number and the control number. Case numbers only identify the case and not the contents of the case. Serial numbers identify the exact item but they are sometimes hard to find, often non-existent and do not always fit into a pattern easily digested by computers. The control tags are easy to peel off, but it seems that the control number system is the best. If we could enlist the support

of everyone to properly identify each instrument and its case, the same numbers could be painted on the instrument and case. Each teacher could be given a small supply of paint to keep the numbers fresh and we need only be wary of those who carry around paint thinners.

Centralized Control: Many teachers rebel at inventories because under the present system each teacher has to write the same information anew every time. Under the modified system the teacher would periodically receive a Consolidated Instrument Receipt which he would only check and sign if it is correct. Of course, this function could be easily computerized and may prove to be one of the higher priority items system-wide for computerization. Regardless how it is done, the teacher receiving a periodic list of what he is supposed to have would be much less likely to overlook items.

Lost or Stolen Equipment: The military has a procedure which may or may not be of use here. It may not because man-hours are so valuable in terms of dollars. It may because it has merit. In addition to notifying police and insurance companies of losses, a disinterested party is appointed to "survey" the loss. That is, he makes an effort to talk to all the persons who have had any access to the equipment over a period of several months prior to the apparent date of the loss. This person completes a report which goes to the Central File for purposes of clarification and to the police or whoever may require it for purposes of clearing the accountable teacher. The main purpose of this is to account for the item as well as possible but often new information is uncovered leading to eventual recovery of the missing items.

Design of Instrument Receipts: Assuming that they could be computerized, but not being familiar with computerized systems, I would not undertake to design an individual instrument receipt. However, here are a few of the things that could be included:

a) Signature of recipient.

b) Initials of person OK'ing the loan.

c) Planned date of student's graduation from WCS. (Could be important)

d) Date equipment is to be returned.

INVENTORIES

Generally, it is a good business procedure to maintain some form of inventory records and inventory control. With computers being more and more a part of a board's standard equipment, it is much easier today to sustain such records and to exercise better use of the distribution of music supplies and music equipment. All sheet music, books, audio-visual materials and recordings should be catalogued and placed on computer cards. This information should then be circulated periodically to remind teachers in a system or county of available resources. It may also serve as a means of checking the board's expenditure to the various school building as well as helping the individual school keep track of its own equipment. (For detailed information and sample inventory forms utilizing computers, see Appendix O, page 216.)

INSURANCE

It is increasingly difficult to acquire insurance at a reasonable rate. In most cases the cost is so prohibitive that schools prefer to take their chances. If students are assigned an instrument for school and home use, it is advisable that they be urged to include the instrument on their home insurance.

Music administrators should confer with their board business agent and determine the advisability of carrying some kind of insurance. This is often overlooked even when it is easily accessible through a board of education total contract with an insurance company.

PROFESSIONAL ETHICS

Administrators have the difficult role of setting the ethical tone for their staff. They are looked to as the example for procedures and behavior. They are responsible for signing attendance payrolls and should not compromise themselves. There is a fine line between human understanding and strict adherence to all rules. One should not confuse what can be handled in an ethically correct manner and what is sometimes done to preserve human dignity in dealing with an outside engagement that does not interfere with learning.

Under no circumstances can a music administrator permit personal interest to interfere with judgment when establishing guidelines, specifications, or standards. He must have administrative courage to take a stand in the best interest of education for his community on matters affecting purchases. He cannot be all things to all dealers. He should use his knowledge to advise appropriately and not base his recommendations on expediency or fear of rejection by business interests.

The National Education Association in its publication, *The NEA Handbook,* specifically establishes the guidelines governing ethical practices in regard to outside employment and compensation affecting school purchases. Every music administrator needs to be fully aware of these guidelines and be certain that they are followed. Those statements were developed to protect the students and the community, and everyone connected with the school system is obligated to follow and enforce them.

In addition, the music administrator must not indulge in practices that are in direct violation of copyright laws. Neither can he knowingly approve of members of his staff committing such acts. This law should be reviewed periodically with the staff to remind them of their responsibility in this matter.

In matters of finance, the music administrator must follow and rigidly enforce the regulations set up by the board of education, no matter how frustrating they may be. These practices have been established to protect all parties, and not following them leaves one open to suspicion. No one conducting school matters can permit this to happen if he is to continue to be effective as an administrator or teacher.

Selected Articles For Supplementary Reading

AEBISCHER, DELMER W., "How to Win Friends and Influence People," *Music Educators Journal* (February, 1971), 45.

BERK, LEE ELLIOT, "Life Styles, Credits, and Moral Rights," *Music Educators Journal* (March, 1971), 69.

————, "Music Education and Copyright Law: Infringements in Copying," *Music Educators Journal* (April, 1971), 55.

BRADEMAS, JOHN, "Government, the Arts, and the Public Happiness," *Music Educators Journal* (April–May, 1966), 41.

"Copyright Crackdown in Wisconsin," *Music Educators Journal* (December, 1968), 92.

"Equipment for Electronic Music Laboratories," *Music Educators Journal* (November, 1968) 176.

"Government Aid to the Arts. How and How Much," *Music Educators Journal* (March, 1970), 107.

GUTHRIE, JAMES, "A Political Case History: Passage of ESEA," *Phi Delta Kappan* (February, 1968), 302.

HARTLEY, HARRY J., "Limitations of Systems Analysis," *Phi Delta Kappan* (May, 1969), 515.

LEHMAN, PAUL, "Federal Programs in Support of Music," *Music Educators Journal* (September, 1968), 51.

Music Educators National Conference, "Music Buildings, Rooms and Equipment," *Music Educators Journal* (September, 1966), 67.

NEA Handbook (Washington, D.C.: National Education Association, 1958–59), pp. 62–63.

124   *Budget and Business*

"New Conservatory at Oberlin College," *Music Educators Journal* (November–Decembers, 1964), 121.

"New School of Music Building, University of Michigan," *Music Educators Journal* (November–December, 1964), 70.

SEAWRIGHT, JAMES, "What Goes Into an Electronic Music Studio," *Music Educators Journal* (November, 1968), 70.

SHOEMAKER, JOHN R., "A Classroom on Wheels for the Circuit Riding Teacher," *Music Educators Journal* (March, 1970), 57.

SHORES, J. HARLAN, "Federal Funds: To Assist or To Control," *Educational Leadership* (October, 1966), 7.

"The Arts and Congress—A Battle Won," *Music Educators Journal* (October, 1970), 63.

"The Arts, The Humanities, and the Budget," *Music Educators Journal* (December, 1969), 68.

Chapter 10

KEEPING THE COMMUNITY
AND SCHOOL INFORMED

As indicated earlier, the schools are supported by and are the property of the public. It is, therefore, advisable to keep the public informed regarding their schools and the music department. This is a matter not merely of information but of education as well.

> In today's world, the competition for men's minds is ever more intense. Millions of individuals make daily choices in terms of money, time and energy. These choices, when combined, add up to public support or rejection of causes, products and personalities. Education, too, is subject to competitive pressures for allocation of time, money and energy. And music education, like all education, must measure up in terms of quality, meaning, impact on lives, and contribution to the total society if it is to survive and advance. Furthermore, music education must be successful in interpreting its true significance to the public.[1]

It is not enough, however, to conduct a public relations program for the community only. It is equally important that the music department maintain an active program of keeping its school administrators informed. Often it is taken for granted that they will be informed and when the administrator learns from an outside source of an event that affects his school, it may prove embarrassing to him as well as to the music staff. This information, incidentally, should not be confined to developments within the department but should include innovations, issues, and trends as they occur within the total music education profession.

> Public relations for music education means, in part, educating the school administration in new ways of thinking about this particular discipline. Such communication deserves high priority among music educators.[2]

[1] Joan Gaines, *Approaches to Public Relations for the Music Educator* (Washington, D.C.: Music Educators National Conference, 1968), p. 10. Permission granted by the *Music Educators National Conference.*

[2] Gaines, *Approaches to Public Relations for the Music Educator,* p. 15.

It is equally essential to keep the music faculty informed about events and developments that occur in public occasions or within the administrative complex. So often music administrators are shaping events in their offices and neglecting to keep informed the very people that are eventually affected by these decisions. Communication and public relations are dependent on interacting, dynamic, open arteries functioning in all directions as the occasions arise. When decisions are being considered that affect teachers, it is much easier to implement these decisions if the faculty is aware of them and permitted to respond to them. Those in administration have often been accused, and with some justification, of involving people after the fact. Under these conditions those most affected by whatever change may be contemplated have little involvement in making the decision. This insensitivity has often been the cause of much of the misunderstanding that has occurred in education between administration, faculty, and community. It is far better to involve these people initially when decisions that affect them are being contemplated.

Good public relations is dependent on the music administrator's understanding the community and its needs. This includes knowledge of the racial make-up of the community as well as its socioeconomic structure. He must be aware of and sensitive to the aspirations of all the people who live in it. He should have knowledge of the businesses and industries that are a part of his community as well as the cultural and social climate in it. Anything or anyone who is involved in any way with education in the school system should be a resource for information or aid. It is important that good relations be established and maintained with all of them.

PURPOSE OF COMMUNITY-STAFF RELATIONS

To maintain a good staff and community relationship, a planned program that reflects the best qualities of the music program and school should be organized. It should be designed to appeal to the best opinions in the community. It should never be intended as a cover-up for errors, ineptitude, or incompetence. The program should be based on good common sense whether dealing with individuals vis-à-vis or with groups through publications and announcements. Its chief functions are as follows:

1. To interpret and inform the community about the school music program
2. To improve the learning experiences offered in the school
3. To promote interest in and support for the school music program

4. To eliminate confusion regarding the role of music in the schools
5. To ascertain whether or not the school music program is meeting the needs of the community
6. To make the public aware of the contributions that music makes to the child's growth and development
7. To include the community in planning and developing desirable music programs
8. To involve the community in helping solve problems that affect music
9. To make the community aware of certain needed changes and what should be done to facilitate desirable growth and progress through music
10. To promote a genuine feeling of cooperation among the school, the music department, and the community

In addition, communication serves to increase the effectiveness of the music administrator. It should make him more accessible to staff and community, and will, if appropriately handled, help him gain support from people both in and out of school. To do this, the music administrator must establish effective contacts between himself, parents, other school personnel, civic groups, and the communications media. He should employ every one of the available media and their resources to accomplish his purpose:

1. Newspapers
2. School publications
3. Administrative publications
4. PTA and similar school service groups
5. Lay advisory committees
6. School-made motion pictures of music activities
7. Students
8. Special school events such as concerts, assemblies, open house, special observances, etc.
9. Performers' bureau
10. Radio and T.V.
11. Personal appearances in public
12. Performances—professional and school
13. Civic service groups
14. Adult education and recreation programs
15. Related professional organizations and their media organs

Probably the most critical individuals in the school organization with whom the music administrator must have good communication, outside of the superintendent and the custodian, are the guidance counselors. Unless the music administration maintains good relations with the guidance department and its personnel, it cannot assist teachers and students when conflicts between guidance and music scheduling occur. It is essential that arteries of communication be kept open with the guidance department so that problems may be solved through joint creative efforts on behalf of the student. Such problem solving can be brought about satisfactorily only when there is mutual understanding of the basic philosophy, function, and purpose of differing views, and this can only be obtained through communication and mutual respect for one another's goals.

A joint committee representing the Ohio School Counselors Association and the Ohio Music Education Association published a pamphlet, "What's Good for the Student?," which was designed to ameliorate some of the misconceptions and conflicts that existed·between counselors and music teachers. The entire focus was on doing what would be in the best interest of students and education generally. This publication represented a positive effort toward improved communications between counselors and music departments. Copies of the pamphlet are available through the Music Educators National Conference. Every music department should develop a similar publication in conjunction with its counseling department if only to open communications between the two groups. The advantage of writing one's own booklet rather than using one emanating from a national office is that one can focus on the needs of the specific community and its students as well as dealing in generalities. The preparation of the document also serves as a unifying force between the counselors and music teachers.

COMMUNITY INVOLVEMENT

A concerned music administrator is civic-minded as well as school oriented. He must take an active role in civic groups that indirectly contribute to the well-being of the schools. It is time-consuming, but it is essential!

Music and music education involve working with people. It is impossible to avoid this function if you wish to have a flourishing music program. It cannot be done in isolation. It is an integral part of school music administration.

Desirable public relations begin in the classroom. Since the signal objective of the entire administrative program is to improve the quality of learning experiences offered the students, even public relations must focus initially upon them. Thus, the school becomes the focal point, and good working relationships must exist within the school as well as within the department.

Through the children, working relationships with parents may be easily established. This affords direct contact with the community for building good will and support for the school music program. As nonmusically oriented people see their children grow and benefit from constructive musical experiences, they will be more supportive of school music programs. Parents do not have to understand the aesthetics of music to know that acquiring aesthetic knowledge and developing good taste will make their children better educated. Focusing on what a program is doing musically for children and the musical child is the best type of public relations.

Another vital segment of the community, often overlooked by the music administration, is the professional musician. If the musical community supports the school music program, the public image of the music department is improved. In the past there has been considerable friction between the two groups. School music and professional music can enhance each other's functions. Both school and professional musicians should utilize all their resources by working together for better music everywhere.

Good working relationships should include members of the music industry as well. The Music Industry Council has prepared a publication, "The Music Educators Business Handbook." It is intended to promote better understanding between the school music department and the industry. In it one can find almost every bit of pertinent information dealing with the industry. It is intended as a service to music education and may be secured through the offices of the Music Educators National Conference.

Often the marching band in a parade or the high school choir at a civic meeting may be the only contact many people have with the music education program. It becomes the music administrator's concern that these groups function with a high degree of efficiency and skill. High standards and good taste should always prevail when dealing with the public. It is an educational responsibility.

OUTSIDE ENGAGEMENTS

Operating a "performers' bureau" for schools can be time-consuming for a music administrator, but it is well worth the effort in school community relations. In a community like Detroit, the music department scheduled between 150–200 outside engagements annually. In smaller communities the number may not be as large, but it is equally important that this service be provided. To avoid exploitation of student time and abuses that could infringe on professional agreements, strict regulations should be established governing these engagements. The head of the music department should administrate the program to take the pressure that might be unduly applied by local school patrons off the individual teacher or school. Teachers and school administrators must face these people on a daily basis, whereas the music administrator can, in a sense, isolate himself from the immediate situation.

All requests for outside engagement by school groups should be submitted in writing with full details as to time, place, nature of the sponsoring organization, type of group requested, admission charged and for what purpose, and any other pertinent information. All responses should be returned in writing so that no misunderstanding may arise. (Forms may be prepared to expedite these matters. See Appendix F.)

No engagement should be approved that is in violation of the code of ethics agreed upon by the American Federation of Musicians, The Music Educators National Conference, and the American Association of School Administrators (see Appendix G). In addition, final acceptance should be made by the school principal in consultation with the school music teacher involved.

Most decisions affecting these engagements are just good common sense. Travel should be at a minimum and loss of class time negligible. The code is quite specific as to the types of activities that may or may not be approved. If handled properly, this service will not only promote good public relations but can be an excellent means for motivating students to participate in school music activities.

KEEPING COMMUNICATIONS OPEN

Most school systems publish some form of official staff paper or bulletin that emanates from the superintendent's office and is distributed to all teachers. Music administrators may use this publication for special events or announcements of city-wide or county-wide interest. Since the space in it is limited, it should be used sparingly and judiciously.

Every music department should publish its own periodical. It could serve as a county-wide publication or, if a sufficient number of schools is involved, be local. It should be distributed to every staff member assigned to the department as well as to key school administrators. It should contain every piece of pertinent information that will help the staff to be better informed about the music activities throughout the school system, including a calendar of school music events. No bit of information should be regarded as too trivial unless it has absolutely no relevance. It is better to make each issue short and distribute it frequently than to limit the number of issues and have them so lengthy that the staff members find it an imposition to read. (See Appendix H.)

In large school systems it is advisable to hold an occasional "information session" with administrators out in the field. A similar program should be utilized for county schools. In addition to informing them about the aims and objectives of the school music program, it is helpful to renew standard information regarding basic equipment, materials, and texts. Always allow time for a question and answer period. Detroit, which was divided into regions, would permit the various departments to do this on occasion. Do not abuse this opportunity and stay well within the allotted time.

ISSUES INVOLVING GOOD RELATIONS

There will be times when the school music administrator will permit students to be involved in activities purely to promote good school-community relations. However, at no time should this be permitted if it involves an abuse of sound educational practices or outright exploitation of the children. One has to be careful that overly ambitious parents' clubs are not permitted to dictate policies regarding "outside engagements" and trips. Tact and firmness must prevail.

Religious and racial questions are difficult to deal with because one cannot arbitrarily set up rules to fit all situations. These problems are usually handled by "human relations" committees within the board of education. However, a music administrator must have a philosophy to assist and guide him in such situations. He should not be placed in a position where he is isolated and forced to make an arbitrary decision on a matter that affects so many people.

No music administrator can permit himself to be racially or religiously prejudiced. He must understand and value people for their differences. Music can enhance human dignity and the music administrator must be the champion of its cause. Regardless of its quality, if music or a performance infringes on an individual's personal beliefs, the individual should be given first consideration. Music or a performance that is offensive or deprecating to a race or group of people should not be permitted. On the other hand, the individual responsible for decisions affecting music must be certain that where music enhances human dignity, without violating the previously stated objections, it has every right to be heard and performed.

Music cannot separate itself from religion; it is an integral part of its history. Until the latter part of the seventeenth century, it received its major financial support and inspiration from the church. However, religion should not be used to undermine the dignity of the people who make up the community.

To assist administrators with this problem, the American Association of School Administrators has prepared a pamphlet, *Religion in The Public Schools,* which is published by Harper and Row. It can be of valuable assistance in helping to understand the complexities of this issue.

Today there are many issues that concern music. A major issue confronting education is integration and decentralization in cities and other areas of the land. The school music administrator is obligated to uphold the board of education, which is his employer, in its prescribed position. He cannot impede its progress in dealing with these problems because of personal bias. Music administrators must not regard a department of music as their personal empire. They must follow whatever course of action is necessary to improve the social and human conditions in their community.

IMPROVING SCHOOL-COMMUNITY RELATIONS

The most significant way to improve relations between school and community is to improve the "product." The better and more inclusive the school music program, the more likely it is to receive community support. Quality education merits better support.

In Warren, Michigan, the instrumental music teachers developed a unique progress report form which was distributed with the child's report card. This form not only enabled the teachers to provide specific information regarding the student's progress, but also informed the parent of the specific instrumental skills being taught in the elementary schools. (See page 133.)

The school music administrator must be personally school-community relations-oriented in the sense that he must keep in mind certain responsibilities that go with his office. He must try to see that all events are publicized and that board of education and school administration officials are invited. He must strive to maintain a high standard of performance both in and out of the classroom and he must work to build a feeling in the total community of pride and commitment to the school music program. Every effort should be exerted to make each citizen feel that it is his program and his accomplishment. It is not just the success of the school music administration, but a result of contributions from the community as a whole.

The Music Educators National Conference, under the direction of Joan Gaines, Director of Public Relations for MENC, has prepared a tape and manual to assist administrators and teachers in holding workshops on "Building Community Support." It contains all the essential information for organizing such a workshop with special instructions to workshop leaders on utilizing necessary space and limiting numbers. The entire presentation is divided into three basic topics: 1) Sharing Images and Cross Perceptions, 2) Problem Analysis through Role Playing, and 3) Ways to Build Community Support. It is a useful unit that every music administrator may use as an in-service device for improving school-community public relations.

WARREN CONSOLIDATED SCHOOLS
Music Department

TO:_____ _____ _____

(Instrumental Teacher)   (School)   (Date)

I, Mr./Mrs._____acknowledge receipt of the Instrumental
Music Progress Report. (Please sign and return with child to next lesson.)

Parent Comments:_____

_____

_____

WARREN CONSOLIDATED SCHOOLS INSTRUMENTAL
MUSIC PROGRESS REPORT (WIND INSTRUMENTS)

STUDENT_____ GRADE_____ DATE_____

INSTRUMENT_____ SCHOOL_____

Individual Progress	1 2 3 4 5 6	Articulation	1 2 3 4 5 6
Comparative Progress	1 2 3 4 5 6	Correct Fingerings	1 2 3 4 5 6
Attendance		Tone Quality	1 2 3 4 5 6
(with equipment)	1 2 3 4 5 6	Playing Position	1 2 3 4 5 6
Attitude	1 2 3 4 5 6	Note Values	1 2 3 4 5 6
Effort	1 2 3 4 5 6	Rhythm	1 2 3 4 5 6
Preparation of Lessons	1 2 3 4 5 6	Time/Key Signatures	1 2 3 4 5 6
Embouchure	1 2 3 4 5 6	Intonation	1 2 3 4 5 6

KEY: 1–2 Needs Improvement; 3–4 Satisfactory; 5–6 Excellent

COMMENTS:_____

1st COPY—Parent (to be distributed by classroom teacher)
2nd COPY—Instructor-school file

_____

(Instructor)

Selected Articles For Supplementary Reading

BENSON, CHARLES, "The Economics of Education in Urban Society," *Phi Delta Kappan* (March, 1967), 316.

BROIDO, ARNOLD and GARY, CHARLES, "Is Your Music Program for Real?" *Music Educators Journal* (March, 1969), 31.

GAINES, JOAN, "Building Community Support for the Music Program," *Music Educators Journal* (January, 1972), 25.

LEONHARD, CHARLES, "The Next Ten Years," *Music Educators Journal* (September, 1968), 48.

MELVIN, KENNETH, "McLuhan the Medium," *Phi Delta Kappan* (June, 1967), 488.

"Music Belongs: MENC Releases a Third Series of Radio Spots," *Music Educators Journal* (May, 1971), 48.

THOMAS, RONALD B., "Rethinking the Curriculum," *Music Educators Journal* (February, 1970), 68.

THOMPSON, WILLIAM, "Music Rides a Wave of Reform in Hawaii," *Music Educators Journal* (May, 1970), 73.

ZIMMERMAN, MARILYN P., "Percept and Concept Implications of Project," *Music Educators Journal* (February, 1970), 49.

Chapter 11

THE CHALLENGE OF ADMINISTRATION

The increasing incidence of social disorder in our society is sufficient evidence of the maladjustment that exists in our schools. There is a need for some change. Administrators in education have traditionally been regarded as deterrents to change within the social structure. This, of course, is not true of all administrators. However, too many of those who represent vested interests have risen through the system and were "successful" products and thereby defenders, of the system. This too is changing. Qualifications for administrative posts in music and music administration have become more stringent in the search for informed, enlightened people. Administrators are expected to be sensitive, imaginative, and flexible. They need to be creative individuals who seek new solutions to unresolved problems in music education. They are expected to be catalysts for change, for they are in the best position to make change.

Music education in the past has not kept pace with most changes that have occurred in society. This was evidenced in the 1967 report of the Tanglewood Symposium and its recommendations for action.[1] The report raised issues that have been with us for far too many years and represent commitments that concerned music educators must face.

Research in administration has established that it takes new ideas or a change in direction approximately fifty years from the moment it is accepted and initiated in a school to fully permeate all of the school systems in our country. The current state of mass media in our society may have reduced this figure. However, this implication is still frightening, especially when one realizes it is usually a direct result of inaction or apathy on the part of an individual. The most obvious approach to

[1] Robert Choate, ed., *Music in American Society: Documentary Report of the Tanglewood Symposium*, chapter IX (Washington, D.C.: Music Educators National Conference, 1968).

improving the schools is through change—change in curriculum, change in human attitudes, and change in behavior in the classroom by either the teacher or the student. There has not been sufficient evidence of this occurring in any major proportion in music education outside of the Contemporary Music Project and its focus on comprehensive musicianship. This project, originally conceived to place contemporary composers in the public schools under a grant from the Ford Foundation and the Music Educators National Conference, not only influenced the way music was taught in many schools, but changed the attitude of many teachers and students who were exposed to these experiences, either through direct contact with composers or by performing their music. The change manifested itself in the support, the added comprehension, and the increased performance of contemporary music in our schools. In its second phase the "Project" embarked upon a program of developing concepts and attitudes for teaching that promote "comprehensive musicianship" as the basic core for all instruction in music.

Habits or ideas that have proven successful in past years often become so imbedded in behavioral patterns that they are accepted as a valid basis for teaching long after the initial purpose or even function has ceased to exist. This is a form of mental or educational atrophy. Evidence of it may be found in certain guides, texts being used in classrooms, subject matter being taught, or even the schedules being utilized. If signs of atrophy are there, the music administrator or his supervisory staff must diagnose them properly and seek remedies that will release the frustrated energies confined by such restrictions.

It doesn't matter when this book will be read; the times are always changing. Unfortunately, what most educators fail to recognize is that the nature and purpose of change is also changing and that it is occurring at a faster rate than ever before. An enlightened music administrator anticipates change; a complacent or frightened administrator will initiate change only when forced to or under the most dire circumstances. The key to successful music administration is knowing how to work with and for change. To do this one must possess *administrative courage*. One must be able to identify stereotype thought and practice and abandon them for the benefit of today's and tomorrow's learners. It is these qualities that enable an individual to act at the propitious moment when motivated by need and conviction.

Music administrators should not fear an occasional failure. Goethe once said that men will always be making mistakes as long as they are striving for something. The best way to avoid criticism is to avoid any responsibility or course of action. Unfortunately, too many administrators, both in and out of music, are satisfied with avoiding criticism.

ISSUES IN MUSIC EDUCATION

Although it is fairly well established that humanities and related or multiple arts courses are desirable at virtually every level of the school experience, these programs are still regarded in many places as experimental. Music administrators should be holding dialogues with administrators in other related disciplines to determine how to implement these programs in their communities.

The concern for the "80 percent" of the students in secondary schools not enrolled in music has taken on the character of struggle between performance and nonperformance. Like so many debates, the basic issues become obscured in the rhetoric. One cannot have music without a performance. It is naive to assume as much. A listening lesson culminates in a performance either live or on a record. What is the issue is that performance for performance's sake is sterile and insufficient. Every performance should bring with it musical comprehension and musical understanding that will contribute to a more musically intelligent human being, one whose attitudes and involvement are reflected in musical behaviors—a comprehensive musician.

The issue affecting the vast number of students who reject music is why they do so and whether or not music education has rejected them. Too many classes in music act as though the music that has ephemeral appeal to their students is nonexistent. Teachers won't even discuss it with their students, as though it were a taboo subject. Certainly it is worth making music programs more meaningful and even more relevant if we can acquire a commitment from this "80 percent" that will involve them in music—past, present, or future—by at least acknowledging the existence of their music through intelligent discussions in a classroom.

Contrary to popular belief, music is *not* a universal language. It *is* a universal form of expression. In our world of change, our shrinking hemispheres, it becomes incumbent upon us to learn the musical forms of expression of other ethnic groups and of other cultures. It is no longer adequate in music education to limit students to one ethos, to one segment of the plurality of people that exist on this earth. Neither is this to be construed as advocating that music education minimize or ignore the plethora of great literature that emanates from the Western European tradition. The music administrator has a tremendous task to educate, inform, and disseminate information in the area of ethnic music if he is to maintain a degree of balance and proportion in the total music picture. On the other hand, he cannot permit those experiences that acquaint students with the great moments that exist in Western music to disappear from the curriculum.

The appearance of electronic music and computer-organized music is another development emanating from the latter half of the twentieth century that cannot be ignored. The students in today's schools will be the supporters of musical events in the twenty-first century. They must develop ears and understanding that enable them to express valid musical judgments in relation to the music of their time. To do this they must be exposed to experimental idioms, new styles, and new developments. It is the responsibility of the music administrator to keep his staff informed as these new idioms occur. He must devise ways and means to provide the necessary exposures.

MASS MEDIA AND CHANGE

Gabriel D. O'Fiesh in his article "Technology, The Road to Freedom," points out that "music educators have not taken full advantage of the available media, of the available work that has been done in programming education."[2] There is an untapped reservoir of individualized learning opportunities for students interested in music that music education is just beginning to explore. Materials and tools have not been developed by commercial firms only because music educators have not demanded them or even seen the potential for individualized instruction in cassettes, portable cameras, video tape, micro-teaching and micro-lessons. Tomorrow's schools are here today. Instead of fearing modern technology, music educators should be putting it to productive use. Electronic instructional devices cannot only implement instruction, but also facilitate learning. Rather than struggle against the technological revolution or resist it by ignorance, music educators should seek ways to utilize instructional technology as a means of making it serve human concerns and improving instruction. The present traditional classroom contains projection equipment, audio-playback, and the usual battery of electronic recording devices. This is hardly innovative today and all future classrooms will involve themselves with video cassettes, video discs which will offer six to twelve minutes of video programming from a television screen, and systems of multichannel sounds that create the illusion of depth by having sound completely surround the listener-viewer. Computer-assisted instruction and programmed learning texts will be some of the prime sources for individual instruction, even in music.

Smaller communities and rural areas will combine efforts to organize

---

[2] Gabriel D. O'Fiesh, "Technology, The Road to Freedom," *Music Educators Journal* (March, 1970), 45.

central audio/video centers which will disseminate and distribute multi-media materials and equipment for their use. It will no longer exist only for the larger or financially independent areas. There will be a central computing system that will be located in a central office and each of the schools in the district or county will be connected to the central computer. (As a matter of fact, it already exists in California.) Such a facility may either help analyze projected plans or participate in instruction. The center in turn might be a link in a series of intra- and interconnected systems that could utilize transcontinental lines with instruction centers across the country.

Unfortunately, music education as it exists in many of the schools of today is much more like the music education programs of 1935 than like the programs needed for 1995. In the schools of tomorrow the tempo of change will accelerate even more rapidly. As this occurs, the role of the music administrator will assume increasing importance in determining the nature and direction of change. Administrators will need to determine what is educationally desirable and then attempt to make it administratively possible.

USE OF COMPUTERS

The future of computer usage in music education is inevitable. It will become a working tool, an instrument, to facilitate learning and teaching in tomorrow's schools. Computers will not necessarily serve as assistants in instruction, but they will be utilized for retrieving information and making unlimited amounts of materials available to teachers in an extremely short period of time. Music educators will see their schools become a part of time-sharing computer terminals that will completely revolutionize the production of educational materials and printed matter.

Music educators of the future will be assisted by "Song Information Retrieval and Analysis Systems." They will handle many of the housekeeping chores that are so burdensome and time-consuming in today's classroom. Halftime marching shows will be planned and stored through computers. They will assist in diagramming and preparing work sheets for bandsmen. Problems of transposition will be handled quickly and efficiently so that scores will be accurate and available almost immediately through computers.

FUTURE OPERATIONAL PATTERNS FOR MUSIC ADMINISTRATION

The core of any program should focus on the students. The source of power emanates from the community which transforms this power

into an action program through its board of education. The superintendent with his administrative staff will develop programs *with teachers* and
lay people in the community that will be translated into desirable learning experiences for children. The patterns of operation will be circular
and contain channels in all directions rather than follow the traditional
line and staff.

FUTURE PLAN OF OPERATION

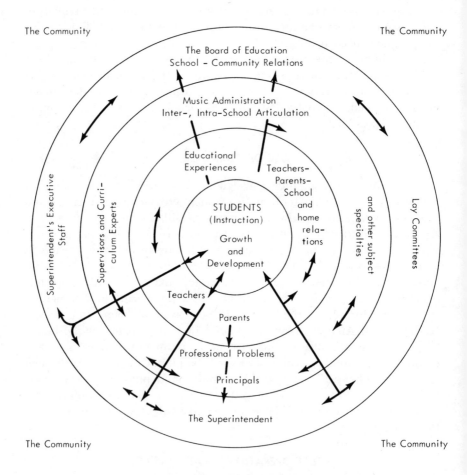

Future changes in plans of operation will also encompass changes
within the supervisory and administrative departments as well as in the
classroom. Larry E. Greiner in his business article on "Patterns of Organ-

izational Change"[3] attempts to dispel certain traditional myths that affect administrative patterns of behavior. To modify these behaviors he identifies four positive actions that are necessary to initiate procedures for progressive change. They are as follows:

1. We must revise our egocentric notions that organizational change is heavily dependent on a master blueprint designed and executed in a fell swoop by an omniscient consultant or top manager [music director or possibly a superintendent].

2. We too often assume that organizational change is for "those people downstairs," [teachers and students], who are somehow perceived as less intelligent and less productive than "those upstairs" [music directors, supervisors, and superintendents].

3. We need to reduce our fond attachment for both unilateral [authoritarian] and delegated approaches [from a committee complex] to change.

4. There is a need for managers [music directors], consultants [music supervisors], skeptics [the classroom teacher], and researchers to become less parochial in their viewpoint.

His plea in item four is basically for constructive dialogue between all persons involved. Joint effort and mutual respect is far more productive than a parochial, isolated attitude.

Tomorrow's music administrator will utilize modern research and data to develop, carry out, and evaluate what is needed to improve instruction in the classroom. Curriculum revision will follow procedures organized in a systematic manner based on a "systems" approach. Objectives will be stated in measurable behavioral terms and instruction will be organized and implemented in such a way that it will be governed by these objectives. Music educators will then evaluate their effort in such a way that the results will be measured in terms of the stated objectives. But even more important, objectives for future learning patterns will emanate out of the needs of students and the community rather than express those arbitrarily determined by the school administration.

The music administrator of the future will comprehend the role of the music educator not only as a "musician-educator" but as a socially sensitive individual. He will understand and appreciate diversity in people whether he is concerned with the inner city, a rural area, Appalachia, or the Northwest. He will be a leader in curriculum development in every sense for every part of the community. He will possess the necessary skills to work with those teachers and elements in the community that obstruct essential change as well as releasing the energies of and guiding those who support it.

[3] Larry E. Greiner, "Patterns of Organization Change," *Harvard Business Review* (May-June, 1967), 119.

Our future music administrator will possess a broad knowledge of the humanities that will enable him to deal with music in relation to other disciplines. He will involve himself with all of the arts activities in the total community so that music in the schools assumes its proper role in the lives of all people.

CONCLUSION

Music is an art and a discipline involving aesthetic, artistic judgment. It is a form of communication for people. Education is a science involving learning experiences based on developing a product with certain behavorial goals. Thus, for tomorrow's schools we will need teachers who are artists, scientists, and humanists. Securing them and implementing their work will be the responsibility of the music administration, made up of individuals who are basically teachers first. As administrators they metamorphose into advisors, teachers, and interpreters of philosophical concepts evolving from all the roles that affect the teacher, the student, and the community. They will be responsible for "quality control" in relation to the emerging concepts as they develop for tomorrow's society.

The music administration of the future will be concerned about creating environments in school that will bring out the latent creativity that exists in teachers and students. They will not be content to rely on past clichés that imply that all individuals are born creative and that they will express their creativity regardless of the situation. This is too easy an escape and makes music educators suspect.

Tomorrow's administrators will permit and even invite informed criticism, for they will understand that it is such enlightened criticism that enhances creativity. In fact, when differing views exist and those who differ try to learn from one another, the benefits are greater for all. Both the art of music and learning will gain.

The full challenge for music education as expressed in the Tanglewood Symposium is as follows:

> Educators must accept the responsibility for developing opportunities which meet man's individual needs and the needs of a society plagued by the consequences of changing values, alienation, hostility between generations, racial and international tensions, and the challenges of a new leisure.[4]

The success of music education in our schools will depend on how well music administrators bring about the necessary change that will effectively meet this responsibility.

---

[4] Choate, *Music in American Society: Documentary Report of the Tanglewood Symposium*, p. 139.

Selected Articles For Supplementary Reading

ANDREWS, FRANCES, "The Preparation of Music Educators for the Culturally Disadvantaged," *Music Educators Journal* (February, 1967), 42.

ARBERG, HAROLD, "Music and the New Federal Legislation: Challenge and Opportunity," *The American Music Teacher* (June–July, 1966), 32.

BLOOM, KATHRYN, "A New Federal Education Program in Arts and Humanities," *Music Educators Journal* (January, 1965), 37.

BRADEMAS, JOHN, "Government, The Arts, and The Public Happiness," *Music Educators Journal* (April–May, 1966), 41.

BROUDY, HARRY S., "A Philosophy of the Arts in an Emerging Society," *Music Educators Journal* (September, 1969), 43.

GRAMBS, JEAN D., "The Culturally Deprived Child," *The Education Digest* (January, 1965), 1.

KRISTY, NORTON F., "The Future of Educational Technology," *Phi Delta Kappan* (January, 1967), 240.

LANDON, JOSEPH, "Music–The Uncommon Denominator in Secondary Education," *Journal of Secondary Education* (February, 1965), 57.

MAYNOR, DOROTHY, "Why Should Whitey Care About the Ghetto?", *Music Educators Journal* (April, 1969), 60.

REIMER, BENNETT, "The Curriculum Reform Explosion and the Problem of Secondary General Music," *Music Educators Journal* (January, 1966), 38.

RICE, JOSEPH P., "Total Talent Development," *Journal of Secondary Education* (January, 1967), 12.

RIESSMAN, FRANK, "The Lessons of Poverty," *American Education* (February, 1965), 21.

"Rock" Issue of *Music Educators Journal* (November, 1969).

ROSS, JERROLD, "Music Education 1966 and Forward," *Music Educators Journal* (January, 1967), 36.

SHETLER, DONALD J., "Breaking Down the Hardware Barrier," *Music Educators Journal* (January, 1971).

THOMPSON, WILLIAM, "New Math New Science, New Music," *Music Educators Journal* (March, 1967), 30.

Appendix A

PUBLIC SCHOOLS ANNOUNCEMENT
OF ADMINISTRATIVE OPENING

*PLEASE GIVE APPROPRIATE PUBLICITY
TO THE FOLLOWING ADMINISTRATIVE OPENING*

Title of Position	Director, Department of Music Education (12 months)

Minimum   Increment
Maximum

A candidate with preparation beyond the Master's degree will be eligible for a salary differential above this maximum:
(1) Master's degree plus 30 hours
(2) Earned Doctorate

Qualifications   *Education.* Candidates for this position must be able to satisfy the legal requirements necessary for teaching in the state and must possess a minimum of a Master's degree from an accredited institution. An earned Doctorate or graduate work beyond the Master's degree is desirable.

Candidates must present evidence of experience and competence in most of the following areas:

1. Teaching in the field of music education at the elementary and secondary levels or experiences of comparable nature acceptable to the examining committee.

2. Demonstrated ability as a performer, conductor, clinician, and teacher in

144

either vocal or instrumental music. Successful experience in both music areas is highly desirable.

3. Supervisory experience in the fine arts field.

4. Special competence and knowledge pertaining to instructional materials for music education.

5. Competence in written and oral communication.

6. Good personal relationships with the public and with associates.

Duties and Responsibilities   The director of the department of music education will have the following duties and responsibilities:

1. Providing leadership to supervisors in the department and to teachers of music throughout the city at both the elementary and secondary levels.

2. Interpreting the total music education program to administrators in the central office, principals and teachers in the schools, and members of the staff of the Office for Improvement of Instruction.

3. Formulating general policies and procedures relating to the music education department.

4. Providing leadership and participating actively in conducting in-service programs, meetings, institutes, clinics, and workshops to improve the instructional program and to promote the professional growth of music teachers.

5. Cooperating with the personnel department in terms of auditioning candidates for teaching and accompanists positions, and making recommendations for assignments and transfers of music department personnel.

6. Supervising music education in the schools.

7. Directing arrangements for out-of-school performances given by school

musical organizations at community functions in the metropolitan area.

8. Supervising the selection of books, equipment, and supplies.

9. Directing the preparation of instructional guides, courses of study, bulletins and other printed materials used as aids for teachers.

10. Providing direction in the general planning of co-curricular and enrichment activities such as special ability classes; opera education program; city-wide vocal and instrumental festivals; and auditioning outstanding high school instrumentalists to perform with the symphony orchestra at a school concert series program each year.

11. Interpreting the total music education program to professional educators and the general public.

Method of Application

Candidates meeting these qualifications and wishing to accept the duties and responsibilities outlined should file a letter of application to the superintendent in charge of personnel indicating their desire for consideration. Application forms and other related information will be mailed to those who apply.

Closing Date
for Applications

ANNOUNCEMENT OF SUPERVISORY OPENING

Title of Position

Supervisor of Vocal Music in Elementary and Junior High School (10 months)

Minimum   Increment
Maximum

A candidate with preparation beyond the Master's degree will be eligible for a salary differential above this maximum:
(1) Master's degree plus 30 hours.
(2) Earned Doctorate.

Qualifications

Education. Candidates for this position must be able to satisfy the legal requirements for teaching in the state of _____ and must possess a minimum of a Master's degree from an accredited institution. Graduate work beyond the Master's degree is desirable. Preparation should include systematic study and competence in the following areas:

1. Specialization in the field of music education.

2. Knowledge of child growth, supervision, curriculum development, and educational research.

3. Knowledge of current curriculum trends and teaching methodology in music education.

147

4. Exhibited ability in written and oral communications.

5. Demonstrated outstanding musical competency.

Experience. The candidate must present evidence of successful experience in several of the following areas:

1. Teaching of music education subjects.

2. Some experience in coordination or supervision would be desirable.

3. A minimum of five years of elementary or junior high school music classroom experience.

4. Participation in curriculum committees, workshops, and/or general school committees.

5. Preparation of written materials, bulletins, and teacher guides.

6. Knowledge of methods of interpreting an instructional program to citizen and professional groups through oral, written, or visual materials.

7. Sound personal relationships, professional leadership, and productive scholarship.

8. Evidence of participation in community affairs and a variety of school experiences, one of which must have been in a school located in a low socioeconomic area.

Duties and Responsibilities

Serving as a staff member of the Office for Improvement of Instruction, department of music education, the supervisor will have the following duties and responsibilities:

1. Supervising the teaching of music in elementary and junior high schools, giving help to teachers when and where needed.

2. Conducting in-service programs, meetings, institutes, and workshops to improve the instructional program.

3. Preparing instructional guides, courses of study, bulletins, and teacher's guides for music education.
4. Assisting in the preparation of TV programs dealing with music education.
5. Assisting in the selection of basic and supplementary books for music education; preparing specifications for the procurement of equipment, materials, and supplies; and assisting in the preparation of budget recommendations.
6. Interpreting the music education program to region superintendents, principals, staff members, and the general public.
7. Assisting with the continuing evaluation and research of the effectiveness of the music education program.
8. Keeping abreast of the current literature and research in the field; helping to improve and strengthen the music program through creative innovative programs.

Method of Application

Candidates meeting these qualifications and wishing to accept the duties and responsibilities outlined should file a letter of application to _____

_____

indicating their desire for consideration. Application forms and other related information will be mailed to those who apply.

Closing Date
for Applications

Letters of application for the position of supervisor of vocal music will be accepted in the office of personnel through

_____.

Appendix B

A CHECK LIST FOR THE EXAMINATION
OF CURRICULUM GUIDES IN MUSIC*

I. Guide Construction and Revision Criteria	Yes	No

(1) There is evidence that the following people have been consulted in the formulation of the guide:

	Yes	No
a. Classroom teachers	____	____
b. Music teachers	____	____
c. Music supervisors	____	____
d. Professional musicians	____	____
e. Parents	____	____
f. Children	____	____
g. Administrators	____	____
[h. Curriculum specialists]	____	____

(2) Provisions are made for further revision; statements are given citing the need for further revision, or that the guide is tentative, or that there is a permanent curriculum committee at work. ____ ____

(3) Opportunity is provided for teachers using the guide to register opinions and suggestions about the value of the guide. A statement may be given encouraging teachers to give their opinions regarding the worth of the guide. A questionnaire sheet may be included in order to elicit the opinions of teachers. ____ ____

(4) The guide is five years old or less. ____ ____

No date given ____

II. Format and Physical Features	Outs	Good	Fair	Poor	Omit
(1) The table of contents is printed in a manner so as to provide for easy location of topics, subjects, and appendixes.	____	____	____	____	____

* Permission granted by Philip McClintock from *An Examination of Curriculum Guides in Music With Reference to Principles of Curriculum Planning* (unpublished dissertation, Indiana University, September 1970), pp. 99.

	Outs	Good	Fair	Poor	Omit
(2) The guide lends itself to quick reference due to the use of such devices as tabs or different colored papers.	___	___	___	___	___
(3) The guide is attractive in appearance.	___	___	___	___	___
(4) The binding is durable.	___	___	___	___	___
(5) The guide is easy to read. It is printed in large type. It uses easy-to-understand language; plenty of space is employed.	___	___	___	___	___

III. Curriculum Planning Procedures

(1) A philosophy of education is stated in a clear, concise manner and generally reflects the ideals of a democratic society. ___ ___ ___ ___ ___

(2) The broad goals of music education are stated in a manner that reflects the current thinking of the music education profession:

    a. The guide stresses the need for development of aesthetic discrimination. ___ ___ ___ ___ ___

    b. The study of non-Western music is recognized as being an important objective. ___ ___ ___ ___ ___

    c. Twentieth-century composers and their music are given consideration in the guides. ___ ___ ___ ___ ___

(3) The immediate goals of music are stated in terms of observable behaviors. ___ ___ ___ ___ ___

(4) Varied activities are included to promote musical learnings. ___ ___ ___ ___ ___

(5) Learning experiences are included that further state aims of music education. ___ ___ ___ ___ ___

(6) Characteristics and needs of children are listed appropriate to the grade level the guide deals with. ___ ___ ___ ___ ___

(7) The basic referents of the child, society, and subject matter are equally considered

	Outs	Good	Fair	Poor	Omit
throughout the guide, either implicitly or explicitly.	___	___	___	___	___
(8) Evaluation is stressed as an important concept, and the guide suggests many appropriate ways of evaluating.	___	___	___	___	___

Number of Guides including the Following Materials

IV. Materials, Equipment, and Aids for Guide Users

(1) A representative list of professional materials is to be found in the guide. For example:

a. Professional books	___
b. Music books for children	___
c. Publishers/manufacturers	___
d. Music lists	___
e. Films	___
f. Curriculum guides	___
g. Records	___
h. Resources of musics of other cultures	

	Outs	Good	Fair	Poor	Omit
(2) Sample lesson plans and units are included in the guide.	___	___	___	___	___

	Yes	No
(3) In the guide, suggestions are given as to the time allotted for instruction.	___	___
(4) Space requirements for music instruction are stated.	___	___
(5) A basic equipment list is included in the guides.	___	___

Appendix C

EVALUATION CRITERIA: MINORITY TREATMENT*

Following is a list of criteria on which educators can evaluate most if not all curriculum materials. It was prepared jointly by the Office for Improvement of Instruction and the Division of School-Community Relations. (This topic was a chief concern of the October 4–6 Waldenwoods Workshop on "Racism in Textbooks.")

While not all fifteen criteria will be applicable in every case, the questions raised by them do focus upon basic considerations in the materials that we use in the education of our children.

Do the curriculum materials

1. Give evidence on the part of writers, artists, and editors of a sensitivity to prejudice, to stereotypes, and to the use of offensive materials?

2. Suggest, by omission or commission, or by overemphasis or underemphasis, that any racial, religious, or ethnic segment of our population is more or less worthy, more or less capable, more or less important in the mainstream of American life?

3. Provide abundant, but fair and well-balanced, recognition of male and female children and adults of Negro and other minority groups by placing them in positions of leadership and centrality?

4. Exhibit fine and worthy examples of mature American types from minority as well as majority groups in art and science, in history and literature, and in all other areas of life and culture?

5. Present a significant number of instances of fully integrated human groupings and settings to indicate equal status and non-segregated social relationships?

6. Make clearly apparent in illustrations the group representation of individuals—Caucasian, Afro-American, Indian, Chinese, Mexican-American, etc.—and not seek to avoid identification by such means as smudging some color over Caucasian facial features?

---

* Permission granted by The Detroit Public Schools. From *The Detroit Schools* (October 29, 1968), 30.

7. Delineate life in contemporary urban environments as well as in rural or suburban environments so that today's city child can also find significant identification for himself, his problems, and his potential for life, liberty, and the pursuit of happiness?

8. Portray racial, religious, and ethnic groups, with their similarities and differences, in such a way as to build positive images?

9. Emphasize the multi-cultural character of our nation as having unique and special value which we must esteem and treasure?

10. Assist students to recognize clearly and to accept the basic similarities among all members of the human race, and the uniqueness and worth of every single individual, regardless of race, religion or socioeconomic background?

11. Help students appreciate the many important contributions to our civilization made by members of the various human groups, emphasizing that every human group has its list of achievers, thinkers, writers, artists, scientists, builders and statesmen?

12. Supply an accurate and sound balance in the matter of historical perspective, making it perfectly clear that all racial, religious and ethnic groups have mixed heritages, which can well serve as sources of both group pride and group humility?

13. Clarify or present factually the historical and contemporary forces and conditions which have operated in the past, and which continue to operate to the disadvantage of minority groups?

14. Analyze intergroup tension and conflict fairly, frankly, objectively, and with emphasis upon resolving our social problems in a spirit of fully implementing democratic values and goals in order to achieve the American dream for all Americans?

15. Seek to motivate students to examine their own attitudes and behaviors, and to comprehend their own duties and responsibilities as citizens in a pluralistic democracy—to demand freedom and justice and equal opportunity for every individual and for every group?

Appendix D

RATING ON
TEACHER COMPETENCE MEMORANDUM

SUBJECT: **Ratings on Teacher Competence**

FROM: Superintendent's Office

TO: All Department Heads and Supervisors

DATE:

I call to your attention section "X" of the new contract which was agreed upon by the Board of Education as a result of collective bargaining.

It should be noted that no specific reference is made to dates on which reports must be in, but the time schedule included in this agreement will apply regardless of the date which is given for reports to be in.

"X" QUESTION OF TEACHER COMPETENCE:
ASSISTANCE AND REPORTING

Before a teacher is rated unsatisfactory in instructional performance the following steps shall be taken:

1. The principal, assistant principal, or department head shall have observed the teacher's classroom performance at least twice.

2. The teacher's supervisor shall have observed the teacher's classroom performance at least twice.

3. A conference between the teacher, the supervisor and at least one school administrator as named above shall be held at least a month before the rating becomes final to put the teacher on notice that his work is unsatisfactory and to discuss with him ways in which he can improve.

4. If the efforts of school administrator, supervisor, and teacher fail to raise the teacher's performance to a satisfactory level, the administrator and supervisor shall each fill out a Form 4045, Special Report on Teacher

Services. The completed forms shall be forwarded to the field executive who, if he approves, will forward them to the head of the division. The teacher involved will be furnished with a copy of the ratings of both school administrator and supervisor.

Appendix E

THE VOCAL MUSIC PROGRAM*

OBJECTIVES

Music education forms a vital part of a well-balanced educational program and provides for the sequential development of the musical growth of young people in the Detroit schools.

The general objectives of the vocal music program are these:

To make music a vital influence in a child's life.

To develop in each child a love for and understanding of music.

To contribute to the personal, social, and cultural development of all children.

To help children use music to express their ideas and emotions.

To afford every child the opportunity to experience the joy of singing.

To teach every child the use of his singing voice.

To develop musical skills and discrimination.

To relate music learnings with other subject-matter areas.

To build a permanent repertory of folk and art songs that will enable children to appreciate the values of a multi-ethnic society.

ORGANIZATION OF THE VOCAL MUSIC PROGRAM

Elementary Division

Under the Detroit plan, vocal music classes in grades three through six meet twice weekly. All classes are taught by music specialists and meet in specially-designated rooms completely equipped with a piano, modern facilities, as well as basic and supplementary materials.

Each elementary school is assigned one or two vocal music teachers.

* Detroit Public Schools. Permission granted by the Detroit Public Schools.

In non-graded primary units, music is taught by the classroom teacher under the helpful guidance, when needed, of the vocal music specialist in the building, or a member of the supervisory staff.

Enrichment of essential music experiences is offered through participation in and performances by special singing organizations such as glee clubs, choruses, and small ensembles.

Junior High School Division

The vocal music program embraces classes in general music and special singing organizations.

Every vocal music room is equipped with a piano, autoharp, and ample materials.

Most performing groups meet daily.

Senior High School Division

A comprehensive music education program is offered in the high schools to meet the needs of the non-performers as well as the students having special interests and musical ability. Classes meet five periods per week for credit in specially-designated rooms that provide necessary facilities and equipment. In addition each Fine Arts Department staff includes a professional accompanist.

All courses are elective and include "Fine Arts Adventure," which is designed primarily for the consumer of music, vocal and instrumental instruction, theory, and performing organizations. Openings at this level are staffed by experienced teachers, *generally* within the school system.

TEACHER QUALIFICATIONS

It is essential that any candidate who wishes to be considered for a vocal music teaching position in the Detroit schools should have adequate preparation in terms of basic musicianship, methods, materials, successful directed teaching experience, and ability to perform both vocally and pianistically.

RESOURCES AND MATERIALS

Numerous opportunities for performances by way of radio, television, region and city-wide festivals, and community functions offer stimulating experiences for students and teachers each year. The Detroit Symphony and Chamber Music Ensembles present school concerts that provide enrichment to the music appreciation program.

Supplementary teaching aids such as films, filmstrips, phonograph records, and leading collections of exhibit materials are available upon request from circulating libraries of the Audiovisual Department and Children's Museum, which are operated by the Detroit Public Schools.

Teachers' guides for developing the vocal music program as well as lists of approved supplementary octavo material are available for use in elementary, junior high schools, and senior high schools.

Inquiries relating to the vocal music program may be addressed to Divisional Director of Music Education, Office for Improvement of Instruction, Detroit Public Schools Center, 5057 Woodward, Detroit, Michigan 48202. Telephone: (313) 833-7900.

THE INSTRUMENTAL MUSIC PROGRAM

OBJECTIVES

A well-articulated program provides for instrumental study and participation in performing groups beginning at the fourth-grade level and continuing through the twelfth grade in the Detroit schools.

General objectives of the instrumental program may be stated as follows:

To discover and foster the development of musically talented children.

To offer an opportunity to achieve self-realization by successful performance on a musical instrument.

To cultivate good human relationships through group participation in orchestras, bands, and ensembles.

To develop civic responsibility through participation in community activities such as concerts, parades, pageants, and other public performances.

To cultivate a better understanding and appreciation of music in our multi-ethnic society, through actual playing experience.

To enrich the cultural background of children and to provide them with wholesome leisure-time activities.

ORGANIZATION OF THE PROGRAM

Elementary Division

Instrumental classes are held during the regular school day. They are organized according to homogeneous groupings of either wind or string instruments and are taught by wind or string instrumental specialists. Pupils receive two lessons per week. An average teaching schedule includes five schools serviced twice weekly. Pre-instrumental training in simple melody instruments is optional at the third and fourth grade level.

District bands and orchestras as well as all-city organizations provide challenging opportunities for advanced players in the elementary and junior high schools.

Limited openings are available in wind instrumental positions. Entry positions in instrumental music are generally at the elementary and junior high level.

Secondary Schools

The instrumental program in the secondary schools is an extension of the work started in the elementary schools. Instruction is offered to beginners as well as advanced players of wind and string instruments. Classes meet for credit five periods per week in specially-designated rooms having all necessary facilities and equipment.

Honors organizations composed of personnel selected on a city-wide basis offer splendid opportunities for talented students to achieve on a mature musical level.

TEACHER QUALIFICATIONS

It is essential that any candidate who wishes to be considered for an instrumental music teaching position in the Detroit schools should have teacher certification and have adequate preparation in terms of basic musicianship, methods, materials, and successful directed teaching experience. He should have the ability to perform skillfully on one or more instruments, and a working knowledge of other wind and string instruments.

RESOURCES AND MATERIALS

Numerous opportunities are available for performances by ensembles, bands, and orchestras at community functions, on radio and television, and as participants in the six city-wide instrumental festivals that are conducted each spring. Clinics and supervisory assistance are also available.

Supplementary teaching aids and materials such as films, film-strips, district supplementary music collections, and Instrumental Teachers Handbook, and a Guide for Teachers of Instrumental Music, Grades 4–6 are available upon request by the teachers.

Inquiries relating to the instrumental program may be addressed to Divisional Director of Music Education, Office for Improvement of Instruction, Detroit Public Schools, Center, 5057 Woodward, Detroit, Michigan 48202. Telephone: (313) 833-7900.

Appendix F

OUTSIDE ENGAGEMENT FORMS

SUBJECT: **Request for Outside Music Engagement and Confirmation**

From:

To:

For:

Date:

We have received a request for music from:

For:

Date:

Time and Place:

Group and type of music required:

If you can accept, will you kindly make necessary arrangements (transportation, etc.) directly with:

Note: Keep this half of the form. It is your confirmation, if the assignment is accepted.

(Please fill in and return promptly to the Music Education Department, Division for Improvement of Instruction.)

We WILL ACCEPT this invitation. ☐

We are UNABLE to accept this invitation. ☐

The engagement requested by_____
(Name of Organization)

will be furnished music by_____ _____
(Type of Group)   (Number)

from_____   on_____
(School)   (Date)

_____   _____
(Director)   (Department Head)

_____
(Principal)

(Date)

Name
and
Address

Dear_____ :

This is to inform you that your request for music from the Detroit Public
Schools has been confirmed. Entertainment will be provided by:

School:
Type of Music:
Director:
Organization:
Date:

I would like to inform you that as a matter of long established policy,
your organization is expected to pay the costs involved in transporting
the members of the performing group. (Director's Name) has been asked
to contact you concerning the various details pertaining to this engage-

ment. If you do not hear from _____ within a few days, please feel free
to call _____ at the school.

Very truly yours

Appendix G

CODE FOR UNDERSTANDING
AND COOPERATION BETWEEN SCHOOL
AND PROFESSIONAL MUSICIANS*

A Code Adopted by the American Federation of Musicians, Music Educators National Conference, and American Association of School Administrators.

The competition of School bands and orchestras in the past years has been a matter of grave concern and, at times, even hardship to the professional musicians.

Music educators and professional musicians alike are committed to the general acceptance of music as a desirable factor in the social and cultural growth of our country. The music educators contribute to this end by fostering the study of music among the children, and by developing an interest in better music among the masses. The professional musicians strive to improve musical taste by providing increasingly artistic performances of worthwhile musical works.

This unanimity of purpose is further exemplified by the fact that a great many professional musicians are music educators, and a great many music educators are, or have been, actively engaged in the field of professional performance.

The members of high school symphonic orchestras and bands look to the professional organizations for example and inspiration; they become active patrons of music in later life. They are not content to listen to a twelve-piece ensemble when an orchestra of symphonic proportions is necessary to give adequate performance. These former music students, through their influence on sponsors, employers and program makers in demanding adequate musical performances, have a beneficial effect upon the prestige and economic status of the professional musicians.

* Permission granted by the Music Educators National Conference. From *The Music Teacher and Public Relations* (Washington, D.C.: Music Educators National Conference, 1958), 44.

Since it is in the interest of the music educator to attract public attention to his attainments for the purpose of enhancing his prestige and subsequently his income, and since it is in the interest of the professional musician to create more opportunities for employment at increased remuneration, it is only natural that upon certain occasions some incidents might occur in which the interests of the members of one or the other group might be infringed upon, either from lack of forethought or lack of ethical standards among individuals.

In order to establish a clear understanding as to the limitations of the fields of professional music and music education in the United States, the following statement of policy, adopted by the Music Educators National Conference and the American Federation of Musicians, and approved by the American Association of School Administrators, is recommended to those serving in their respective fields:

I. MUSIC EDUCATION

The field of music education, including the teaching of music and such demonstrations of music education as do not directly conflict with the interests of the professional musicians, is the province of the music educator. It is the primary purpose of all the parties signatory hereto that the professional musician shall have the fullest protection in his efforts to earn his living from the rendition of music; to that end it is recognized and accepted that all music performances by school students under the "Code of Ethics" herein set forth shall be in connection with non-profit, non-commercial enterprises. Under the heading of "Music Education" should be included the following:

(1) School Functions initiated by the schools as a part of a school program, whether in a school building or other building.

(2) Community Functions organized in the interest of the schools strictly for educational purposes, such as those that might be originated by the Parent-Teacher Association.

(3) School Exhibits prepared as a part of the school district's courtesies for educational organizations or educational conventions being entertained in the district.

(4) Educational Broadcasts which have the purpose of demonstrating or illustrating pupils' achievements in music study, or which represent the culmination of a period of study and rehearsal. Included in this category are local, state, regional and national school music festivals and competitions held under the auspices of schools, colleges, and/or educa-

tional organizations on a non-profit basis and broadcast to acquaint the public with the results of music instruction in the schools.

(5) Civic Occasions of local, state or national patriotic interest, of sufficient breadth to enlist the sympathies and cooperation of all persons, such as those held by the G.A.R., American Legion, and Veterans of Foreign Wars in connection with their Memorial Day services in the cemeteries. It is understood that affairs of this kind may be participated in only when such participation does not in the least usurp the rights and privileges of local professional musicians.

(6) Benefit Performances for local charities, such as the Welfare Federations, Red Cross, hospitals, etc., when and where local professional musicians would likewise donate their services.

(7) Educational or Civic Services that might beforehand be mutually agreed upon by the school authorities and official representatives of the local professional musicians.

(8) Audition Recordings for study purposes made in the classroom or in connection with contest or festival performances by students, such recordings to be limited to exclusive use by the students and their teachers, and not offered for general sale or other public distribution. This definition pertains only to the purpose and utilization of audition recordings and not to matters concerned with copyright regulations. Compliance with copyright requirements applying to recording of compositions not in the public domain is the responsibility of the school, college or educational organization under whose auspices the recordings are made.

II. ENTERTAINMENT

The field of entertainment is the province of the professional musician. Under this heading are the following:

(1) Civic parades, ceremonies, expositions, community concerts, and community-center activities (see I, paragraph 2 for further definition); regattas, non-scholastic contests, festivals, athletic games, activities or celebrations, and the like; national, state and county fairs (see I, paragraph 5 for further definition).

(2) Functions for the furtherance, directly and indirectly, of any public or private enterprise; functions by chambers of commerce boards of trade, and commercial clubs or associations.

(3) Any occasion that is partisan or sectarian in character or purpose.

(4) Functions of clubs, societies, civic or fraternal organizations.

Statements that funds are not available for the employment of professional musicians, or that if the talents of amateur musical organizations cannot be had, other musicians cannot or will not be employed, or that the amateur musicians are to play without remuneration of any kind, are all immaterial.

Appendix H

PUBLICATIONS

Uigo County School Corporation

667 Walnut Street   Terre Haute, Indiana

The task of our educational system is to take a lot of live wires and see that they are well grounded.   Pauline Glenn

Newsletter

3   *Volume 11 – Number 4   April 1970*

MUSIC PROMOTES HARMONY

FIFTH GRADE STRING STUDENTS AT MEADOWS – rehearse with their teacher, Mrs. Rosemary Funkhouser, for the Elementary Music Festival, April 26 at 3:15 p.m. in the ISU Arena. Seated, Terry Jones, cello. Standing left to right, Kevin Snyder, bass viol; Becky Hanks, violin; David Bindley, violin; and Diana Fortune, violin.

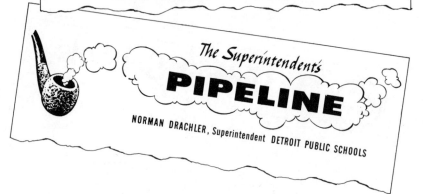

The Superintendent's

PIPELINE

NORMAN DRACHLER, Superintendent DETROIT PUBLIC SCHOOLS

City School District
Rochester, New York
Music Education Department

VOL. I No. 2   May 1970

Appendix I

PROMOTIONAL FORMS FOR
MUSICALLY TALENTED STUDENTS

SUBJECT: **Promotional Forms for Musically Talented Students**

FROM: Department of Music Education

TO: All Department Heads, Counselors, and All Music Teachers, Elementary, Junior High, and Senior High Schools

DATE: March 12, 1970

IMPORTANT—FOR IMMEDIATE ACTION

Uninterrupted musical activities for students interested and talented in music are important. Every effort should be made to help such students schedule in secondary schools the specific musical offerings for which they are qualified.

To simplify and streamline the programming and scheduling of the student when he transfers to a secondary school, it is important that there be cooperation of the secondary school music teachers, counselors, the elementary music teachers, and all who have a part in programming and scheduling.

PROCEDURE

The High School Music Teachers

Early in the semester, assume the responsibility and take the initiative in:

1. Knowing your contributing schools and establishing personal contact with the music teachers in those schools.
2. Acquainting the teachers with the required performing ability suitable for each high school musical activity.

171

3. Acquainting the teachers in contributing schools with the musical offerings in your high school.

4. Following through on the recommendations of the teachers in contributing schools, and providing some musical experience for each student who has expressed interest in music. The Department Heads will receive the lists in duplicate, and will be responsible for the use made of them in their schools, and determine the policies to be followed in effecting the most satisfactory solution to departmental scheduling.

5. Invite teachers to attend high school programs and festivals. THE COUNSELORS CAN BE MOST HELPFUL, and will be able to assist effectively if preliminary planning and preparation has been made.

The lists of recommended students must be accurate when they reach the counselors, and the students must have expressed the desire to continue music study in specific classes offered in the secondary schools.

The Junior High School Music Teachers

1. Assume the same responsibility as the High School Music Teachers in establishing personal contacts with elementary schools.

2. Know the class designation of the High School offerings.

3. Discuss these classes with the students, and individually with those students whom you wish to recommend.

4. List only those students who know that you are listing them and who want music in the High School. Do not limit your lists to outstanding talent but include the names of all who express interest in further musical activities.

5. Through the proper channels in line with policies operating in your building, try to have the specific music offering on the students' program.

    Example: *Vocal*—Glee Club, Chorus, Choir

                 Instrumental—A Band, B Band, A Orchestra, B Orchestra

    On the form where students may express a preference for electives, be sure that the students list specifically the music they are interested in; and if music is the first preference, put it first on the list because the counselor will be guided by this information.

6. Begin early in the semester to work on this project and return the lists according to the dates indicated.

The Elementary School Teachers

Follow the same procedure in sending students to secondary schools as the junior high school music teachers. Read instructions to junior high school teachers. Stimulate interest. Most all your glee club singers would profit by Vocal I in high school or Glee Club in junior high school.

Important—For All Teachers

1. Fill out forms listing the names of students whom you recommend and

who have indicated that they want music in the secondary school, if possible.

2. Use a separate form in duplicate, for each secondary school to which students are going. (Be sure this is checked with the student.)

3. Under *Comments*, indicate the type of organization in junior high or senior high school which would be most suitable. Examples:

> Has played trumpet for two years—good—B Band
> Has played clarinet six months—instrumental class
> Has studied privately for two years—A Band
> Contralto voice—reads well—Glee Club or Choir
> Soprano—light but musical—voice class

These comments will be most important in getting the pupil enrolled in the most suitable musical activity.

4. Keep a record of this information and do all you can to see that a suitable musical activity is placed on the preliminary program made out in your school for the school to which students will be promoted. *This is very important.*

5. Send both copies *directly* to the department head of the receiving school.

6. WHEN: Not later than Wednesday, March 25, 1970. Please do *not* be late. A return from every school is required.

SUBJECT: **Promotional Forms for Musically Talented Students**

FROM: Department of Music Education

TO: All Principals, for Department Heads, Counselors, and all Music Teachers in Elementary, Junior, and Senior High Schools

Relates to All Divisions

Promotional forms for musically talented students are being sent to all elementary, junior, and senior high schools as related material.

To All Music Teachers:

Please read carefully and immediately the entire bulletin, as procedure may take some time to effect an accurate and helpful list. Note that the return date is *Wednesday, March 25, 1970.*

To All Teachers in Contributing Schools:

The procedure outlined in the bulletin has been in effect for some time. Reports from high schools indicate that the lists have been most helpful. The comments indicate that some teachers are still too conservative, listing only the very talented, while others have recommended all who were able to carry a tune. Perhaps a compromise between these two extremes would be desirable.

Observe especially the important items:

1. The student must know he is being recommended for music and be prepared to accept music on his program.
2. He must indicate his first preference as instrumental or vocal music on his promotional form.

Send *two* copies of the vocal form and *two* copies of the instrumental form to the principal of the secondary school to which pupils will be going.

Please note that the lists should be made out in duplicate. One original and one carbon copy would be acceptable, even if written by hand. If you need more forms, call the Music Department office.

We shall greatly appreciate your interest and cooperation.

PROMOTIONAL FORM FOR VOCAL MUSIC STUDENTS

Region _____   Vocal Music Teacher _____   Date _____

The following vocal music students will transfer from the _____

School to the _____ School, and should continue their study of vocal music:

Name	Grade	Voice	*Musical Aptitude	Interest and Achievement in Music	Recommended for the following class

Please make out *two* forms for each situation and send them both directly to the principal of the receiving school not later than Wednesday, March 25, 1970.

* Rating Scale: Excellent, Good, Fair

_____
Principal

PROMOTIONAL FORM FOR INSTRUMENTAL MUSIC STUDENTS

Region _____   Instrumental Music Teacher _____   Date _____

The following instrumental music students will transfer from the _____

School to the _____ School, and should continue their study of instrumental music:

Name	Grade	Instrument	*Musical Aptitude	Interest and Achievement in Music	Recommended for the following class

Please make out *two* forms for each situation and send them both directly to the principal of the receiving school not later than Wednesday, March 25, 1970.

* Rating Scale: Excellent, Good, Fair

_____
Principal

Appendix J

LETTER FROM MICHIGAN
EDUCATION ASSOCIATION

October 1, 1970

Dear M.M.E.A. Member:

The enclosed represents an answer to needs relative to music education programs and working conditions as expressed by teachers of music. This material should be brought to the attention of your local education association negotiation committee.

It is recognized that some teaching assignments within a given bargaining unit are considerably different from others. Therefore, in order to be properly represented by the recognized bargaining agent, an effort should be made to set forth these particular conditions of employment in the master agreement.

The Michigan Music Educators Association (including its affiliate, Michigan School Vocal Association), and the Michigan School Band and Orchestra Association as departments of MEA have recognized this need and have taken upon themselves the development of such proposed language in an effort to assist local negotiating teams and their concerns regarding the best interests of the members of the bargaining unit.

It is very difficult to prepare guidelines which will apply to every situation. However, if special consideration is needed under certain unusual conditions, you should contact the Board of Directors of the above named organizations.

Sincerely,

Tom Patterson
Assistant Executive Secretary
Office of Professional Negotiations

Appendix K

SPECIFICATIONS FOR
INSTRUMENT PURCHASES

The various instrument manufacturers cited here are used merely as examples of how one school system is exacting in determining its specifications. They do not represent any endorsement or recommendation of a particular product. Each school must determine for itself the type of instrument that it feels will satisfy the educational standard that it sets for itself (*R. K.*).

PICCOLO, C and Db (HIGH SCHOOL)

New, Boehm system with covered holes and closed G sharp. Complete with standard plush lined Keratol (or equal) covered case, including swab. Case must be standard equipment as supplied by manufacturer for the instrument. Instrument and case to be delivered in perfect condition with key action, intonation, and general playing response of the instrument *subject to the approval of the purchaser.* Instrument must be engraved with phrase "DET. BD. OF ED." on main body of instrument. Letters to be 1/8″ to 3/16″ high.

Artly Philharmonic No. 22-P-30
Or Approved Equal

PICCOLO, C (JUNIOR HIGH and ELEMENTARY)

New, student line quality, closed G sharp, nickel silver alloy body, silver plated. Complete with swab, tuning rod, and standard plush or velvet lined Keratol (or equal) covered case. Case must be standard equipment as supplied by manufacturer for the instrument. Instrument and case to be delivered in perfect condition with key action, intonation, and general playing response of the instrument *subject to the approval of the purchaser.* Instrument must be engraved with the phrase, "DET. BD. OF ED." on the back of the body. Letters to be 3/16″ to 1/4″ high.

Armstrong No. 204
Gemeinhardt Model No. 4
Artley Prelude No. 15-P-30 (5-26-67)
Or Approved Equal

FLUTE (JUNIOR HIGH and ELEMENTARY)

New, student line quality, nickel silver alloy body, silver plated. Covered holes, closed G sharp. Complete with swab and standard plush lined Keratol (or equal) covered case. Case must be standard equipment as supplied by manufacturer for instrument. Instrument and case to be delivered in perfect condition with key action, intonation, and general playing response of the instrument *subject to the approval of the purchaser.* Instrument to be engraved with the phrase, "DET. BD. OF ED." on the back of the body. Letters to be 3/16" to 1/4" high.

Artley Prelude No. 18-0-30 (5-26-67)
Gemeinhardt Model No. 2
Armstrong No. 104
Beselor-Stangnane
Or Approved Equal

CLARINET, Bb (Wood) (HIGH SCHOOL)

New, wood, Boehm system, 17 keys, 6 rings, complete with ligature, cap, mouthpiece, three Ricco or Symmetricut reeds, #2 strength, lyre, and French style case. 2 barrels: 1 standard and 1-4 mm shorter. Case must be standard equipment as supplied by manufacturer for the instrument. Instrument and case to be delivered in perfect condition with key action, intonation, and general playing response of the mouthpiece and instrument *subject to the approval of the purchaser.* Instrument to be engraved with phrase, "DET. BD. OF ED." on back of both joints. Letters to be 3/16" to 1/4" high.

Buffet No. R-13
LeBlanc No. 476
Selmer No. B-15
Evette Schaeffer E10
Or Approved Equal

CLARINET, Bb (Wood or Plastic) (JUNIOR HIGH)

New, student line quality, 17 keys, 6 rings, complete with ligature, cap, Selmer HS Star mouthpiece, lyre, and French style case. Case must be standard equipment as supplied by manufacturer for the instrument.

Instrument and case to be delivered in perfect condition with key action, intonation, and general playing response of the mouthpiece and instrument *subject to the approval of the purchaser.* Instrument to be engraved with the phrase "DET. BD. OF ED." on the back of both joints. Letters to be 3/16″ to 1/4″ high.

Bundy No. Resonite 1400
Boosey Hawkes Resotone 1-10 Series Model 81
Conn Director Model 17N
Vita Resotone Model 14
Or Approved Equal

CLARINET, Bb (Metal) (JUNIOR HIGH and ELEMENTARY)

New, student line quality, metal, silver, nickel-silver, or nickel plated finish, 17 keys, 6 rings, complete with ligature, cap, mouthpiece, lyre, and Keratol (or equal) covered plywood, plush lined case. Case must be standard equipment as supplied by manufacturer for the instrument. Instrument and case to be delivered in perfect condition with key action, intonation, and general playing response of the mouthpiece and instrument *subject to the approval of the purchaser.* Instrument to be engraved with the phrase "DET. BD. OF ED." on the back of the body. Letters to be 3/16″ to 1/4″ high.

Noblet No. 18 with LeBlanc mouthpiece
Carl Fischer No. 225
Or Approved Equal

OBOES (HIGH SCHOOL)

New, wood, full conservatory system, single action octave keys (not automatic), covered holes, F-resonance key, complete with French style plush lined case including reed case, three Meeson reeds, medium strength, and one box of joint grease. Case must be standard equipment as supplied by manufacturer for the instrument. Instrument and general playing response of the instrument *subject to the approval of the purchaser.* Instrument to be engraved with phrase, "DET. BD. OF ED." on back of both joints. Letters to be 3/16″ to 1/4″ high.

Chauvet Professional
Platz
Benwall, Plateau model
Conn Artist Model 12Q
Lucerne No. 210
Or Approved Equal

OBOE (JUNIOR HIGH)

New, student line quality, full conservatory system, open or closed tone holes, single action octave key, F-resonance key. Must have low "Bb" key. Complete with French style case including reed case, three Meeson reeds, joint grease, and cleaning feather. Case must be standard equipment as supplied by manufacturer for the instrument. Instrument and case to be delivered in perfect condition with key action, intonation, and general playing response of the instrument *subject to the approval of the purchaser*. Instrument must be engraved with the phrase, "DET. BD. OF ED." on the back of the body. Letters to be 3/16" to 1/4" high.

Malerne No. I-6
Linton No. HRS
La Marque No. LM-7
Buffet—R7 (5-10-68)

BASSOON (HIGH SCHOOL)

New, wood, full Heckel system with whisper key, F sharp trill key, and the following roller keys: low F to A flat, low D sharp to C sharp. Complete with three bocals (corked, not wound), reed case, three Meeson reeds, soft strength, joint grease, swab, and French fitted plush-lined leather, Keratol (or equal) covered case, with compartments for bocals and accessories. Case must be standard equipment as supplied by manufacturer for the instrument. Instrument and case to be delivered in perfect condition with key action, intonation, and general playing response of the instrument *subject to the approval of the purchaser*. Instrument to be engraved with the phrase "DET. BD. OF ED." on boot joint. Letters to be 3/16" to 1/4" high.

Linton, Model K
Puschner Artist Model
Or Approved Equal

BASSOON (JUNIOR HIGH and ELEMENTARY)

New, student line quality, full Heckel system with whisper key, F sharp trill key, and the following roller keys: low F to A flat, low D sharp to C sharp. Complete with three bocals (corked, not wound), reed case, three reeds, joint grease, swab, and French fitted plush lined leather, Keratol (or equal) covered case, with compartments for bocals and accessories. Case must be standard equipment as supplied by manufacturer for the instrument. Instrument and case to be delivered in perfect condition with key action, intonation, and general playing response of the instrument *subject to the approval of the purchaser.* Instrument to be engraved with the phrase "DET. BD. OF ED." on both wing and tenon joints. Letters to be 3/16″ to 1/4″ high.

Mollenhauer No. 1-1456
Schreiber No. R-86
Cabart No. 11X
Lescher Model LSB
Or Approved Equal

SAXOPHONE, *Eb Alto (HIGH SCHOOL)*

New, satin finish, silver plate, complete with mouthpiece, cap, ligature, three Ricco or Symmetricut reeds, #2 strength, lyre, leather strap, and standard plush-lined Keratol (or equal) covered case. Case must be standard equipment as supplied by manufacturer for the instrument. Instrument and case to be delivered in perfect condition with key action, intonation, and general playing response of the instrument and mouthpiece *subject to the approval of the purchaser.* Instrument to be engraved with phrase "DET. BD. OF ED." on back of body. Letters to be 3/16″ to 1/4″ high.

Selmer No. 52
King, regular No. 1004
LeBlanc No. 39
Or Approved Equal

SAXOPHONE, *Eb Alto (JUNIOR HIGH and ELEMENTARY)*

New student line quality, satin silver finish, silver bell, complete with mouthpiece, three reeds, cap, ligature, lyre, leather strap, and standard plush lined Keratol (or equal) covered case. Case must be standard equipment as supplied by manufacturer for the instrument. Instrument and case to be delivered in perfect condition, with key action, intonation, and general playing response of the mouthpiece and instrument *subject to the approval of the purchaser.* Instrument to be engraved with phrase "DET. BD. OF ED." on the bell section. Letters to be 3/16″ to 1/4″ high.

Cleveland No. 613
Buescher Aristocrat No. 1033
Conn Model 50M
Vito No. 37
Or Approved Equal

TRUMPET, Bb (HIGH SCHOOL)

New, satin silver, silver bell, complete with Carl Fischer 7C star mouthpiece, lyre, bottle of valve oil, and standard plush-lined Keratol (or equal) covered case. Case must be standard equipment as supplied by manufacturer for the instrument. Instrument and case to be delivered in perfect condition with valve action, intonation, and general playing response of the instrument *subject to the approval of the purchaser.* Instrument to be engraved with phrase "DET. BD. OF ED." on back of bell. Letters to be 3/16″ to 1/4″ high.

Conn No. 22-B
Holton Revelation No. T302
Olds Super No. S-10 (in new case available April 1, 1968)
King "Liberty" No. 1045
Martin Committee No. 3300 (without trigger)
Or Approved Equal

TRUMPET, Bb (JUNIOR HIGH and ELEMENTARY)

New, student line quality, satin silver, silver bell, complete with mouthpiece, lyre, bottle of valve oil, and standard plush-lined Keratol (or equal) covered case. Case must be standard equipment as supplied by manufacturer for the instrument. Instrument and case to be delivered in perfect condition with valve action, intonation, and general playing response of the instrument *subject to the approval of the purchaser.* Instrument must be engraved with phrase "DET. BD. OF ED." on bell. Letters to be 3/16″ to 1/4″ high.

Olds "Ambassador" No. A-10 (in new case available April 1, 1968)
Holton "Collegiate" Model T602
Martin Imperial
Besson Model 235
Cleveland No. 600
Conn Director Model 15B
Evette Schaeffer American
Or Approved Equal

CORNET, Bb (HIGH SCHOOL)

New, satin silver, silver bell, complete with Carl Fischer 7C star mouthpiece, lyre, bottle of valve oil, and standard plush-lined Keratol (or equal) covered case. Case must be standard equipment as supplied by manufacturer for the instrument. Instrument and case to be delivered in perfect condition with valve action, intonation, and general playing response of the instrument *subject to the approval of the purchaser.* Instrument to be engraved with phrase "DET. BD. OF ED." on back of bell. Letters to be 3/16" to 1/4" high.

Conn "Victor" No. 80-A
Martin "Committee" No. 2300
Olds Super No. S-5 (in new case available April 1, 1968)
King "Master" No. 1065
Or Approved Equal

CORNET, Bb (JUNIOR HIGH and ELEMENTARY)

New, student line quality, satin silver plate, silver bell, complete with mouthpiece, lyre, bottle of valve oil, and standard plush lined Keratol (or equal) covered case. Case must be standard equipment as supplied by manufacturer for the instrument. Instrument and case to be delivered in perfect condition with valve action, intonation, and general playing response of the instrument *subject to the approval of the purchaser.* Instrument must be engraved with phrase "DET. BD. OF ED." on bell. Letters to be 3/16" to 1/4" high.

Olds "Ambassador" No. A-5 (in new case available April 1, 1968)
Holton "Collegiate" Model C602
Cleveland No. 602
Conn "Director" No. 15A
Besson Model 245
Buescher Aristocrat—No. 229
Evette and Schaeffer American

FRENCH HORN (Double) (HIGH SCHOOL)

New, nickel silver, complete with mouthpiece, lyre, and standard plush-lined Keratol (or equal) covered case. Case must be standard equipment as supplied by manufacturer for the instrument. Instrument and case to be delivered in perfect condition with valve action, intonation, and general playing response of the instrument *subject to the approval of the purchaser.* Instrument to be engraved with phrase "DET. BD. OF ED." on back of bell. Letters to be 3/16" to 1/4" high.

Conn No. 8-D
King No. 1160
Holton-Karkas Model No. H177
Or Approved Equal

FRENCH HORN in F (JUNIOR HIGH and ELEMENTARY)

New, student line quality, gold, or clear lacquer, complete with mouthpiece, lyre, and standard plush lined Keratol (or equal) covered case. Case must be standard equipment as supplied by manufacturer for the instrument. Instrument and case to be delivered in perfect condition with valve action, intonation, and general playing response of the instrument *subject to the approval of the purchaser.* Instrument must be engraved with phrase "DET. BD. OF ED." on bell. Letters to be 3/16" to 1/4" high.

Holton "Collegiate" Model H-600
Conn Director 14D
Zalzer No. PX 2325
Elkhorn Model 412
Carl Fischer No. C-2
Or Approved Equal

TROMBONE, TENOR (Medium Bore)
(JUNIOR HIGH and ELEMENTARY)

New, student line quality, satin silver finish, silver bell, complete with mouthpiece, lyre, bottle of oil, and standard plush-lined Keratol (or equal) covered case. Case must be standard equipment as supplied by manufacturer for the instrument. Instrument and case to be delivered in perfect condition with slide action, intonation, and general playing response of the instrument *subject to the approval of the purchaser.* Instrument to be engraved with phrase "DET. BD. OF ED." on bell. Letters to be 3/16" to 1/4" high.

Holton Collegiate Model TR602
Olds "Ambassador" A-15 (in new case available April 1, 1968)
Conn Director Model 14H
Besson Stratford Model 255
Buescher Aristocrat No. 500
Evette and Schaeffer American 17
Or Approved Equal

TROMBONE, TENOR (HIGH SCHOOL)

New, satin silver finish with silver bell, complete with Carl Fischer 12C star or Bach 12C mouthpiece, lyre, bottle of slide oil, and standard plush-lined Keratol (or equal) covered case. Case must be standard equipment as supplied by manufacturer for the instrument. Instrument and case to be delivered in perfect condition with slide action, intonation and general playing response of the instrument *subject to the approval of the purchaser.* Instrument must be engraved with phrase "DET. BD. OF ED." on back of bell. Letters to be 3/16″ to 1/4″ high.

Olds Studio No. T-15 (in new case available April 1, 1968)
King "Liberty" No. 1403
Conn 78G
Martin Committee No. 4300
Besson 10-10 No. 55
Or Approved Equal

BARITONE (Bellfront) (HIGH SCHOOL)

New, euphonium type single bell, satin silver finish, silver bell, complete with Carl Fischer 12C star mouthpiece, lyre, bottle of valve oil, and standard plush-lined Keratol (or equal) covered case. Case must be standard equipment as supplied by manufacturer for the instrument. Instrument and case to be delivered in perfect condition with valve action, intonation, and general playing response of the instrument *subject to the approval of the purchaser.*

Conn No. 20-I
Besson 3-Valve, compensating model No. 175
King "Artist" No. 1165
Olds "Studio" No. T-30
Or Approved Equal

BARITONE (Bellfront) (JUNIOR HIGH and ELEMENTARY)

New, student line quality, euphonium type single bell, satin silver finish, silver bell, complete with mouthpiece, lyre, bottle of valve oil, and standard plush-lined Keratol (or equal) covered case. Case must be standard equipment as supplied by manufacturer for the instrument. Instrument and case to be delivered in perfect condition with valve action, intonation and general playing response of the instrument *subject to the approval of the purchaser.* Instrument must be engraved with phrase "DET. BD. OF ED." on bell joint of instrument, letters to be 3/16″ to 1/4″ high.

Olds "Ambassador" No. A-25
Holton Collegiate B-601
Conn Director, Model 14I
Or Approved Equal

TUBA BBb Upright (HIGH SCHOOL)

New, gold, or clear lacquer, complete with mouthpiece and lyre, and bottle of valve oil. Instrument to be delivered in perfect condition with valve action, intonation, and playing response *subject to the approval of the purchaser.* Instrument to be engraved with phrase, "DET. BD. OF ED." on main body of instrument. Letters to be 3/16″ to 1/4″ high.

King No. 1240
Conn Co. 21J
Or Approved Equal

TUBA, BBb Upright (Small Size)
(JUNIOR HIGH and ELEMENTARY)

New, student line quality, gold, or clear lacquer or silver finish, complete with mouthpiece and lyre. Instrument to be delivered in perfect condition with valve action, intonation, and general playing response of the instrument *subject to the approval of the purchaser.* Instrument to be engraved with the phrase "DET. BD. OF ED." on bell. Letters to be 3/16″ to 1/4″ high.

Besson Stratford No. 588
Holton Collegiate Model 660
Or Approved Equal

SNARE DRUM, Orchestra (HIGH SCHOOL)

New, separate tensions, self-aligning tension rods, full-flanged counter hoops. All metal shell, chrome plated. Wire snares, calf skin heads. Complete with mackintosh zipper cover. To be delivered in perfect condition and *subject to the approval of the purchaser.* Instrument to be engraved with phrase "DET. BD. OF ED." near vent hole. Letters to be 3/16″ to 1/4″ high.

Ludwig Super Sensitive 4 in 1 Model 411 (6½″×14″)
Rogers Dyna-Sonic Model 37
Or Approved Equal

SNARE DRUM, Orchestra (5″ × 14″)
(JUNIOR HIGH and ELEMENTARY)

New, student line quality, separate tension, self-aligning tension rods, full-flanged counter hoops, collar screw must go through counter hoops, metal shell, nickel plated hardware, wire snares, plastic heads. Complete with mackintosh zipper cover. To be delivered in perfect condition and *subject to the approval of the purchaser.* Instrument to be engraved with phrase "DET. BD. OF ED." near vent hole. Letters to be 3/16″ to 1/4″ high.

Ludwig Acrolite No. 404
Or Approved Equal

BASS DRUM, Concert (HIGH SCHOOL)
(14″ × 28″, 16″ × 32″,
16″ × 36″, 16″ × 34″)

New, (size to be specified) separate tension, wood shell, white lacquer finish (or school color upon request), chrome plated hardware, calf skin heads. Complete with double end beater, web sling, and mackintosh water proof zipper cover. To be delivered in perfect condition and *subject to the approval of the purchaser.* Instrument to be engraved with phrase "DET. BD. OF ED." near vent hole. Letters to be 3/16″ to 1/4″ high.

Ludwig Concert— 14″ × 28″ — 801L
                 16″ × 32″ — 804L
                 16″ × 34″ — 805L
                 16″ × 36″ — 806L

Or Approved Equal

BASS DRUM, Concert (JUNIOR HIGH and ELEMENTARY)
(14″ × 28″)

New, student line quality, 14″ × 28″ size. Separate tension, wood shell, white lacquer finish, chrome plated hardware, plastic heads. Complete with double end beater, web sling, and mackintosh water proof zipper cover. To be delivered in perfect condition and *subject to the approval of the purchaser.* Instrument to be engraved with phrase "DET. BD. OF ED." near vent hole. Letters to be 3/16″ to 1/4″ high.

TYMPANI (Pedal-Tuned) (HIGH SCHOOL)

New, one pair (25″ and 28″ kettles) complete with two pairs standard professional felt mallets, 2 fibre head protectors, and short skirt mackintosh cover for each tympani. All equipment to be delivered in perfect condition with playing response of tympani *subject to the approval of the purchaser.* Bowls to be engraved with the phrase "DET. BD. OF ED." Letters to be 3/16″ to 1/4″ high.

Leedy Model 5517
Slingerland Standard Pilharmonic No. 400
Supplementary Units (1 each)
    23″—Slingerland Philharmonic #400W-23
    30″—Slingerland Philharmonic #400W-30
Or Approved Equal

TYMPANI *(Machine-Tuned,* 25″ and 28″) *(JUNIOR HIGH)*

New, machine-tuned kettles, heavy grade copper fiberglass. Chrome plated hardware and legs, telescoping. Complete with head covers and professional felt beaters. Equipment to be delivered in perfect condition, *subject to the approval of the purchaser.* Bowls to be engraved with phrase "DET. BD. OF ED." Letters to be 3/16″ to 1/4″ high.

Ludwig 871
Or Approved Equal

CYMBALS *(HIGH SCHOOL)*

Size 17″ to 21″—High School   Weight: Medium
                                                   Medium-Heavy
                                                   Heavy

New, one pair, genuine Avedis Zildjian matched cymbals, complete with leather strap and pad-type holders. To be delivered in perfect condition and *subject to the approval of the purchaser.*

CYMBALS *(JUNIOR HIGH)*

Size 15″ and 16″
New, one pair, medium heavy weight, genuine Avedis Zildjian cymbals, complete with strap and pad type holders. To be delivered in perfect condition and *subject to the approval of the purchaser.*
See High School regarding straps.

CYMBALS *(ELEMENTARY)*

Size 14″
New, one pair, medium weight, Avedis Zildjian matched cymbals, complete with wood handle holder with adjustable strap. To be delivered in perfect condition and *subject to the approval of the purchaser.*

VIOLIN SPECIFICATIONS *(HIGH SCHOOL),* 4/4 *SIZE ONLY*

Violin Outfits: To consist of: New violin. American-made thermo plastic shaped plush-lined case. Fiberglass bow. Chinrest. Extra set of strings. Cake of rosin.

Violin:

Made of properly loft-seasoned curly maple back and sides. Medium grain spruce top. Equipped with full genuine ebony fittings, correctly graduated fingerboard, chinrest, genuine Caspari or DeJacques or Lewis self-holding non-slip pegs, glued in bass bar. Body to have four solid corner blocks. Instrument expertly adjusted. Fingerboard "dressed" in USA with proper curvature and string heights. Fingerboard nut of correct height and properly spaced. Soundpost fitted in the United States. Hand-rubbed oil-finished neck. No varnish on neck handle. Violin varnished with soft textured varnish. To be equipped with strings as listed below, with adjusters on E and A strings. 1 cake of RAO rosin to be included. All instruments with label inside showing model number, serial number, date of adjustment in USA, certifying adjustment to MENC specifications. Instrument must be engraved with the phrase "DET. BD. OF ED." on scroll. Letters to be 3/16" to 1/4" high.

Acceptable Brands:
Roth 303C
Lewis Sarasate #176
Schroetter-Roman Teller, Model 220/240 (with either of above pegs)

Chinrest:

Becker or Walter model, deep cup, ribbed.

Bow:

Fiberglass bow with correct resilience, firmness, and proper weight and balance. Guaranteed not to warp. Stick should have metal reinforcing core. Genuine wire winding soldered at both ends with genuine leather thumb grip. Screw to turn freely. Bow must be dusted and rosined, ready to play.

Natural hair for High School line outfits.

Acceptable Brands: Roth C202 or *Accepted Equal*

Case:
Strong durable thermo plastic vacuum form-fitted, with snug fitting aluminum valance. Two bow pockets and at least one enclosed compartment. Equipped with nickel long lasting latches—sturdy nickel bumpers, three heavy type hinges. Heat-resisting, waterproof. Plush lined interior. Bow clips may not be plastic.

Acceptable Brands:
Roth B126
Boltaron #900
or *Approved Equal*

Strings:
E—Pirastro Ultrasensitive #401
A—Pirastro Ultrasensitive #402
D—Pirastro Wondertone Black Label #485
G—Pirastro Wondertone Black Label #486

Instrument and bow must be expertly shop adjusted and assembled ready to play with bridge set up.

VIOLIN SPECIFICATIONS (JUNIOR HIGH and ELEMENTARY), 1/2, 3/4, 4/4 SIZES

Violin Outfits:
To consist of: New violin. American-made thermo plastic shaped plush-lined case. Fiberglass bow. Chinrest. Extra set of strings. Cake of rosin.

Violin:
Made of properly loft-seasoned curly maple back and sides. Medium grain spruce top. Equipped with full genuine ebony fittings, correctly graduated fingerboard, chinrest, genuine Caspari, De-Jacques or Lewis self-holding non-slip pegs, glued in bass bar. Body to have four solid corner blocks. Instrument exertly adjusted. Fingerboard "dressed" in USA with proper curvature and string heights. Fingerboard nut of correct height and properly spaced. Soundpost fitted in the United States. Hand-rubbed oil-finished neck. No varnish on neck handle. Violin varnished with soft textured varnish. To be equipped with strings as listed below,

with adjusters on E and A strings. 1 cake of RAO rosin to be included. All instruments with label inside showing model number, serial number, date of adjustment in USA, certifying adjustment to MENC specifications. Instrument must be engraved with the phrase "DET. BD. OF ED." on scroll. Letters to be 3/16″ to 1/4″ high.

Acceptable Brands:
Roth 301C-DeJacques Pegs
Lewis Kayser No. 134
Schroetter No. 50

Chinrest: Becker model, deep cup, rubbed.

Bow: Fiberglass bow with correct resilience, firmness, and proper weight and balance. Guaranteed not to warp. Stick should have metal reinforcing core. Genuine wire winding soldered at both ends with genuine leather thumb grip. Screw to turn freely. Bow must be dusted and rosined, ready to play.

Acceptable Brands:
Roth C202 or *Accepted Equal*

Case: Strong durable thermo plastic vacuum form-fitted, with snug fitting aluminum valance. Two bow pockets and at least one enclosed compartment. Equipped with nickel long last latches—sturdy nickel bumpers, three heavy type hinges. Heat-resisting, waterproof. Plush-lined interior. Bow clips may not be plastic.

Acceptable Brands:
Roth B126
Boltaron #900
or *Approved Equal*

Strings: E—Pirastro Ultrasensitive #401
A—Pirastro Ultrasensitive #402
D—Pirastro Wondertone Black Label #485
G—Pirastro Wondertone Black Label #486

Instrument and bow must be expertly shop adjusted and assembled ready to play with bridge set up.

VIOLA SPECIFICATIONS (HIGH SCHOOL)

Viola Outfit: To consist of: New viola made of properly loft-seasoned curly maple back and sides. Medium grain spruce top. American-made thermo plastic shaped plush-lined case. Fiberglass bow. Chinrest. Cake of RAO rosin.

Viola: New, imported German model, made to correct size measurements. Equipped with genuine high-grade ebony fittings. Fingerboard correctly graduated according to MENC specifications with proper curvature and string height. Fingerboard nut of correct height and properly spaced. Four solid corner blocks. Lower and upper rib edges fully lined. Glued in bass bar. New soundpost fitted in USA. Equipped with genuine Caspari, DeJacques or Lewis non-slip pegs. Hand-rubbed oil-finished neck. No varnish on neck handle. Viola varnished with soft textured varnish. To be equipped with chinrest of proper size. To be equipped with strings as listed below. All instruments with label inside showing model number, serial number, date of adjustment in USA, certifying adjustment to MENC specifications. Stradivarius imported model. Instrument must be engraved with the phrase "DET. BD. OF ED." on the scroll. Letters to be 3/16″ to 1/4″ high.

Acceptable Brands:
High School—15½, 16″, 16½ (to be specified)
Roth 407C—DeJacques Pegs
Lewis
Schroetter Roman Teller, Model 660 (with either of above pegs)

Bow: Fiberglass bow with correct resilience, firmness, and proper weight and balance. Guaranteed not to warp. Stick should have metal reinforcing core. Genuine wire winding soldered at both ends with

genuine leather thumb grip. Screw to
turn freely. Bow must be dusted and
rosined, ready to play.

Natural hair for High School line outfits.

Acceptable Brands: Roth E301

Case:

Strong, durable thermo plastic vacuum
form-fitted with snug fitting aluminum
valance. Two bow pockets and at least
one enclosed compartment. Equipped
with nickel long lasting latches—sturdy
nickel bumpers, three heavy type hinges.
Heat-resisting, waterproof. Plush-lined
interior.

Acceptable Brands:
Roth No. E50 (Standard Size) or
Equal or

Three-ply veneer keratol or equivalent
cover. Silk plush-lined. Two bow pockets
with ribbons, at least one accessory
pocket. No plastic bow clips. Three
sturdy hinges. Nickel bumpers and heavy
duty locks and hardware.

Acceptable Brands: Roth No. E41
Lifton 3102P

Strings:

A—Pirastro Flexocore #931
D—Pirastro Black Label #496
G—Pirastro Black Label #497
C—Pirastro Black Label #498

Adjusters on A and D strings. Instrument and bow must be expertly shop-
adjusted and assembled ready to play
with bridge set up.

VIOLA SPECIFICATIONS (JUNIOR HIGH and ELEMENTARY)

Viola Outfit:

To consist of: New viola made of properly loft-seasoned curly maple back and
sides. Medium grain spruce top. American-made thermo plastic shaped plush-
lined case. Fiberglass bow. Chinrest. Cake
of RAO rosin.

Viola:

New imported German model made to
correct size measurements. Equipped

with genuine high-grade ebony fittings. Fingerboard correctly graduated according to MENC specifications with proper curvature and string height. Fingerboard nut of correct height and properly spaced. Four solid corner blocks. Lower and upper rib edges fully lined. Glued in bass bar. New soundpost fitted in USA. Equipped with genuine Caspari, De-Jacques or Lewis non-slip pegs. Hand-rubbed oil-finished neck. No varnish on neck handle. Viola varnished with soft textured varnish. To be equipped with chinrest of proper size. To be equipped with strings as listed below. All instruments with label inside showing model number, serial number, date of adjustment in USA, certifying adjustment to MENC specifications. Stradivarius imported model. Instrument must be engraved with the phrase "DET. BD. OF ED." on the scroll. Letters to be 3/16″ to 1/4″ high.

Acceptable Brands:
13″—Roth 107C (DeJacques Pegs)
Lewis (Lewis Non-slip Pegs)
Schroetter Model 75 (either of above pegs)
14″—Roth 105C (DeJacques Pegs)
Lewis (Lewis Non-slip Pegs)
Schroetter Model 75 (either of above pegs)
15″—Roth 100C (DeJacques Pegs)
Lewis (Lewis Non-slip Pegs)
Schroetter Model 75 (either of above pegs)

Bow: Fiberglass bow with correct resilience, firmness, and proper weight and balance. Guaranteed not to warp. Stick should have metal reinforcing core. Genuine wire winding soldered at both ends with genuine leather thumb grip. Screw to turn freely. Bow must be dusted and rosined, ready to play.

Acceptable Brands: Roth E301

Case: Strong, durable thermo plastic vacuum

form-fitted with snug fitting aluminum valance. Two bow pockets and at least one enclosed compartment. Equipped with nickel long-lasting latches, sturdy nickel bumpers, three heavy type hinges. Heat-resisting, waterproof. Plush-lined interior. Model: Roth No. E45 (Intermediate size), No. E47 (Junior size), No. E50 (Standard size), or *Equal.*

or

Three-ply veneer keratol or equivalent cover. Flannel-lined. Two bow pockets with ribbons, at least one accessory pocket. No plastic bow clips. Three sturdy hinges. Nickel bumpers and heavy duty locks and hardware.

Acceptable Brands:
15"—Roth E40
Lifton 3102F
14"—Roth
Lifton
13"—Roth
Lifton

Strings: 13" Viola—Pirastro Wondertone Ultrasensitive—Medium gauge Set 701
14" Viola—Pirastro Wondertone Ultrasensitive—Medium gauge Set 501
15" Viola—
A—Pirastro Flexocore #931
D—Pirastro Black Label #496
G—Pirastro Black Label #497
C—Pirastro Black Label #498

Adjusters on all four strings. Instrument and bow must be expertly shop adjusted and assembled ready to play with bridge set up.

CELLO SPECIFICATIONS (HIGH SCHOOL LINE), 4/4 SIZE ONLY

Cello Outfit: To consist of: Instrument, bow, bag, and Rock-stop endpin rest. Cake of RAO rosin, mute, tuner.

Cello: Imported Stradivarius model. Two-piece properly loft-seasoned curly maple back.

Medium grain spruce top. Genuine ebony fittings of high grade. Fingerboard "dressed" and correctly graduated according to MENC specifications with proper curvature and string height. Fingerboard nut of correct height and properly spaced. Four solid corner blocks. Glued in bass bar. New soundpost fitted in USA. Equipped with genuine Caspari, DeJacques or Lewis self-holding non-slip pegs. With adjustable endpin, nickel-plated steel rod and rubber tip. Endpin rest. Hand-rubbed oil-finished neck. No varnish on neck handle. Soft textured varnish. To be equipped with strings listed below. Instrument must be engraved with phrase "DET. BD. OF ED." on scroll. Letters to be 3/16″ to 1/4″ high.

Acceptable Brands:
Roth 55C (DeJacques Pegs)
or *Accepted Equal*

Bow: Fiberglass with correct resilience and proper weight, firmness and balance. Guaranteed not to warp. Equipped with genuine wire winding soldered at both ends and with genuine leather thumb grip. Or: High grade pernumbuco bow with fully lined ebony frog and genuine wire winding.

Acceptable Brands:
Roth No. F401 (fiberglass) or
Roth No. F320 (Pernumbuco)
Bow to be dusted and rosined, ready to play.

Bag: Extra heavy canvas, bound edges, reinforced neck area. Zipper fasteners and protector. Bow pocket, string and music pocket. Sturdy handle.

Acceptable Brands:
Roth No. 5
Artistic
or *Approved Equal*

Strings: A—Pirastro Flexocore #951
D—Pirastro Flexocore #952

G—Pirastro Black Label—Silverplated wire wound #490
C—Pirastro Black Label—Silverplated wire wound #491
Adjusters for A and D strings. Instrument, bow, and bag to be expertly shop adjusted and assembled ready to play with bridge set up.

CELLO SPECIFICATIONS (JUNIOR HIGH and ELEMENTARY), 1/2, 3/4, 4/4 SIZES

Cello Outfit:

To consist of: Instrument, bow, bag, and Rockstop endpin rest. Cake of RAO rosin, mute, tuner.

Cello:

New, imported, German- or French-made with genuine ebony purfling, fingerboard and fittings. Fingerboard "dressed" and correctly graduated according to MENC specifications with proper curvature and string height. Fingerboard nut of correct height and properly spaced. Four solid corner blocks. Glued-in bass bar. New sound post fitted in USA. Equipped with DeJacques or Lewis self-holding non-slip pegs. Adjustable endpin, nickel-plated steel rod and rubber tip. End pin rest. Hand-rubbed oil-finished neck, no varnish on neck handle. Soft textured varnish. To be equipped with strings listed below. Instrument must be engraved with phrase "DET. BD. OF ED." on scroll. Letters to be 3/16″ to 1/4″ high.

Acceptable Brands:
Roth Model No. 50 (with DeJacques pegs)
Schroetter Model No. 100 (with either DeJacques or Lewis pegs)

Bow:

Fiberglass with correct resilience, proper weight, firmness, and balance. Guaranteed not to warp. Equipped with genuine wire winding soldered at both ends and genuine leather thumb grip.

Acceptable Brands:
Roth-Glasser No. F401
or *Approved Equal*

Bow must be dusted, rosined, and ready to play.

Bag: Extra heavy canvas, bound edges, reinforced neck area. Zipper fasteners and heavy protector. Bow pocket, string and music pocket. Sturdy handle. Flannel lined.

Acceptable Brands:
Roth No. 5
Artistic
or *Approved Equal*

Strings: A—Pirastro Flexocore No. 951
D—Pirastro Flexocore No. 952
G—Pirastro Black Label—Silverplated wire wound No. 490
C—Pirastro Black Label—Silverplated wire wound No. 491

Adjusters for A and D strings.

Instrument, bow, and bag to be expertly shop-adjusted and assembled ready to play with bridge set up.

STRING BASS (HIGH SCHOOL, JUNIOR HIGH and ELEMENTARY) 3/4 and 1/2 SIZES

String Bass Outfit: Fiberglass (standard ¾ or ½ size), to consist of instrument, bow, bag, and rosin.

Instrument: American-made fiberglass bass in brown violin finish. Scientifically fused construction, guaranteed against cracking or splitting. Adjustable endpin. Model: Roth No. G 662, or acceptable equal. Instrument to be engraved with phrase "DET. BD. OF ED." on scroll. Letters to be 3/16″ to 1/4″ high.

Bow: Fiberglass with correct resilience and proper weight and firmness, guaranteed *not* to warp. Equipped with genuine wire winding soldered at both ends and genuine leather thumb grip. Or: high grade brazilwood with genuine ebony frog, nickel silver trimmings. Equipped with genuine wire winding soldered at both ends and genuine leather thumb grip. Pre-rosined. Bow screw must turn freely. Natural hair, must be dusted and rosined ready to play. Model: Fiberglass: Roth G 501 (Butler Model), G 502 (French model), Lewis Steinman Model 2320 (French or German), or accepted equal.

Bag: High grade canvas with zipper fastener and reinforced edges. Roth—Model #1, Artistic, or accepted equal.

Strings: Four, flat, chromium wire strings (G, D, A, and E), wound on steel.

"A" Pirastro Flexocore #973
"D" Pirastro Flexocore #972
"G" Pirastro Flexocore #971
"E" Pirastro Flexocore #974

Rosin: Minimum 1¼ cubic inches in telescoping cardboard box.

All instruments with label inside showing model number, serial number, and date of adjustment in USA, certifying adjustment to MENC specifications.

All instruments assembled, ready to play, bridge set up, instrument pre-tuned.

STRING BASS (JUNIOR HIGH and ELEMENTARY) 1/2, 3/4 SIZES

See specifications for String Bass (High School).

Appendix L

SPECIFICATION FOR PIANOS
(CONSOLE STYLE)

These specifications are intended to cover all labor, materials, and transportation necessary to furnish, deliver, unpack, and set up in locations as directed.

1. *Over-All Size*

    Height to be at least 44 inches.

    Keyboard shall have full seven and one-third octaves (88 keys).

2. *Key Bed*

    The piano key bed shall be of "panelled" construction, made of kiln-dried lumber and measuring at least 1-9/16 inches thick. Underside of key bed shall be at least 24 inches from the floor to allow proper knee room for pianist.

3. *Action*

    Action to be positive, and responsive to power and lightness of touch. No plastic parts are to be used. Entire action to be mothproofed. Pratt Reed, Wood and Brooks, or other approved. (Bidder to state name of manufacturer.)

4. *Keys*

    All "natural" keys shall be made of either pine or basswood, with ivory or white plastic tops and ends. If ivory, then nothing less than No. 3 grade shall be used. "Sharp" keys shall be either black plastic or ebonized hard maple.

5. *Pedals*

    Solid brass. Two or three; if three, one to be a bass sustaining pedal. Height at top of pedals (area of contact) to be not more than 2¾ inches from the floor, adjusted or installed to compensate for any added height resulting from the use of large-sized casters.

6. *Case and Finish*

    Case to be made of suitable hard wood, preferably oak.

Music rack: Full length, permanently fixed at the proper angle, for ease of reading.

Top: Single-piece top to be constructed with a fixture at each end to prevent opening at more than a 90-degree angle.

Finish: Blond color. Not less than two coats of good-grade lacquer or varnish in addition to the stain and filler, and rubbed to a dull, satin lustre.

Sample: Showing color and quality of finish to be submitted by the successful bidder and approved before proceeding with contract.

7. *Casters*

Heavy duty, free running, double-wheel casters of hard rubber (or other approved). To be of double ball bearing, swivel type (plate with spindle) contruction. Bidder to state name of manufacturer. Faultless, Darnell, or other approved.

8. *Bass Strings*

Bass strings to be copper wound.

9. *Bench*

Piano bench to match piano in style and finish to be furnished and included in price submitted.

10. *Back and Pin Plank*

The piano back shall be made of at least five hardwood posts, securely anchored to the plate.

The pin plank shall be laminated with at least four sections of hard maple. It may or may not be exposed.

11. *Tuning Pins*

Piano tuning pins shall be threaded and properly sized, made of blued steel. Pickled or brass pins will not be accepted.

12. *Hammers*

Weight shall be in keeping with the scale design, but not less than 12-pound felt made of 100% top grade wool to be used. Felt to be chemically treated to resist moths.

13. *Plate and Scale*

Plate to be what is known as "full cast plate" made of gray iron with either a bronze or silver finish.

Scale to be scientifically balanced so as to produce consistently resonant and clear tone quality in all registers of the instrument.

14. *Sound Board*

The sound board to be made of close-grained, hard texture, quarter-sawed mountain spruce, properly ribbed and crowned.

15. *Voicing and Tuning*

All pianos to be voiced "medium brilliant" subject to the approval of the purchaser prior to delivery.

Each piano to be tuned by the vendor's own tuner within one week after delivery, plus three additional tunings to be given at approximately 75-day intervals. Vendor to tune the pianos during school hours and to furnish the Purchasing Department with a copy of a signed service report showing the date of tuning and approval.

All such "voicing" and "tunings" to be included in the price submitted by the vendor.

16. *Locking Device*

A locking device should be installed on each piano which would lock both the top lid of the piano cabinet and the fall board in one operation. A piano lock must protect not only the piano keyboard, but also the sounding board, strings, hammers, and the like found inside the piano so that the inner workings of the various parts will be protected from vandals.

17. *Tone Quality*

The piano shall possess, throughout the entire range of the keyboard (scale) a musical tone of sufficient depth and power to warrant the written approval of the Music Education Department and the Piano Evaluation Committee of the Public Schools. *No piano shall be accepted which fails to qualify for this written approval, even though such piano complies with all other requirements and may be entered as the lowest bid.*

18. *Guarantee*

Each piano to be guaranteed as to workmanship and parts for one full year from date of delivery.

Pianos to be delivered in perfect condition with all foregoing factors subject to the approval of the purchaser.

19. *Delivery Date*

To be indicated on bid blank in terms of the number of days after receipt of order.

20. Pedal linkage, rods, studs and brackets shall be strongly built and so designed that the sustaining pedal damper lifter rod arm is not subjected to excessive torque to cause breakage. The total pedal linkage design shall be one that has been successfully used in _____ and has not resulted in broken damper lifter rod arms and studs.

21. Pianos quoted to be [List acceptable instruments] or other approved.

22. **Vendor must show in writing in space provided any deviations of product quoted from listed specifications and failure to so indicate**

in writing may disqualify said vendor from further invitations to bid. Existing deviations, from listed specifications, not shown by vendor in writing on the bid form must be corrected at the vendor's expense and the item quoted must be made to comply when delivered in every respect to the listed specifications.

DEVIATIONS:_____

_____

_____

_____

_____

Appendix M

TABLE OF ALLOWANCE FOR
FAIRFAX COUNTY SCHOOLS
ADOPTED DECEMBER 12, 1966

The Table of Allowance listed below was originally established to establish a minimal or basic support level for each program in the curriculum, and to try to develop standardization in purchasing. It was definitely used as the guideline for equipping new schools and for guiding teachers and principal in their program budgeting. It could not be a static document, however, because program requirements differ from school to school and the TA, in order to be an effective instrument, was diminished or expanded according to needs and available money.

Fairfax County has since gone into the PPBS budgeting, which places the responsibility for budgeting with the Program Manager and in the case of Fairfax County the P.M. is the principal of the school. Under this system the TA is a guide for developing support for the program within a school, but it is not an inviolate instrument.

Philip J. Fuller
Music Curriculum Specialist
Fairfax County Schools
January 21, 1972
(excerpt from personal letter)

INSTRUMENTAL MUSIC

ITEM	ELE-MENTARY	INTER-MEDIATE	HIGH SCHOOL
PICCOLO	—	1	2
OBOE	—	2	3
ENGLISH HORN	—	—	1
BASSOON	—	2	3
CLARINET—Eb Soprano	—	1	1

ITEM	ELE-MENTARY	INTER-MEDIATE	HIGH SCHOOL
CLARINET—Eb Alto	—	4	6
CLARINET—Bb Bass	—	2	3
CLARINET—Bb Contra Bass	—	1	1
CLARINET—Eb Contra Bass	—	1	1
SAXOPHONE—Bb Tenor	—	2	2
SAXOPHONE—Eb Baritone	—	2	2
SAXOPHONE—Bb Bass (With Stand)	—	—	1
FRENCH HORN—Single F	2	—	—
FRENCH HORN—Double F & Bb	—	4	8
ALTONIUM	—	—	6
TROMBONE—Bass Bb & F	—	1	2
BARITONE	1	4	1
EUPHONIUM	—	—	4
BASS—Upright Tuba	1	3	—
BASS—Recording (With Stand)	—	—	5
SOUSAPHONE	—	—	8
DRUM—Concert Bass	1	1	1
DRUM—Scotch Bass	—	—	2
DRUM—Field	—	—	3
DRUM—Concert Snare	1	2	2
DRUM—Tenor	—	—	2
TYMPANI—(one pair 26" & 29")	—	1	1
GLOCKENSPIEL	—	—	4
ORCHESTRA BELLS—(With Stand)	—	1	1
GONG—(With Stand)	—	1	1
CHIME	—	—	1
MARIMBA	—	—	1
CELESTE	—	—	1
CYMBAL—16" Marching	—	—	1
CYMBAL—18" Concert	—	1	1
CYMBAL—20" Concert	—	—	1
CYMBAL—18" Suspended with Stand	—	1	1
VIOLIN—1/2 Size*	3	—	—
VIOLIN—3/4 Size*	3	—	—
VIOLA—13" Elem. 14" Int.	3–13"	2–14"	—

ITEM	ELE-MENTARY	INTER-MEDIATE	HIGH SCHOOL
VIOLA—15″	—	3–15″	—
VIOLA—Full*	—	—	4
CELLO—1/2 Size*	3	—	—
CELLO—3/4 Size*	3	4	—
CELLO—Full*	0	2	10
BASS VIOL—1/2 Size*	1	4	—
BASS VIOL—3/4 Size**	—	2	10 (80/2B)
HARP*	—	—	1

* Instruments used in the string program only.
** Instruments used in both band and orchestra: (80 = 8 Orchestra: 2B—2 Band)

ELEMENTARY GENERAL MUSIC

ITEM	PER SCHOOL	PER CLASSROOM
AUTOHARP		1
MELODY BELLS	2	
RESONATOR BELLS	2	
RHYTHM INSTRUMENT SET—25	1	
RHYTHM INSTRUMENT SET—35	1	
RECORD PLAYER—STEREO	1	1—Gen. Music
TAPE RECORDER—STEREO	2	
ORGAN, ELECTRIC		1 per 2 3rd grade clsrm. 1 per Gen. Music Room
PIANO	2	

INTERMEDIATE GENERAL MUSIC

PIANO	2	
ORGAN, ELECTRIC		1 per Gen. Music
AUTOHARP		1 per Music Classroom
LATIN AMERICAN INSTRUMENT SET	1 (Gen. Music)	
RECORD—PLAYBACK SYSTEM		1 per Music Room

Appendix N

PPBS SAMPLE BUDGET

The following is a sample budget from the Bartholomew Consolidated School Corporation (Columbus, Indiana) based on PPBS. All of the descriptive material does not appear in the example since it will vary from community to community. For reference purposes only, we have traced the plan for the elementary schools. The same procedures for planning and budgeting would apply to individual schools at all levels.

1972 PROGRAM BUDGET

Program Title: ___Music___ ___K–12___
               Subject-Area   Grade(s)

Program Code_____

Goals, K–12: (Attach sheet if needed)

1. To give students understandings in music.
2. To give all students the opportunity to perform by moving, reading, singing, playing, and listening.
3. To enable students to use knowledge to understand new materials.
4. To allow students to create.
5. To allow students to develop special skills in vocal and instrumental classes.

DESCRIPTION OF EXISTING PROGRAM

Present Elementary Program

Kindergarten music is taught by music teachers in some schools.
Grades 1–6 classes meet twice a week for 25 minutes each.
Nine out of nineteen schools have choir on the school day.

Mary Helen Richards Charts are available in all schools.
Orff instruments are available in six schools.
Doolin bell sets—ten sets available.
Tonettes used in three schools.
Music listening is presented with tests.
An achievement test on fundamentals is given in all six grades.
Students are given the opportunity to perform.

Junior High [to be filled in by the appropriate administrator]

Senior High [to be filled in by the appropriate administrator]

PROGRAM CHANGES

Program Title: <u>   Music   </u>   <u>   K–12   </u>
                   Subject-Area   Grade(s)

Program Code <u>   </u>

Briefly indicate the nature of the program change in terms of personnel, materials, equipment, and facilities. (Attach sheet if needed.) Indicate how many years it will take to fully implement the program. If no change, indicate "Program is same as previous year."

Elementary Program Changes

The program as listed will be the same except for the extension of the work with Doolin Bells and Orff Instruments.

The program will be expanded with the addition of strings before school, after school, during activity periods, and at noon hour.

The present elementary staff will be used.

The elementary teachers that will assume this additional assignment will do the teaching.

PLAN I   Staff Utilization for Next Year with the Present Staff

[To be filled in by the appropriate administrator.]

10 4/5   Teachers
    1/5   Supervision

PLAN II [Alternate Plan]   **Staff Utilization for Next Year if We Have Staff Member Resign. A 3/5 Time Teacher Will Be Hired to Replace This Full Time Teacher.**

[To be filled in by the appropriate administrator.]

10 9/10   Teachers
 1/5   Supervision

The number of schools that have strings will depend upon the number of teachers that will teach and the program that can be arranged.

The program will have to be arranged with the principals. Mr. Dale Spurlock will serve as the in-service leader of the string teachers. He will lead weekly leader sessions with the teachers.

Classes will be taught in the present music class location.

Students in grades five and six will receive instruction. Full practices may be held on Saturday later in the year.

Materials, Equipment, and Facilities Needed to Fully Implement the Program.

Classes will be taught in the present facilities.

Materials, equipment, staff needs listed below. (Replacement and costs will be reduced 40% by bids.)

Year		New Staff	
1971–1972		None	6

At the end of the first year, there are two options available.

1. The students that go into the junior high schools can receive their only instruction in private lessons outside of school—and the one a week youth orchestra under Pro-Music.
2. An additional one-half or one full time teacher will be needed. An additional one-half will allow a class at each junior high to be added. A full time teacher will allow additional elementary schools to be served.

1972–1973

Option 1	*Option 2*	
	New Staff	7
	½ or 1	

An additional one-half will be needed if only one-half was added the year before.

1973–1974	(½)	8
1974–1975	0	9
1975–1976	1	10
1976–1977	0	11
1977–1978	0	12
1978–1979	0	

At this time a complete evaluation of the program will be necessary if it has not been made earlier.

Using Option 1—The program over eight years will cost _____ or _____ + a year. There will be no string program beyond the sixth grade.

Using Option 2—The program over eight years will cost _____ or _____ a year and the addition of two teachers. The program will be through all three junior high schools and the two high schools.

I recommend that this program be accepted for this next year with the decision to pick and an option delayed until the first year's experience can be evaluated.

Junior High [to be filled in by the appropriate administrator]

Senior High [to be filled in by the appropriate administrator]

Prepared by_____ Date_____
                   Chairman

Reviewed by Principals
(Comments may be attached)   Date   Reviewed by Principals   Date

Eastern District		Central	
South Central		Northside	
North Central		Southside	
Southwest		Senior High—North	
		Senior High—East	

(Signature of Principal is required.)

Program Title: _____ Subject-Area: Music Grade(s): K–12 Program Code: _____

CERTIFICATED PERSONNEL
(indicate in 10ths if needed)

	1971		1972		Difference
	No. of Certificated	No. of Non-Certificated	No. of Certificated	No. of Non-Certificated	
Elementary					
Classroom Teachers					
Supervisor					
Total					
Junior High					
Classroom Teachers					
Dept. Chairmen					
Supervisor					
Total					
Senior High					
Classroom Teachers					
Dept. Chairmen					
Supervisor					
Total					
Grand Total					

OTHER INSTRUCTIONAL COSTS

	1971		1972	Difference
Supplies 233		+		
AV 232		+		
General 241		−		
241 Festivals		+		
		+		
Equipment, Maintenance, 741P.T.		+		
Replacement or Repair 741.8P.		+		
741.		+		
741. AV		+		
New Equipment 1233		−		
1233 AV		+		
Consultant Services and Curriculum Supplies 269		+		
Travel		+		
GRAND TOTAL		+		

213

ELEMENTARY STAFF

Burdell Sell	.16	Supervisor
Marjory Fritz	.20	Supervisor
Lydia Bohn	.50	
DeVon Cunningham	.50	
Phyllis Edson	1.00	
Marjory Fritz	.80	
Helen Galbraith	1.00	
Karen Grasch	1.00	
Roger Helman	1.00	
Grace Pentzer	1.00	
Leah Hooker	1.00	
Elaine Long	1.00	
Pauline Miller	.50	
Dale Spurlock	.50	
Barbara Taylor	1.00	
Total	11.16	

Students Served		*Budget*	
		1971	*1972*
K– 135			
1–6–6523	232.1		
Total 6658	232.2		
	232.3		
	241.5000		
	741. AV		
	741.		
	1233. AV		
	1233.6000		
	Totals		

MUSIC BUDGET: SYNOPSIS

	ELEMENTARY		JUNIOR HIGH		HIGH SCHOOL		TOTAL	
	71	72	71	72	71	72	71	72
232.1								
232.2								
232.3								
233.3								
241.								
741.								
741. AV								
1233. AV								
1233.								
Totals								

STUDENTS SERVED

Elementary	6,658
Junior High	1,946
High School	369
Total	8,973

215

Appendix O

APPLICATION:
MUSICAL INSTRUMENT INVENTORY*

TABLE OF CONTENTS

Unit	Title	Page
I	Overview	100
II	How to make Additions, Deletions, Replacements and Changes to the Inventory	200
III	Data Processing Procedures and Operations	300
IV	Program Documentation (Units II and III are not included in user's manual.)	400

UNIT I—OVERVIEW

The purpose of this application is to simplify and improve the accuracy of the District's inventory of musical instruments. Three kinds of inventories are provided:

a. System-Wide,
b. Building Level, and
c. Teacher.

Additions, changes, and deletions may be made at any time during the year; however, the inventory reports are produced at the beginning of each semester.

* Warren Consolidated Schools, Warren, Michigan.

216

Each inventory item contains the following data:

a. *Case Number* The number assigned to the case housing the instrument.
b. *Instrument* The name of the instrument followed by two descriptors; i.e., SAX C MELL.
c. *Manufacturer*
d. *Serial Number*
e. *Purchase Price*
f. *Purchase Date*
g. *Teacher Number* Each music teacher is assigned a unique number.
h. *Building Number* Each building is identified by the same number used in the payroll and accounting systems.
i. *Student* Name of student having custody of the instrument.
j. *Remarks* A notation for lost or stolen instruments.
k. *Record Number* A record number used by Data Processing to retrieve a specific inventory item in the file.

Separate tabulations are provided for instruments on hand, stolen, and lost. Dollar amount totals reflect the purchase price of instruments on hand.

A SUGGESTED SCHEDULE OF SCHOOL YEAR EVENTS FOR INVENTORY MAINTENANCE

FALL SEMESTER

Week   *Event*

1   Music Coordinator distributes two copies of the official inventory from the previous semester to each music teacher.

4   Teachers record student assignments and return one copy of report to Music Coordinator for review.

5   Music Coordinator forwards all teacher returns to Data Processing. Data Processing produces an updated inventory report.

6   Music Coordinator distributes fall semester official inventory reports.

6–17 Teachers and Music Coordinator record lost, stolen, deletions*, and changes to inventory. Warehouse reports any replacements that had occurred during the semester.

18   Music Coordinator collects all building inventories and forwards to Data Processing.

19   Data Processing produces an end of semester inventory. Copies are sent to teachers for Spring semester student assignments.

*An inventory item is deleted when the Music Coordinator desires that the item should not appear on subsequent inventories.

SPRING SEMESTER

Week   Event

1–18   Teachers and Music Coordinator record lost, stolen, deletions, and changes occurring to the inventory on the inventory report. Warehouse reports any replacements that have occurred.

19   Music Coordinator collects all building inventories.

Music Coordinator forwards inventories to Data Processing two weeks preceding the opening of the fall semester. Data Processing produces an updated inventory and sends to Music Coordinator one week prior to the opening of school.

UNIT II—HOW TO MAKE ADDITIONS, DELETIONS, REPLACEMENTS, AND CHANGES TO THE INVENTORY

An inventory must be accurate and up-to-date to merit any worthiness. Therefore, four methods are provided to maintain the musical instrument inventory. Each method is clarified below.

Additions: Inclusion of a musical instrument in the inventory which enlarges the number of instruments available for District use.

Deletions: Removal of a musical instrument from the inventory.

Replacement: Removal of musical instrument and replacing that instrument with another like instrument, i.e., replacing a worn violin with a new violin. The new violin bears the same case number as the replaced instrument.

Changes: The correction of erroneous data to better identify the inventoried item, i.e., incorrect serial number on inventory report is changed to reflect actual serial number of instrument.

The following table denotes those persons responsible for each method of maintaining the inventory.

Additions	Music Coordinator
Deletions	Music Coordinator
Replacements	Warehouse
Changes	Teacher

HOW TO MAKE ADDITIONS

A special form is used to notify Data Processing to add a new entry to the inventory. The form is illustrated on page 220. The form should be completed from left to right and then each entry should be reviewed to make certain no vital data has been omitted. The sequence of steps in completing a new entry are detailed below.

1. Print the current date in the upper left corner.
2. Assign a unique five-digit number to the entry. This number is used by Data Processing. Make certain duplicates *have not* been assigned.
3. Record the Case Number. Use three digits. A preceding zero may be necessary.
4. The instrument is described using standardized nomenclature. Acceptable nomenclature is shown on page 202.
5. Print the name of the manufacturer. A maximum of ten characters can be used.
6. Print the serial number. Use seven digits. Preceding zeros may be necessary.
7. Record the purchase price. Use six digits; two digits for cents and four for dollars. Preceding zeros may be necessary to complete the field.
8. Indicate the purchase month and year. Each field must contain two digits. For example, January 1971 would be shown as 01 71.
9. Use two digits to record the building. A list of building codes is on the next page.
10. Teacher number denotes the teacher responsible for the custody of the instrument. The Music Coordinator maintains an up-to-date directory of music teaching stations.
11. If the student to whom the instrument will be assigned is known, his last name, first and middle initials are printed.

Additions can be submitted any time to Data Processing. However, if additions are to be shown in the next inventory report, they must be submitted two weeks prior to the scheduled inventory run.

HOW TO MAKE DELETIONS

Draw a line through the system-wide inventory. The person making the deletions will write his initials in the left-hand column.

HOW TO MAKE REPLACEMENTS

Follow same procedure for Additions and Deletions. Deletions must be made on system-wide inventory.

HOW TO MAKE CHANGES

Draw a line through incorrect data and print above the line the correct data. Building inventory reports have been double spaced especially for this purpose.

CORD NO. (5)	CASE NO. (3)	INSTRUMENT			MFG. (10)	SERIAL NO. (7)	PRICE (6)	PURCH. DATE		BLDG. NO. (2)	TCHR. NO. (3)	STUDENT		
		SUBJ. (9)	DESCR. 1	DESCR. 2				MO. (2)	YR. (2)			L. NAME (10)	FI	MI

INSTRUMENTAL VOCABULARY

Subject	Descr. 1	Descr. 2	Subject	Descr. 1.	Descr. 2
ALTONIUM			FLUTE		
BARITONE	EUPH		FR HORN	DOUBLE	F
BARITONE	REC		FR HORN	SINGLE	BB
BARITONE	UPR		FR HORN	SINGLE	F
BASSOON			GONG		
BASS	REC		GUIRO		
BASS	SOUSA		MARACAS		
BASS	STR				
BASS	UPR		OBOE		
BELL LYRE			PICCOLO		
BELLS	ORCH		RATCHET		
BELLS	SLEIGH				
BLOCK	TEMPLE		SAX	ALTO	
BLOCK	WOOD		SAX	BAR	
			SAX	SOP	
CASTANETS			SAX	TENOR	
CELLO	1/2		STAND	SNARE	
CELLO	3/4		STAND	TIMBA	
CELLO	4/4		TROMBONE		
CHIMES			TROMBONE	BASS	
CLARINET	ALTO		TROMBONE	VALVE	
CLARINET	BASS		TUNER	STROBO	
CLARINET	BB	SP	TUNER	TEMPO	
CLARINET	CONTRA	ALTO	TYMPANI		
CLARINET	CONTRA	BB	TYMPANI	20	
CLARINET	EB	SP	TYMPANI	23	
CLAVES			TYMPANI	25	
CORNET			TYMPANI	26	
COWBELL	4		TYMPANI	28	
COWBELL	5		TYMPANI	29	
CRADLE	DRUM	BASS	TAMBOUR		
CYMBAL	RIDE		TIMBALES		
CYMBAL	15		VIOLA	14	
CYMBAL	17		VIOLA	15	
CYMBAL	18		VIOLA	16	
CYMBAL	19		VIOLIN	1/2	
			VIOLIN	3/4	
DRUM	BASS		VIOLIN	4/4	
DRUM	BONGO		WHIPCRACK		
DRUM	PARADE		WHISTLE	SLIDE	
DRUM	SNARE		XYLOPHONE		
DRUM	TENOR				

CODE	BUILDING	CODE	BUILDING
11	Warren High School	20	Butcher Junior High School
12	Cousino High School	21	Fuhrmann Junior High School
13	Mott High School	22	Hartsig Junior High School

CODE	BUILDING	CODE	BUILDING
23	Melby Junior High School	48	Wilde Elementary
24	Carter Junior High School	49	Wildwood Elementary
25	Beer Junior High School	50	Lean Elementary
26	Grissom Junior High School	51	Rockwell Elementary
31	Bever Elementary	52	Black Elementary
32	County Line Elementary	53	Haitema Elementary
33	Cromie Elementary	54	Susick Elementary
34	Green Acres Elementary	55	Wilkerson Elementary
35	Hesse Elementary	56	Fillmore Elementary
36	Marshall Elementary	57	Angus Elementary
37	Murthum Elementary	58	Holden Elementary
38	North Elementary	60	Administration
39	Pennow Elementary	64	Radio Station
40	Rinke Elementary	65	Textbook Stockroom
41	Shepard Elementary	74	Harwood Elementary
42	South Elementary	76	Willow Woods Elementary
43	Warner Elementary	77	Hatherly Elementary
44	Weber Elementary	90	Library Processing
45	Frost Elementary	96	St. Annes Elementary
46	Holland Elementary	98	Bus Garage
47	Siersma Elementary	99	Warehouse

Transfer of instruments among teachers may occur during the semester. Procedures for making such transfers are detailed below.

INSTRUMENT RECEIPT

	Use this column if applicable
Recipient: MARY BROWN	Student's Name: MARY BROWN
Address: 12345 FOURTEEN MILE RD.	School: WARREN HIGH SCHOOL
	Expected Date of Graduation
Date: 10–20–70 Phone: SL 7–0123	Month: JUNE Year: 1972
(Signature of Recipient)	Date Equipment to be Returned
Lender: MR. MUSIC MAN	Month: JUNE Day: 12 Year: 1970
Location: WARREN HIGH SCHOOL (11)	Rental Fee: $

CASE NO.	ITEM	SERIAL NO.	CONTROL NO.	COMMENTS
007	CELLO 4/4	002468	Do not use this space	

White Copy: Lender
Yellow Copy: Recipient
Pink Copy: Music Office

SAMPLE OF INDIVIDUAL INSTRUMENTAL
RECEIPT FORM

Individual Instrument Receipt Forms are used primarily as a means of identifying the location and use of all system-wide musical instruments. The form acts as a formal contract with parents in accepting responsibility for the proper care and use of school property.

The Instrumental Receipt Form is printed in triplicate. Copies are retained in this manner: 1) The original (or white) copy is kept by the person *Lending* the equipment, 2) The second (or green) copy is retained by the *Receiver* of the equipment, and 3) The third (or pink) copy is sent to the *Music Education Office* on the first school day of each month. Any movement of system-wide equipment or change of responsibility is recorded on the individual Instrument Receipt Form, whether between teacher and student, teacher and teacher, or teacher and equipment manager.

The Instrumental Receipt Form becomes a valuable means of maintaining an accurate inventory only when the information being transferred is thorough and accurate. Here are some recommendations which will assist the process.

1) Printing of information is preferable to handwriting (except in the case of the signature).
2) Bear down on the copy when printing so that the third copy is legible.
3) The information should be as complete as possible. Use of the vocabulary as determined by your manual.
4) It is preferable that only *one* instrument be recorded on the I.R.F.
5) Rental fees are used only in the case of students loaning an instrument during the summer. A maintenance fee is charged elementary students loaning an instrument normally purchased by the beginning students.

The teacher bearing responsibility for instruments will maintain an organized file of all receipts, and transmit this information to the System-wide Inventory on those calendar dates designated in your manual.

After completing this form, follow Steps 1–4.

1. The white copy is retained by the "Lender" as part of his personal inventory record.
2. The yellow copy is given to the "Recipient" of the instrument.
3. The pink copy is sent to the Music Education office on the first day of each month.
4. The "Lender" will draw a line through the instrument on his inventory and record the name of the receiving teacher under "Remarks." The receiving teacher will add the acquired instrument to his inventory list.

UNIT III—DATA PROCESSING PROCEDURES AND OPERATIONS
MUSICAL INSTRUMENT INVENTORY: FLOW CHART

(This job is run in August and January)

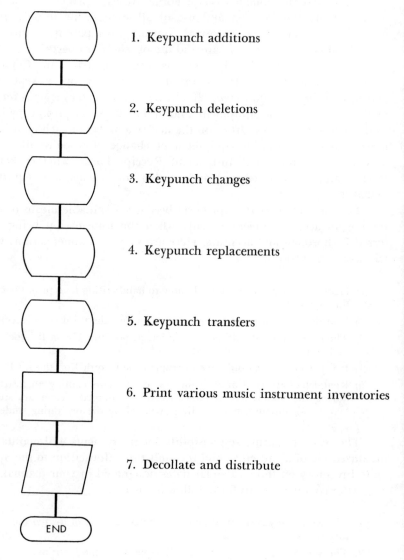

1. Keypunch additions

2. Keypunch deletions

3. Keypunch changes

4. Keypunch replacements

5. Keypunch transfers

6. Print various music instrument inventories

7. Decollate and distribute

END

CARD LAYOUT

MUSICAL INSTRUMENT INVENTORY RECORD

CARD NO.

RECORD NO. | BLANK | CASE NO. | BLANK

INSTRUMENT
SUBJECT | BLANK | DESCR. 1 | DESCR. 2

MANUFACTURER

SERIAL NO.

PRICE

PURCH DATE — MO | YR

STATUS

BLDG. NO.

TCHR. NO.

STUDENT
LAST NAME | FI | MI

BLANK

REMARKS   Status Code: 1 = Lost
2 = Stolen

E-O-J

CARD NO.

"99"

BLANK

REMARKS

The Music Coordinator will indicate the transfer on the System-Wide inventory by changing the building and teacher number for the transferred item.

STEPS 1–5

KEYPUNCH OPERATOR

1. *Additions* are keypunched from the "Addition to Musical Instrument Inventory" form.

2. *Deletions*: Remove cards from the file which have the same record number as those entries that have a line drawn through them on the System-Wide inventory. The margin on the inventory report should contain the initials authorizing the deletion.

3. *Changes*: Any of the inventory reports will contain changes whereby new or correct identifying data is punched into the inventory record card. Duplicate the card and punch changes where indicated.

4. *Replacements*: Remove card for old instrument and replace with card for new instrument. Record number and case number on new card should be identical to old card. Replacements are shown on System-Wide and Building inventory reports.

5. *Transfers* are shown on System-Wide inventory. Change Building and Teacher numbers.

Card format is shown on next page.

STEP 6

CONSOLE OPERATOR

1. Set up system as shown on next page.
2. Execute MUSIC.
3. Observe console messages. Enter date that next semester begins.
4. Place E-O-F (9's in cc 1-2) after last inventory card.

STEP 7

MACHINE OPERATOR

1. Decollate last two carbons. Do not burst.
2. Forward all copies to Music Coordinator.

IBM 1130 MACHINE SETUP SHEET						

PROGRAM NAME: Music

PROGRAM NUMBER:

PROGRAM DESCRIPTION:

APPROXIMATE RUNNING TIME:

PRINTER	TYPE OF PAPER		NO. OF COPIES		CARRIAGE TAPE	
	Standard		4-Ply		Standard	

DISKS	DRIVE NUMBER:	0	1	2	3	4
	CARTRIDGE ID:	0001	0113			

SWITCH SETTINGS

SWITCH UP _____ DOWN all down

SWITCH UP _____ DOWN \

SWITCH UP _____ DOWN _____

INPUT CARDS

99 EOF

INVENTORY FILE

XEQ

XEQ MUSIC

XEQ

SOURCE OF INPUT: _____

DISPOSITION OF OUTPUT: _____

FOR PAUSES AND ERROR MESSAGES SEE ERROR RECOVERY SHEETS

Appendix P

DATA PROCESSING FOR
INSTRUMENTAL MUSIC
LIBRARY CATALOGS

Before any new music is issued to buildings, the teachers complete this data processing card, in order to keep information in the music library catalog current.

WARREN CONSOLIDATED SCHOOLS
INSTRUMENTAL MUSIC LIBRARY

ADD | X | NO. S 43

DELETE | | DATA SHEET

CHANGE | | DATE
                    1 - 3 - 72

| B | E | G | I | N | | T | H | E | | B | E | G | U | I | N | E | | | | | | |
TITLE

∇
| P | O | R | T | E | R | | | K | R | A | N | C | E | | | | 0 | 8 | 7 |
COMPOSER   ARRANGER   PUBLISHER NO.

| 1 | 5 | 9 | | 0 | 5 | 6 | 3 | | E | 2 | 3 | 8 |
TYPE   CLASS PERIOD DIFFICULTY   FILE NO.

APPROVED BY _____
              (Teacher's Name)

228

EXPLANATION OF THE INSTRUMENTAL MUSIC LIBRARY CATALOG

Example of Codes

Title of Music	Composer	Arranger	File	Pub	Type	Class
Begin The Beguine	Porter	Krance	E 238	087	159	0563

File .... E — Harms Inc
Drawer 2
Folder 38
Publisher No. .... 087 — 087
Type Left .... 1 — Full
    Middle .... 5 — Band
    Right .... 9 — Misc
Classification .... 05 — Beguine
Period .... 6 — Contemporary
Difficulty .... 3 — Difficult

Arranger	File	Pub	Type	Class
Walters	C 358	163	457	4862

File .... C — Rubank Inc
Drawer 3
Folder 58
Publisher No. .... 163 — 163
Type Left .... 4 — Solo
    Middle .... 5 — Band
    Right .... 7 — Trombone Baritone
Classification .... 48 — Popular Standard
Period .... 6 — Contemporary
Difficulty .... 2 — Medium

Asleep In The Deep Petrie

NOTE: Each four-drawer file is designated with an alphabetical letter (e.g. E). Each drawer is numbered and each envelope is given a number.

E 2 3 8

Drawer   Envelope

PUBLISHERS INDEX

1 ABC MUSIC
2 ADVANCED MUSIC
3 AFFILIATED MUSIC
4 AGER YELLEN BORNSTEIN INC

5 J E AGNEW
6 HARRY ALFORD MUSIC
7 ALFRED MUSIC
8 THORNTON W ALLEN CO
9 AM RUS MUSIC CORP

10 EMIL ASCHER INC
11 ASSOCIATED MUSIC
12 AVANT MUSIC
13 BANDLAND INC
15 THE BAND SHED

19 BERKELEY PUB C L BARNHOUS
20 IRVING BERLIN MUSIC
21 BER MAR
22 BIBS MUSIC
23 THE BIG THREE

24 BLAKE
25 BOOSEY AND HAWKES
26 BOSTON MUSIC
27 BOURNE INC
28 BREGMAN JOCCO AND CONN

29 BREITKOPF AND HAERTEL
30 GEORGE F BRIEGEL INC
31 BROADCAST MUSIC INC
32 BROUDE MUSIC
33 BUXTON HILL MUSIC

34 BYRON DOUGLAS PUBLICATION
35 SLUCIAN CALLET
36 CANTON PUB CO
37 CARLIN MUSIC PUB CO
38 CENTURY
39 CHAPPELL AND CO

This represents only one page of the publishers index.

TYPE LEFT DIGIT

MISC

1 FULL
2 COLLECTION
3 METHOD AND TECHNIQUE
4 SOLO
5 DUET

6 TRIO
7 QUARTET
8 QUINTET
9 SEXTET

TYPE MIDDLE DIGIT

MISC OR NOT APPL
1 WOODWIND
2 BRASS
3 PERCUSSION
4 STRINGS

5 BAND
6 ORCHESTRA
7 BAND W CHORUS
8 ORCHESTRA W CHORUS
9 MIXED

TYPE RIGHT DIGIT

FLUTE OBOE VIOLIN
1 CLARINET
2 VIOLA
3 BASSOON CELLO

4 SAXOPHONE
5 TRUMPET CORNET
6 FRENCH HORN
7 TROMBONE BARITONE
8 TUBA STRING BASS

9 MISC OR NOT APPL

CLASSIFICATIONS

1 ANTHEM
2 ARIA
3 BALLAD
4 BALLET

5 BEGUINE
6 BOLERO
7 CANZONA AND CANZONETTA
8 CAPRICE
9 CHORALE

10 CHRISTMAS
11 CONCERT MARCH
12 CONCERT MUSIC
13 CONCERTO
14 DANCE

15 EXCERPT
16 FANFARE
17 FANTASIA
18 FANTASY
19 FOOTBALL SHOW

20 FOXTROT
21 FUNERAL MARCH
22 GALOP
23 GRANDE MARCH
24 GAVOTTE

25 HYMN
26 INTERMEZZO
27 JAZZ
28 LATIN AMERICAN
29 LOVE SONG

30 LULLABYE
31 MARCH
32 MAZURKA
33 MEDLEY
34 MINUET

35 NARRATOR WITH ENSEMBLE

PERIOD

MISC
1 RENAISSANCE
2 BAROQUE

3 CLASSICAL
4 ROMANTIC
5 IMPRESSIONISTIC
6 CONTEMPORARY

DIFFICULTY

MISC
1 EASY
2 MEDIUM
3 DIFFICULT

PAGE NO 2	JAN 68		FILE	PUB	TYPE	CLASS
AIR FOR G STRING	BACH	WILHELMS	S 123	066	140	1223
AIR BOUREE SUITE NO 3 D	BACH	CARSE	X 303	077	140	5822
SLOW MOVEMENT FIRST SYM	BEETHOVEN CARSEF		S 348	077	140	5932
TWENTY FIVE XMAS CAROLS	CLARKE		S 318	026	140	7002
FINALE SYMPHONY IN C	HAYDN	CARSE	S 158	130	141	5943
TWO PASSEPIEDS	BACH	DOUGLAS	S 164	207	142	1222
NOCTURN FOR VLA STR OR	LOPRESTI		S 346	066	142	1263
HOLLOW MEN	PERSICHETTI		S 118	062	145	1263
STRING MASTERS BK ONE	GOEHRING		S 130	118	149	0001
MUSIC FOR STRING INSTRUTS	RUSH		S 135	025	149	0001
SUNFLOWER ALBUM POLYCHRDIA	BROWN		S 224	077	149	0001
ARUNDEL SUITE	BROWN		S 225	077	149	0001
MULBERRY ALBUM POLYCHORDIA	BROWN		S 226	077	149	0001
GOLLIWOG ALBUM POLYCHRDIA	BROWN		S 227	077	149	0001
KANGAROO ALBUM POLYCHRDIA	BROWN		S 228	027	149	0001
PELICAN ALBUM POLYCHDRDIA	BROWN		S 229	077	149	0001
CHARIOT ALBUM POLYCHORDIA	BROWN		S 230	077	149	0001
MORTLAKE ALBUM POLYCHRDIA	BROWN		S 231	077	149	0001
SILKEN STRINGS	OVANIN		S 242	130	149	0001

JAN 68

			FILE	PUB	TYPE	CLASS
TWO SONATINAS	PLEYEL	BROWN	S 107	077	149	0002
SERENADE	CARSE		S 223	077	149	0002
LITTLE CLASSIC SUITE	AKERS		S 237	066	149	0002
FOUR EARLY AMER TUNES	ADLER		S 239	167	149	0002
OSTERLY ALBUM POLYCHORDA	BROWN		S 250	077	149	0002
LAUREL ALBUM	HANDEL	BROWN	S 108	077	149	0021
TWO GRIEG SONGS	GRIEG	STEPHAN	S 241	103	149	0042
IM BALLADENTON	GRIEG	MADDY	S 249	158	149	0342
CANZONETTA	MOZART	STEG	S 109	186	149	0732
FIDDLERS JIG	COWELL		U 116	011	149	0862
CORELLIANA	HUNT		U 115	066	149	0922
CHORATE AND FUGUE	SIENNICKI		S 247	106	149	0962
MEDITATION		STEPHAN	U 113	103	149	0962
SUITE OF CAROLS	ANDERSON		S 134	130	149	1002
XMAS CONCERTO	CORRELLI	SCHERNG	S 161	011	149	1012
CHRISTMAS PASTORALE	CORELLI	CARSE	S 312	077	149	1012

This Catalog has a "Type" Index, an Alphabetical Index, and a Composer Index.

A COPY OF THIS CARD IS KEPT IN EACH FILE DRAWER WITHIN THE INSTRUMENTAL MUSIC LIBRARY (CENTRAL). AS MUSIC IS SELECTED AND USED, TEACHERS INDICATE THIS INFORMATION ON THIS CARD.

INFORMATION FORM ON USE OF MUSIC

TITLE: _____   COMPOSER: _____   FILE: _____   DRAWER: _____

Date Used	Organization	Occasion	*Use	Comment

*Indicate by Number in Above "Use" Column

1. Prepared and Performed at Festival.
2.   "   "   " Concert.
3. Prepared to degree that it could be played on concert program.
4. Prepared to limited extent.
5. Used for sight reading only.

Comment

	Jr. High	Sr. High	Etc.
Good for		"	"
Fair for	"	"	"
Poor for	"	"	"
Too Easy	"	"	"
Too Difficult	"	"	"

236

ALL MUSIC FOR THE INSTRUMENTAL MUSIC LIBRARY IS ORDERED THROUGH THE OFFICE OF MUSIC EDUCATION. THIS FORM IS USED. TEACHERS ARE GIVEN AN ALLOCATED AMOUNT OF MONEY FOR PURCHASES.

REQUISITION: INSTRUMENTAL MUSIC DEPARTMENT

☐ – Music Library

☐ – Music Book Store—Resale

☐ – Music Supplies—Not Resale

Req. No._____

Date_____

19__-19__

(Please Use One Requisition For Each Type of Order—e.g. Do Not Mix System-wide Music with Resale)

Quantity	Title	Composer-Arranger	Arrange-ment	Publisher

WHEN THE MUSIC ORDERED IS RECEIVED, IT IS STAMPED AND PROCESSED IMMEDIATELY.

WITH AN OPEN PURCHASE ORDER, THE PROCESS IS A QUICK AND EFFICIENT ONE.

Do not write in this space.

Order Received:_____(Date)

Ordered:_____(Date)

Signed:_____

_____
Originator

_____
School

1. Original—Music Coordinator
2. Instrumental Teacher—File Copy

BIBLIOGRAPHY

Administration and Supervision

BENNIS, WARREN G., *Organizational Development: Its Nature, Origins, and Prospects.* Reading, Mass.: Addison-Wesley Publishing Co., Inc., 1969.

BESSON, MALCOLM, *Supervising the Successful Music Program.* West Nyack, N.Y.: Parker Publishing Co., 1969.

CALLAHAN, RAYMOND E., *Education and the Cult of Efficiency: A Study of the Social Forces That Have Shaped the Administration of the Public Schools.* Chicago: University of Chicago Press, 1962.

CAMPBELL, RONALD F., JOHN E. CORBALLY, and JOHN A. RAMSEYER, *Introduction to Educational Administration.* Boston: Allyn & Bacon, Inc., 1966.

CHAMBERLAIN, LEO M. and LESLIE W. KINDRED, *The Teacher and School Organizations* (4th ed.). Englewood Cliffs: Prentice-Hall, Inc. 1966.

COLWELL, RICHARD, *The Evaluation of Music Teaching and Learning.* Englewood Cliffs: Prentice-Hall, 1970.

DOLL, RONALD C., *Curriculum Improvement: Decision Making and Process.* Boston: Allyn & Bacon, 1964.

Evaluative Criteria for the Evaluation of Secondary Schools (4th ed.). Washington, D.C.: National Study of Secondary School Evaluation, 1969.

HANDY, H. W., and K. M. HUSSIAN, *Network Analysis for Educational Management.* Englewood Cliffs: Prentice-Hall, Inc., 1969.

HARTLEY, HARRY J., *Educational Planning-Programming-Budgeting: A Systems Approach.* Englewood Cliffs: Prentice-Hall, Inc., 1968.

SNYDER, KEITH D., *School Music Administration and Supervision.* (2nd ed.) Boston: Allyn & Bacon, Inc., 1965.

238

WEYLAND, RUDOLPH H., *A Guide To Effective Supervision.* Dubuque: William C. Brown Company, Publishers, 1960.

Business in Education

OPTNER, STANLEY, *System Analysis for Business and Industrial Problem Solving.* Englewood Cliffs: Prentice-Hall, Inc., 1965.

ROY, ROBERT H., *The Administrative Process.* Baltimore: The Johns Hopkins Press, 1965.

SCHEIN, EDGAR H., *Organizational Psychology.* Englewood Cliffs: Prentice-Hall, Inc., 1965.

UMANS, SHELLEY, *The Management of Education.* Garden City, N.Y.: Doubleday & Company, Inc., 1970.

Elementary School Curriculum

BEAUCHAMP, GEORGE A., *Planning the Elementary School Curriculum* (2nd ed.). Boston: Allyn & Bacon, 1956.

BERGETHON, BJORNAR, and EUNICE BOARDMAN, *Musical Growth in the Elementary School.* New York: Holt, Rinehart and Winston, Inc., 1970.

NYE, ROBERT E., and VERNICE T. NYE, *Music in the Elementary School* 3rd ed.). Englewood Cliffs: Prentice-Hall, Inc., 1970.

SMITH, ROBERT B., *Music in the Child's Education.* New York: The Ronald Press Company, 1970.

General and Philosophical

ANDREWS, FRANCES, and CLARA E. COCKERILL, *Your School Music Program: A Guide to Effective Curriculum Development.* Englewood Cliffs: Prentice-Hall, Inc., 1946.

BRUNER, JEROME S., *The Process of Education.* New York: Alfred A. Knopf Inc., 1963.

CARLSON, RICHARD O., *Change Processes in the Public School.* Eugene: Center for the Advanced Study of Educational Administration, University of Oregon, 1969.

ERNST, KARL, and CHARLES GARY, eds., *Music in General Education.* Washington, D.C.: Music Educators National Conference, 1965.

GOODLAD, JOHN I., *The Changing School Curriculum.* New York: The Georgian Press, Inc., 1966.

KOWALL, BONNIE, ed., *Perspectives in Music Education.* Washington, D.C.: Music Educators National Conference, 1966.

MIEL, ALICE, *Changing the Curriculum: A Social Process.* New York: Appleton-Walker, 1946.

MURSELL, JAMES L., *Music Education: Principles and Programs.* Morristown, N.J.: Silver Burdett Co., 1956.

OLIVER, ALBERT I., *Curriculum Improvement. A Guide to Problems, Principles and Procedures.* New York: Dodd, Mead & Co., 1965.

REIMER, BENNETT, *A Philosophy of Music Education.* Englewood Cliffs: Prentice-Hall, Inc., 1970.

SCHWADRON, ABRAHAM, *Aesthetics: Dimensions for Music Education.* Washington, D.C.: Music Educators National Conference, 1963.

SPRAGUE, CARLETON, and WILLIAM C. HARTSHORN, *The Study of Music: An Academic Discipline.* Washington, D.C.: Music Educators National Conference, 1963.

TABA, HILDA, *Curriculum Development: Theory and Practice.* New York: Harcourt Brace Jovanovich, 1962.

TRUMP, J. LLOYD, *New Direction To Quality Education.* Washington, D.C.: National Association of Secondary School Principals, National Education Association, 1969.

———, and DORSEY BAYNHAM, *Focus on Change: Guide to Better Schools.* Chicago: Rand McNally & Co., 1961.

Improving Instruction

ALLEN, DWIGHT, and KEVIN RYAN. *Microteaching.* Reading, Mass.: Addison-Wesley Publishing Co., Inc., 1969.

CHOATE, ROBERT A., ed., *Tanglewood Symposium.* Washington, D.C.: Music Educators National Conference, 1968.

LEEPER, ROBERT R., ed., *Role of Supervisor and Curriculum Director in Climate of Change.* Washington, D.C.: ASCD Yearbook, National Education Association, 1965.

MAGER, ROBERT F., *Developing Attitude Toward Learning.* Belmont, Calif.: Fearon Publishers, 1968.

————, *Preparing Instructional Objectives.* Belmont, Calif.: Fearon Publishers, 1962.

————, and PETER PIPE, *Analyzing Performance Problems or "You Really Oughta Wanna."* Belmont, Calif.: Fearon Publishers, 1970.

Miscellaneous

BARTHOLOMEW, WILMER T., *Acoustics of Music.* Englewood Cliffs: Prentice-Hall, Inc., 1946.

BERANEK, LEO LEROY, *Music, Acoustics, and Architecture.* New York: John Wiley & Sons, Inc., 1962.

CHISMORE, DALE W., and JOHN F. PUTNAM, *Standard Terminology for Curriculum and Instruction in Local and State School Systems.* Washington, D.C.: U.S. Department of Health, Education and Welfare, 1970.

CULVER, CHARLES, *Musical Acoustics* (4th ed.). New York: McGraw-Hill Book Company, 1956.

FUCHS, ESTELLE, *Pickets at the Gates: The Challenge of Civil Rights in Urban Schools.* New York: The Free Press, 1966.

GAINES, JOAN, *Public Relations.* Washington, D.C.: Music Educators National Conference, 1968.

GARY, CHARLES L., ed., *Music Buildings, Rooms and Equipment.* Washington, D.C.: Music Educators National Conference, 1966.

HARTSHORN, WILLIAM C., *Music For the Academically Talented Student.* Washington, D.C.: Music Educators National Conference, 1960.

KLOTMAN, ROBERT H., ed., *Scheduling Music Classes.* Washington, D.C.: Music Educators National Conference, 1968.

McLUHAN, MARSHALL, *Understanding Media: The Extensions of Man.* New York: McGraw-Hill Book Company, 1964.

Religion in the Public Schools. Report by the American Association of School Administrators. New York: Harper & Row, Publishers, 1964.

SHETLER, DONALD J., *Film Guide for Music Educators,* Washington, D.C.: Music Educators National Conference, 1961.

TURNEY, BILLY L., *Catcher in the Wrong,* Itasca, Illinois: F. E. Peacock Publishers, Inc., 1968.

Secondary School Curriculum

ANDREWS, FRANCES, and JOSEPH LEEDER. *Guiding Junior High School Pupils in Music Experiences.* Englewood Cliffs: Prentice-Hall, Inc., 1953.

BROUDY, HARRY S., B. O. SMITH, and JOE A. BURNETT, eds., *Democracy and Excellence in American Secondary Education.* Chicago: Rand McNally & Co., 1964.

GLENN, NEAL E., WILLIAM B. McBRIDE, and GEORGE H. WILSON, *Secondary School Music: Philosophy, Theory, and Practice.* Englewood Cliffs: Prentice-Hall, Inc., 1970.

HOFFER, CHARLES, *Teaching Music in the Secondary Schools.* Belmont, Calif.: Wadsworth Publishing Co., Inc., 1964.

INDEX

A

Accountability, 1, 82
Accounting. *See* Budget
Acoustics, 113
Administration:
  function, 13-23
  process, 5-12, 139
  public relations, 130, 132
Administrators, types of, 31-32, 135-36,
  142, 144
  authoritarian, 31
  democratic, 31
  laissez faire, 31
  permissive, 31
Aesthetics in music, 6, 77, 104
  objectives, 84
  values, 85
Aims of music education, 49, 82, 95
Akron, Ohio, 3, 92, 115, 118
Allen, Dwight, 56
Allen, Wendell C., 40
American Association of School Admin-
  istrators, 131
American Federation of Musicians, 130
American String Teachers Association,
  40
Amos, David, 96
Andrews, Frances M., 85
Appelson, Wallace, B., 23
Arts combined. *See* Humanities
Assignments, teachers', 78, 91-94
Audio-visual aids, 54, 55, 62, 138
Audition, faculty interviews, 62
Authority, delegated, 1, 17

B

Band, 42-43, 97, 129, 139
Barro, Stephen N., 83
Basic music book series selection proce-
  dures, 51
Baynham, Dorsey, 41
Behavior, 13, 49
Bids, 114
Board of Education, 1, 24, 32, 39, 60, 73
Budget, 75, 100-123
  categories, 110-11
  equipment, 110
  planning, 80, 100-101
  PPBS (Planning-Programming-Bud-
   get System), 101-8, 208
Buildings, 111-12
Bulletins, 169
Business and industry influence, 4, 7,
  101
Business department procedures, 115

C

Caldwell, Michael, 86
Callahan, Raymond E., 7
Catalogs (Computer), 228
Chamberlain, Leo M., 36
Characteristics for administration (per-
  sonal), 20-21, 67
Chismore, Dale, 33n, 42n, 43n
Choate, Robert, 135, 142
Choruses, 42. *See also* Vocal music pro-
  gram

Class, size, 73, 177
Classrooms, 112
Classroom teachers (elementary music), 51, 91
Cleveland, Ohio, 14, 44
Code of ethics, 165
Columbus, Indiana, 92, 108, 208
Communications, 130-31
  bulletins, 169
  mass media, 39, 127, 138
  public relations, 131
Communities and administration, 15, 21-23, 24, 28, 88
  resources, 127
  social structure, 126
  understanding, 80, 87
Comprehensive music teaching, 14, 41-44
Computers, 3, 35, 99, 102-5, 139
  music, 138-39
Conferences:
  professional, 54
  teacher, 61
Consultant, 54
  textbooks, 51
Contemporary Music Project, 41, 88, 136
  Richard Felciano, 88
Context Evaluation (Context, Input, Process and Product-CIPP), 86
Coordinator of music, 19
Copyright law, 123
Courses of study, 47
Creativity, 12, 44, 142
Critical Path Method (CPM), 8
Curriculum, 33-44
  balance, 42-44
  centers, 53-54
  change, 34-35, 40-41
  colleges and universities, 38-39
  custom and tradition, 37
  evaluation, 80-82
  guides, 49, 150-52
  interrelationships between curriculum and instruction, 40-42
  legal requirements, 39
  mass media, 39
  philanthropic foundations, 38
  pressure groups, 38
  professional influences, 38-39
  public opinion, 39

Curriculum (*cont.*)
  standard terminology, 35-36
  textbooks, 37, 51-53

D

Daily schedule, 90
Dearborn, Michigan, 38
Decentralization, 83
Decisions and decision making, 7-12, 55
Democratic procedures, 1, 47
Demonstration lessons, 50
Detroit Public Schools, 14, 44, 51, 70, 88, 109, 129, 153, 157-64
Director of music, 17, 29
Doolin, Howard A., 98

E

Economy, 100
Educational leadership, 86
Efficiency, 100
Electronic piano, 16
Elementary music, 51, 64, 74, 93
Elementary-Secondary Education Act, 78, 109
Equipment, 114
  maintenance and repair, 115
  purchasing, 114
  records, 115
  replacing, 114
  specifications, 114, 178-204
Ernst, Karl, 41
Ethics, 165
  business practices, 122
  outside engagements, 67
  school performances, 165
Ethnic music, 74, 137
Evaluation, 77-89
  of curricula, 80, 87, 153
  of performance, 84
  of personnel, 61, 78, 155

F

Facilities:
  building, 112
  planning, 110

Fairfax County, 205
Financial responsibility:
  foundation, 109
  local, 108
  national government, 108
  state, 109
Flexible schedules, 94-99
Folk music, 16
Ford Foundation, 136
Fritz, Marjorie, 92
Fuller, Philip J., 205
Funds:
  foundations, 108, 136
  fund-raising, 109
  sources, 108

G

Gaines, Joan, 125, 132
Gardiner, John, 68
Gary, Charles, 41, 95
General music, 42, 75, 115, 137
Goals and objectives, 80, 84, 101-4
Greiner, Larry, 140
Grid, managerial, 71
Griffiths, Daniel, 7
Guidance counselors, 99, 127
Guides, curriculum, 47-50

H

Handy, H. W., 7
Hartley, Harry J., 102-8
High school, 74, 86, 137
Humanities (related arts), 17, 38, 44, 113, 142
Human relations, 7, 131, 153
Humidity control, 113
Hussain, K. J., 7

I

Improving instruction, 17, 27, 33, 46-59
  curriculum centers, 53-54
  demonstration lessons, 50-51
  guides, 47-50
  microteaching, 50, 55-59
  organizational structure, 21

Improving instruction (*cont.*)
  professional meetings, 54-55
  programmed instruction, 138
  research and advanced study, 53
  technology, 138
  textbook adoptions, 51-53
  workshops, 46-47
Incompetency, 66
Indiana-Oregon test, 6
Individual instruction, 138
Inner-city, 16, 87
In-service training, 46-47
Instruction. *See* Improving instruction
Instrumental music, 42, 74, 93, 118, 160, 205
Instruments:
  basic instrumentation, 112, 205
  maintenance and repair, 115-16,
  specifications for purchase, 114-15, 178
Insurance, 122
Interpreting the music program. *See* Public relations
Interviews with teacher candidates, 62
Inventories, 119-22, 216-37
Issues in music education, 137-38
  computer music, 139
  "eighty percent" (youth music), 17, 137
  ethnic music, 137
  programmed instruction, 138

J

Jazz, 87
Junior high school, 41, 52, 70, 98

K

Keller, Robert, 96
Kindred, Leslie W., 36
Klotman, Robert H., 95

L

Law, copyright, 123
Leadership in music administration, 2, 13, 17-19, 30

Leadership in music administration
(*cont.*)
artistic-musical, 84
decision-making, 7-12, 55
educational, 41
human relations and human dynamics, 71-72
personal qualities, 20
support for change in, 13, 15
Library, 54
Line and staff relationship, 6, 24-29, 110
in city, 26
in department of music education, 27
in Office for Improvement of Instruction, 27
in small school or community, 28
Listening activities, 97, 137
Literature, music course, 44
Loads, pupil-teacher, 73-75
Loan agreements, instruments, 118-21

M

McClintoch, Philip, 49, 150
McLuhan, Marshall, 39
Managerial grids, 71
Marching band, 129
Mass media, 39, 127, 138
Mayer, Robert F., 77
Michigan Music Educators Association, 74, 177
Michigan School Band and Orchestra Association, 74, 177
Michigan School Vocal Association, 74, 177
Microteaching, 55-59, 138
Modular scheduling, 96-99
Music consultant, 20, 91
Music coordinator, 19
Music courses:
history and literature, 44
theory, 44
Music Educators National Conference, 40, 96, 113, 128, 130, 132, 136, 165
Music Industry Council, 129

N

NEA (National Education Association), 122

Negotiations, 74
News. *See* Public relations

O

Objectives of the school music program, 80, 84-85, 88, 101
Observations, 50-51, 61-62
O'Fiesh, Gabriel, 138
Ohio Music Education Association, 128
Open-door policy, 21
Operational patterns, 139-42
Optner, Stanley, 8
Orchestra, 40, 42, 81
Ordering music and material, 111, 114
Organizational development, 67-71
Outside work, 67
school's performers' bureau, 129
by teachers, 67
trips, 130

P

Parden, Robert H., 107
Parma, Ohio, 17
Patterson, Tom, 74, 177
Performers' bureau (school), 129, 162
Personnel practices, 60-75
criteria for selection, 62-65
evaluation, 60, 71-73, 78-80
inter-staff, 67
teaching load, 73
Phi Delta Kappan, 22, 102
Philadelphia, Pa., 44
Philosophy (of administrator or supervisor), 5
Pianos, 115
specifications, 201
tuning, 115
Planning-Programming-Budget-Systems (PPBS), 101
Press. *See* Public relations
Principal, 40, 50, 52, 54, 61
Process of music administration, 5-12
Professional growth. *See* In-service training
Professional musician, 129
Program evaluation and review technique (PERT), 8
Progress Reports, 133

Publicity:
  inside the school system, 130
  outside the school system, 128, 132
  through publications, 169
Public relations, 125
  community, 125, 128
  press, 127
  purpose, 126-28
  understanding community needs, 126
Purchasing, 114-15
Purpose of music administration, 13
Putnam, John F., 33, 42, 43

Q

Qualifications:
  music administrators, 144-49
  music teachers, 155, 158, 161
Quinmester Plan, 98

R

Rating programs, 80
Rating teachers, 66, 78, 155
Recruiting teachers, 65
Related arts, 17, 44, 137. *See also* Humanities
Relevance, 3, 88
Religion in music, 131
Rental agreements, 118-20
Repairs, 115-18
  budgets, 111
  selecting shops, 117
Research, 53, 141
Responsibility of music administrators, 29-30
  delegation, 17
Rockefeller Panel Report, 38
Rooms, music, 112
Roy, Robert, 11, 28
Rural, 3, 16, 54
Ryan, Kevin, 56

S

Salary, 53, 73
Scheduling, 90-99
  in Akron, Ohio, 92
  computer, 99

Scheduling (*cont.*)
  in Dade County Schools, 98
  in Ekstein Junior High School, 98
  for elementary music teachers, 91
  flexible, 94
  modular, 96
  Quinmester plan, 98
  role of guidance counselors in, 99, 128
School-community relations. *See* Public relations
School publications, 127, 169
Scientific management, 7-10
Secondary schools, 74, 137
Specialists, music, 51, 92
Special music groups, 42, 74
Specifications for music equipment, 114
  instrument repairs, 118
  instruments, 178-204
  piano tuning, 116
Staff organization, 6, 24, 69-70
State's role, 39
  in certification, 39
  in providing funds, 108
Storage of instruments and equipment, 113
Student's needs, 5, 13, 33, 36, 40, 50, 100
  public relations, 128
Superintendent of Schools, 16, 24, 28, 40, 70, 91, 110
Supervision, 15-17
Supervisor of music, 5-7, 15, 17, 147
  definition, 1, 30
  evaluation, 78
  in-service education, 46
  microteaching, 55-59
  role, 12
  school visits, 60-61
Supplies, 118
Systems and systems analysis, 8, 33-34, 101
  evaluation, 141
  objectives, 101
  retrieval, 105

T

Tanglewood Symposium, 135, 142
Tape recorders, use of, 61
Taste, musical, 84

Taxation as source of money, 108
Taylor, Frederick, 7
Teachers:
  classroom, 52, 91
  dealing with incompetencies, 66
  evaluation, 61
  morale, 68-72
  orientation, 47
  selection, 62
  self-appraisal, 61
  See also Improving instruction
Television, 96, 127, 138
Temperature control, 113
Tenure, 66
Textbooks, 51
Titles, 19
  consultant, 20
  coordinator of music, 19
  department head, 20
  director of music, 19
  junior teacher, 20
  supervisor of music, 19
Transfer forms, 43, 172

Trump, J. Floyd, 41

U

Umans, Shelley, 86n
United States Office of Health, Education, and Welfare, 36

V

Ventilation, 113
Video tape, 50, 56, 62, 138
Visitations, 50, 59, 60-61, 64
Vocal music program, 44, 74, 93, 157

W

Warren, Michigan, 118, 132, 216, 228
White, Elizabeth, 74
Wichita, Kansas, 44, 70
Workshops, 46-47

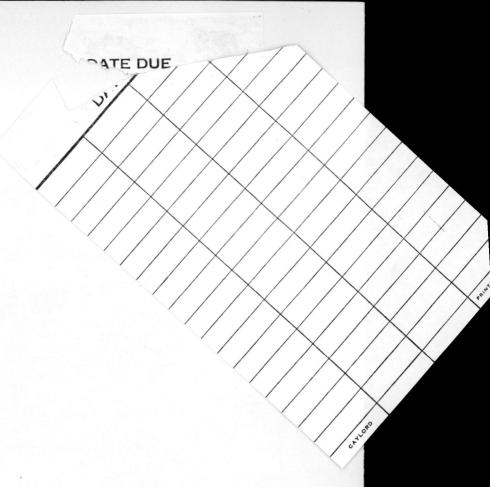